THE UPPER ROOM DISCIPLINES

1991

THE UPPER ROOM

Disciplines
1991

Coordinating Editor
Tom Page

Editorial Advisors
Mary Ruth Coffman
Janet R. McNish
John S. Mogabgab
Mary Lou Redding

Editorial Assistants
Lynn W. Gilliam
Robin Philpo Pippin
Beth A. Richardson

Copy Editors
Lynne M. Deming
Greg Ottarski

UPPER
ROOM BOOKS
NASHVILLE

The Upper Room Disciplines 1991

ISBN 0-8358-0607-3

The scripture quotations not otherwise identified are from the Revised Standard Version of the Bible, copyrighted 1946, 1952, and © 1971 by the Division of Christian Education, National Council of the Churches of Christ in the United States of America, and are used by permission.

Scripture quotations designated NEB are from *The New English Bible,* © The Delegates of the Oxford University Press and the Syndics of the Cambridge University Press 1961 and 1970, and are reprinted by permission.

Scripture quotations designated TEV are from the *Good News Bible, The Bible in Today's English Version,* copyright by American Bible Society 1966, 1971, © 1976, and are used by permission.

Scripture quotations designated NKJV are from the *Holy Bible, The New King James Version.* Copyright 1972, 1984 by Thomas Nelson, Inc., Publishers.

Scripture quotations designated NIV are from the *Holy Bible: New International Version.* Copyright © 1973, 1978, 1984 International Bible Society. Used by permission of Zondervan Bible Publishers.

Scripture quotations designated JB are from *The Jerusalem Bible,* copyright © 1966 by Darton, Longman, & Todd, Ltd., and Doubleday & Co., Inc.

Scripture quotations designated NJB are from the *New Jerusalem Bible,* copyright © 1985 by Darton, Longman & Todd, Ltd. and Doubleday & Company, Inc. Used by permission of the publisher.

The designation KJV is used throughout this book to identify quotations from the King James Version of the Bible.

Any scripture quotation designated AP is the author's paraphrase.

The week of September 30–October 6 is reprinted from *Disciplines 1982.*

CONTENTS

This spring my sister and her husband and two daughters came to visit. To accommodate them, we had to do some rearranging. My daughter cleaned her room (sort of) so she and her older cousin could share it. I moved my things downstairs to allow my sister and brother-in-law to use my larger bedroom. We made room in the closets and bathrooms for them, too, and I shopped for things I know they like to eat. Making these changes were part of making our guests feel comfortable and welcome.

Making space in our lives for others requires something of us. All of us lead busy lives, and it is not automatic that there is time and room for relationships. Good friendships require that we learn what is important to our friends and what they need from us. Good relationships require time.

That is as true of our relationship with God as with other relationships: we must make a space to welcome God into our lives. We must spend time with God in order to build a close friendship with God. In my own life, the primary way I have done that is by reading the Bible and reflecting on what God is saying to me through it. This volume of *Disciplines* can help us spend time with God, reading scripture and hearing God speak to us. God's message—God's challenge and comfort—may come to us through the words of the Bible or through the comments of the writers. As we do the rearranging that is necessary to spend time with God, God will speak. All we have to do is listen.

And so we welcome you to the 1991 edition of *Disciplines*. Some of you have received this book this year for the first time; to you, a special welcome. Some of you are regular readers, having used *Disciplines* in your devotional time for several or even many years; to you, welcome back. Some of the weeks' meditations may speak directly to you; some may not seem to relate as well to your life. More important than the specific words written for any particular day, though, is our commitment to place ourselves regularly and deliberately in God's presence.

Disciplines offers a structure to consciously welcome God into our lives each day. It asks us to clear out a space for that relationship. And as we do, God welcomes us, lovingly, into closer and closer friendship.

Mary Lou Redding

—Mary Lou Redding
Managing Editor
The Upper Room

YOUR LIGHT HAS COME

January 1-6, 1991   **John S. Mogabgab†**
Tuesday, January 1   Read Isaiah 60:3-6.

The prophet's words to Israel combine promise and command: The light that comes to you is to become the light that comes from you. This vision of light emerged from a time in Israel's history when many "sons and daughters" of Israel remained in exile. Social problems and the deterioration of religious practice clouded the lives of those who had returned. Hope in Yahweh's promised salvation flickered.

As we lean into a new year, we do so with keen awareness that too many sons and daughters of the human family live in the exile of poverty, violence, political intimidation, homelessness, or substance abuse. Too many of earth's ecosystems have been ravaged by their human stewards. At the heart of this aching world is a hope for the ingathering of all that has been lost, forsaken, downtrodden.

When we arise from the slumber of sin and allow the fiery glory of God's love to warm us into new life, we become beacons of light and hope in a darkening world. This occurs as we move from a surface reflection of God's truth to such a deep immersion in it that it becomes the very truth of our being. Here is the shining summons extended to each Christian and to the whole church. As we live into the light, God is glorified and the world receives assurance that its longing is not vain.

Suggestion for meditation: *Envision a person, group, or situation in need of reconciliation surrounded and penetrated by the light and warmth of God's presence. Pray that God might mend what is broken, heal what is hurt, restore what is lost, renew what is worn.*

---

†Editor of *Weavings, A Journal of the Christian Spiritual Life*, published by The Upper Room, Nashville, Tennessee.

Wednesday, January 2   Read Psalm 72:1-4.

The people of Israel understood that what is most personal and what is most universal are intimately related. The God of Israel was known as a personal God whose dominion embraced heaven and earth. Israel's hope for salvation was shaped by this convergence of the personal and the universal. The reign of King Solomon, celebrated in our text for today, offered a partial portrait of the fully realized reign of universal peace and well-being (*shalom*) that would flow from the promised messianic king.

What unites the personal and the universal facets of *shalom*? The psalmist recognizes that the answer lies in the righteousness of God, which expresses itself in compassion and justice. God's righteousness is God's original and persistent will for unmarred intimacy with the whole creation. The personal expression of this righteousness is compassion, that profound suffering with another that can release the one in need into new life. The universal expression of God's rghteousness is justice, that comprehensive ordering of social relationships that assures the dignity and liberty of all.

To immerse ourselves in God's truth so deeply that its light shines from our inmost relity means to live compassionately and to work for just social arrangements. But above all, to shine with the light of God's truth means to realize that living compassionately and working for justice are not so much tasks we must shoulder as gifts provided by the overflowing bounty of God's righteousness.

Prayer: *Gracious God, give us your own righteousness, that we may embody the light of compassion and justice before all people. Amen.*

Thursday, January 3   Read Psalm 72:5-14.

The shining light of the messianic reign will endure "like the sun and moon." It will be as welcome as rain showers to thirsty soil. How different this is from our typical experience of ruling regimes, whether political or religious, international or local. The reign of the worldly leader employs authority to augment and channel power for self-serving ends. Such "kingdoms" rely upon coercion, whether subtle or blunt, to sustain themselves. They are acknowledged but never welcomed; they are endured but finally do not endure.

The reign of the messianic king will endure because it depends not upon coercion but compassion. This reign is concerned not with the protection of power but the precious value of every person. This reign does not perpetuate "exploitation and outrage" but redeems the lives of those in need. This reign does not deface the geography of the land or of the soul but causes virtue to flourish throughout the entire web of created life. So attractive is this reign, so true to what is deepest and most authentic in our humanity, that a remarkable thing happens. All the representatives of the world's reigns approach the messianic king with gifts instead of garrisons. And all the forces that feed on enmity toward God and God's creatures recognize their final defeat.

Is our witness to God's reign as welcome as steady rain in the sub-Sahara or as hurtful as torrential rain in a flood plain? Do we shine with a light that will endure or a beam that must be endured?

Prayer: *Holy God, may our witness to your saving purpose cultivate virtue and not villainy, foster compassion rather than coercion, and promote justice instead of just us. In Jesus' name. Amen.*

Friday, January 4   Read Ephesians 3:1-6.

Recent decades have seen a rediscovery of the humanity of Jesus. Whether presented by religious activists as the exemplar of social responsibility, or portrayed by novelists and film makers as a tormented soul in search of personal identity, Jesus has been heartily welcomed into the ranks of our common humanity. But the quest for the human Jesus may have eclipsed something that Paul perceived with special clarity and force: the depths in the mystery of Christ. Paul saw a mystery that reaches back to the roots of the ages and forward to the consummation of God's saving purpose. Universal in scope, the mystery is nevertheless fully embodied in Jesus Christ.

What is this mystery? It is that in Jesus Christ we glimpse not only the model of our true humanity but the new creation in which that humanity flowers. In him we encounter the mystery of a love so utterly unfettered that it not only seeks but accomplishes reconciliation at the most intractable fracture points of the world. In him new pathways to the neighbor are opened. In him new connections between heaven and earth are established. For Paul the most vivid image to evoke the depths of this mystery was that of Jews and non-Jews being parts of one body. In Paul's day no image could have been more radical or more comprehensive.

The light that comes to us is not merely a spiritual spotlight that can guide us to a fuller humanity. Rather, this light is the new sun that gives life and definition to a transfigured human landscape.

Suggestion for meditation: *What image from contemporary life would convey the radical and comprehensive character of the mystery Paul saw in Christ?*

Saturday, January 5   Read Ephesians 3:7-12.

The psalmist whose poetry expressed Israel's hope for the kingdom of *shalom* evoked a vision so universal yet so personal, so attractive yet so authentic, that the powers of evil simply had to acknowledge their own inferiority. Paul believed that this vision had become reality in Jesus Christ. But more astonishing is Paul's conviction that this same magnificent reality is manifested in the church, the Body of Christ. By the faith that sustains it, the hope that guides it, and the love that empowers it, the church proclaims to the sovereignties and powers the decisive overthrow of their dominion. The church is the means God has chosen to reveal the true scope of God's wisdom, a wisdom that confounds completely the ploys of the powers of division and destruction.

It is a matter for serious reflection that Paul's understanding of the church should bear such slight resemblance to the workaday churches of our experience. The reason for concern is clear as Paul continues his line of thought: Insofar as the church embodies the new creation wrought in Jesus Christ, it authenticates and reinforces Paul's confidence in God and in his own ministry. Confident prayer and confident action are rooted not only in the soil of personal religious experience but, more importantly, in the richer humus of the church's life. And such confidence is critical in face of the trials the sovereignties and powers will inflict in their desperate effort to discredit the wisdom of God.

The light that comes to us becomes the light that comes from us as the corporate life of the church nourishes confident ministry in its members. Such confidence confirms the wisdom of God and confounds the powers of evil.

Suggestion for meditation: *Reflect with gratitude upon the ways in which your church has encouraged your confidence in God and in your ministry.*

Sunday, January 6 (Epiphany)
Read Matthew 2:1-12.

Matthew's account of the Magi's visit gathers at the birth of Jesus all the rich symbols of Israel's messianic hope. For the early Christian writers, however, Matthew's story did more than affirm that Jesus was indeed the longed-for Messiah. It also depicted a pattern of the spiritual journey.

Jesus is the light that has come to us, the morning star of the dawning kingdom of God. The marvelous star that guides the Magi to the holy infant reveals that in all our searching for the reality of Jesus he is already with us, guiding us toward himself. The gift of gold acknowledges that Jesus is the king whose reign ushers in the triumph of God's peace. Gold is also a symbol of wisdom (see Prov. 21:20), which we have to offer others as we recognize the wisdom of God in the mystery of Christ. Frankincense is a burnt sacrifice to God, fittingly presented to the one who is God-with-us in human flesh. Yet it also calls to mind the life of prayer (see Ps. 141:2), in which we honor God through offerings of praise and thanksgiving. Myrrh anoints the bodies of the dead and is given to Jesus as the one who would die for all that all might live. The gift of myrrh is therefore a sign of our ongoing conversion, through which we die to all that inhibits fullness of life with God in the kingdom of peace.

The Magi returned home by a different way. Having encountered the light of Israel, we cannot return home by any former paths. The new road to our true home with God is marked by spiritual insight, prayer, and conformation to the dying and rising of Christ. As we travel this road, the light that comes to us becomes the light that comes from us.

Suggestion for meditation: *Imagine yourself before the newborn Jesus. What gifts symbolizing your own spiritual journey do you wish to give him?*

FROM BEGINNING TO BEGINNING—AGAIN

January 7-13, 1991 **Mary Rose O'Reilley†**
Monday, January 7 Read Genesis 1:1-2.

"In the beginning. . . ." In the beginning of what? In the beginning of form, light, evening, morning, days, time, and consciousness, God's Spirit begins to play. What are the materials at hand? A "formless wasteland . . . darkness . . . the abyss" (AP). And a mighty wind sweeping the waters.

In northern Minnesota, watching Lake Superior ice sheets pile against granite in the teeth of a winter gale, it's easy to imagine primal chaos. Landscape becomes an inward, psychic state: frozen, waiting for the freeing dance of spirit.

One black winter night, when the temperature was ten below zero, I skied across a frozen lake. Half a mile from shore, I felt my skis catch, and then begin to drag in-slush. *Slush,* half a mile from shore, at ten below zero. This is my image of elemental terror. What could be ahead? A freak current? A break in the ice? Indeed, where was I? Overhead there were chips of stars, but not a human light on shore. Wasteland, darkness, and abyss. This is my image of the chaos described in Genesis.

Now, it's January. The bright fires of Christmas are behind us, even the promising flares of the new year's resolutions. February is yet to come. We are in the heart's long night, when something deep goes on, like a dream we can't even bring into consciousness, that changes everything. We are at the soul's edge, bone's edge, where God's Spirit begins to dance.

Suggestion for meditation: *Here on the edge of winter, let's try to reframe the idea of new year's resolutions. What does your experience tell you about God? How can you be faithful to what you know?*

---

†Professor of English, theology, and peace studies, St. Thomas College; member, Twin Cities Friends Meeting (Quaker), St. Paul, Minnesota.

Tuesday, January 8   Read Genesis 1:3-5.

"In the beginning," for the ancient Israelites, God defined himself by an act of organizing. He separated day from night. Then God exulted over the result: it was good.

This part of the Genesis account was written during the Babylonian captivity, a time of grieving and chaos for Israel. When a good system is in place—benevolent rulers, a reasonable scheme of social and familial relationships—it's agonizing to see it destroyed by the impious, unsubtle, vulgar, and barbarous force of an alien culture. And yet this has been, more often than not, the fate of "civilized societies." Think of the Irish monks copying their precious books all through the dark ages, and losing them in the end to barbarian pillagers; think of the burning of the Torah scrolls in the Warsaw ghetto. Such desecrations violate our deepest need for order in the universe. Where is the meaning in this destruction? *How long, O Lord?*

In their exile, the Jews envisioned a God who knew how to put things in place, who knew night from day. They needed to cling to a hope of order, though everything in the external world made a mockery of hope.

Some say that our contemporary world culture is going through a "paradigm shift." We feel, in different degrees, a sense of excitement about the future and a grief for old, outdated structures of meaning that seemed to hold the world in place. Liberal and conservative voices prepare to oppose each other, often within the individual psyche. And we are wise to ask ourselves as we move into this new year, this new paradigm, what is worth conserving? What should we freely release?

Suggestion for meditation: *How much order do you need? How much can you let go of? What might happen then? What prayers would make you feel safe? What image of God?*

Wednesday, January 9   Read Psalm 29:1-9.

Psalm 29 puts before us another elemental religious situation. Divine power is revealed in a sound-and-light show of natural energy—flood, devastation, the trees stripped of their branches. Faced with such a scene, the more primitive parts of our brain may send out a signal to cower. Who is in charge here? Are we safe in the universe? The psalmist exhorts us at the very least to "ascribe to the LORD the glory of his name."

Do these primitive attitudes have a place in modern religious consciousness? These days, we are not even much impressed by the power of nature to flood us or strip our trees—it's worth, at best, a few minutes on the evening news. We know a lot; we "control" a lot. *We* light the fuses. *We* strip the forests.

Let's try to go more deeply into the text, to see whether the prayer of awe has a place in our understanding of Spirit. This psalm seems to be speaking about *holy ground:* the places where the Spirit slips through the spaces between matter and reveals something about itself. One way to describe that condition is by analogy with the most intense natural phenomena: earthquake, wind, fire, and flood—the most extreme manifestations of the elements that make up our world.

Most displays of force, then as now, are not happy events. They shake our world and make us cry out in fear. The point of the psalm, though, is not terror, but ecstasy. The cry of "Glory!" in God's temple seems to merge with the quaking and straining of the physical world.

On holy ground, terror and ecstasy are delicately balanced. What can make us feel safe enough there to center ourselves and carry on?

Suggestion for meditation: *Where do you feel awe? Can you interpret that place as holy ground? Can you "keep your feet?"*

Thursday, January 10   Read Psalm 29:10-11;
                                              *Wisdom 7:22-30.

Have you been feeling uncomfortable with the texts we have studied so far this week? The Book of Genesis takes us back into the prehistory of the race and into our own prehistory as well: the child-mind. The child understands power, authority, and might, and it was as children that most of us were influenced by images of an elderly, white-bearded God. As adults, the journey home is not always an easy one. Now many of us are wary of power, questioning of authority, and inclined to subvert the rule of the fathers, that is, patriarchy. Have we outgrown this God?

Psalm 29 assures us that we can feel safe if we trust in a benevolent and impregnable king, who will "give strength to his people" and "bless his people with peace." However, because we find it hard to imagine a king who is either impregnable or benevolent, the psalmist's image may not be meaningful for us.

In our reinterpretation of God's fatherhood and rule, we need to recapture images of masculinity that are powerful but safe. At the same time, we need to recognize that patriarchy is not the whole story. The Eastern church, traditionally, and the Western church, more recently, have learned to honor the wisdom principle as feminine incarnation of God: holy Sophia. Let us claim her, too! "For in her there is a spirit that is intelligent, holy, unique, manifold, subtle, mobile, clear, unpolluted, distinct, invulnerable, loving the good, keen, irresistible, beneficent, humane, steadfast, sure, free from anxiety, all-powerful, overseeing all."

Suggestion for meditation: *What if we were to let* her *into our lives, this Spirit of light, clarity, and agility? How is that different from letting* him *into our lives?*

---

*The Wisdom of Solomon, one of the books of the Apocrypha.

Friday, January 11   Read Mark 1:4-11.

"I [John] have baptized you with water; but he [Jesus] will baptize you with the Holy Spirit."

How are these two baptisms different? we may wonder. What is the relationship between them? Is one "better"? And what do these questions have to do with modern readers, christened (perhaps) undramatically, wearing the family lace? There was no journey into the desert, no meeting with a wild man—that figure who, in folklore, often represents radical change and deep healing from the pollutions of "culture." How tame we are!

Let us look first at what John is offering: "a baptism of repentance for the forgiveness of sins." This is not a congenial message to many modern people, debased as it has been by so many evangelical caricatures: "Repent! Be saved!"—complete with visions of damnation and an appeal for funds. Perhaps we want to leave John to his locusts and his leather girdle and go on to the more inviting prospect of baptism in the Spirit.

Yet, since Jesus does not repudiate John's baptism, we will have to come to terms with it as a stage on the spiritual journey. What is required of us here?

For the hellenized Jewish world, the Greek words *metanoia* ("repentance") and *hamartia* ("sin") had a sense that may be lost to us. *Metanoia* suggests a reflective process; to repent is to change one's mind because of an inner debate, and thus to come to know more. *Hamartia*—a word derived from the vocabulary of archery—means "to miss one's mark." John invites us, then, to allow our minds to be changed and our vision corrected.

Suggestion for meditation: *If John the Baptist calls us to an inner debate, to question the nature of reality, and to sharpen our ethical aim, how can we open ourselves to this process? How can we arrange our lives to receive the wild man? How much will we let him upset us?*

Saturday, January 12   Read Acts 19.

If John the Baptist calls us to inner debate, to question the nature of reality, and to sharpen our ethical aim, what, beyond this, is Jesus calling us to do?

Theologians have filled libraries trying to answer that question. We don't need to read those books—helpful as some of them may be. We need to look within ourselves. What is the claim of the Spirit on each of us? John calls us to a state of mind that is open, questioning, and committed—the only kind of space into which the Spirit can descend.

When Paul asked the disciples at Ephesus whether they had been baptized in the Holy Spirit, they replied, "We have never even heard that there is a Holy Spirit." They found out soon enough, for Paul's preaching put the city in turmoil. Civil dissent and rioting broke out, each faction claiming the authority of its magic, its silver idol, and its way of making a living. Some things never change. Those are pretty much like the things we find ourselves hanging on to when we resist the promptings of the Spirit in our lives.

The way of the Spirit is never boring. This feminine principle of fluidity and change, spontaneity and flux, tends to outrage the status quo. Realizing this situation, we can come to value the wholeness of Judaeo-Christian revelation, which joins spontaneity and order. But we will probably never get comfortable with the spontaneity. Nor will we always overcome the pain of being pulled between the two principles—in our minds, in our churches, and in our society.

Suggestion for meditation: *We have prayed this week for the courage to let go of whatever old paradigms and old structures of meaning impede the flow of the Spirit in our lives. Where now is the growing edge? Where in your life do you detect the stirrings of holy wisdom?*

Sunday, January 13   Read John 1:1-5;
                                                    Proverbs 8:22-31.

This week's scripture passages frame a religious experience, holding it still so that we can take in a bit of the uncontrollable whole. We have gone not from beginning to end but from beginning to beginning—again. John's prologue echoes Genesis; it retells the story with a little updating, a little amplification.

In the beginning was the Word, the *logos*. As a classics student, I used to ask my teachers what that meant. I knew the dictionary definition of "word." But what did it *mean* to the Greek mind, to the Jewish world, to the Johannine author? I was not "religious" in those days, but I liked texts to be coherent. I felt that if I could recover a true sense of that "word," all the difficulties of John's Gospel would be resolved. Finally one of my teachers said, "It means, simply, *meaning. Intelligibility.*"

What a promise: *things make sense!* "In the beginning was meaning, and meaning was identified with, inseparable from, the nature of God. All things were made intelligibly, coherently, and nothing existed without meaning. (*Nothing!*) Life has meaning, and life is light, and light is stronger than darkness—meaninglessness—and meaninglessness cannot overcome meaning" (AP).

In Jesus, meaning becomes incarnate; the Christ-energy is pure intelligence, the principle of reconciliation between God-strength and God-love. John's prologue also echoes wisdom literature from the Apocrypha: " . . . a breath of the power of God, and a clear effluence of the glory of the Almighty" (Wisdom 7:25).

Suggestion for meditation: *What difference does it make to us if we know that things make sense, that everything is exactly as it should be?*

EMPOWERMENT FOR LIFE AND MINISTRY

January 14-20, 1991   **M. Robert Mulholland, Jr.**†
Monday, January 14   Read 1 Sam. 3:1, 7; Matt. 7:22-23.

The power of relationship

What an amazing situation! "Samuel was ministering to the LORD," yet "Samuel did not yet know the LORD, and the word of the LORD had not yet been revealed to him." Jesus seems to touch upon the same reality in Matthew 7:22-23. He does not contradict the claims of those who have been ministering in his name. He questions neither their methods nor their effectiveness. Instead he probes their motives. He lays bare the deep inner dynamics upon which their ministry has been built, and he finds a fatal flaw. Although they have been ministering "in his name," their ministry is not an incarnation of God's presence in their lives. Their service is not the consequence of a vital relationship with God. Although their outward activity conforms to what is expected of those ministering in his name, something of radical essence is missing.

Obviously, Samuel was caught up in the same kind of ministry, and we see its fruitless consequences: "The word of the LORD was rare in those days; there was no frequent vision." Ministry must flow from a vital and growing relationship with God if it is to become a channel through which the presence of God is released into the world. Such ministry touches the persons and situations involved with God's transforming power.

Prayer: *O God, before we act may we adore you; before we serve may we surrender ourselves to you; before we "do" may we devote ourselves unconditionally to you, that our lives may be available for you to make them an incarnation of your presence in the world. Amen.*

---

†Vice-president/Professor of New Testament, Asbury Theological Seminary, Wilmore, Kentucky.

Tuesday, January 15   Read 1 Samuel 3:1-8.

The power of purity

Isn't it interesting that it took three times for Eli to realize that God was speaking to Samuel? It may explain why "the word of the LORD was rare in those days." Obviously Eli was not expecting God to speak, even though he was receptive to a word from God, even a word which destroyed his whole matrix of existence (1 Sam. 3:11-18). We would expect Eli to at least question the validity of Samuel's message, if not reject it outright, especially in light of the fact that the word of the Lord was rare.

It seems that Eli's sensitivity to God had been dulled by his toleration of evil. There is no evidence that Eli himself engaged in the evil practices of his sons, who viewed the priesthood as the means for gratifying their own desires (1 Sam. 2:12-17) and lusts (1 Sam. 2:22). Eli even chastized his sons for their actions. But, even after being warned by a prophet (2:27-36), Eli took no action to remove the evil from his life and ministry. This may well be the cause of his insensitivity to God's action in speaking to Samuel.

Is our sensitivity to God dulled by the toleration of evil in our life or ministry? Perhaps tolerating evil is an "innocent" habit in which we indulge. Perhaps it is something we do away from our ministry to insure that it will not taint our witness. Perhaps it is an unwholesome relationship we nurture yet keep at arm's length. Perhaps it is something God is speaking to us about but, like Eli, we haven't taken action to remove that evil from our life.

From Eli we can learn the tragic consequences of tolerating evil: a loss of sensitivity to God and, ultimately, the destruction of our life or our ministry.

Prayer: *O God, convince us of the need for purity of life and ministry if we are to remain sensitive to you and effective in our service. Amen.*

Wednesday, January 16   Read 1 Samuel 3:10-21.

The power of faithfulness

Have you ever considered what courage it took for Samuel to convey the word of God to Eli? Eli was the high priest, the representative of the covenant people before God. Eli was, in a sense, the one who sustained the entire structure of covenant relationship with God. Eli was Samuel's superior who held Samuel's future in his hands. Eli was also Samuel's mentor, the one who had trained him for ministry and who was nurturing him for a life of service in the sanctuary at Shiloh. And Eli was, for all practical purposes, a father for Samuel, who had been placed in Eli's care as soon as he had been weaned (1 Sam. 1:22). So how could Samuel tell Eli that God has decreed his doom? It was no wonder that "Samuel was afraid to tell the vision to Eli." Even when Eli demanded that Samuel relate what God had said, the temptation must have been strong for Samuel to tone down the harshness of the message.

But Samuel took his life in his hands and recounted for Eli everything God said. Samuel was completely faithful to the word God had entrusted to him. Only then does the account reveal the results of such faithfulness: 'The LORD was with him and let none of his words fall to the ground. . . . Samuel was established as a prophet of the LORD. . . . for the LORD revealed himself to Samuel at Shiloh by the word of the LORD." Faithfulness to the word God gives results in empowerment for the ministry God gives.

Prayer: *O God, enable us by your grace to be courageously faithful to the word you speak into our lives, that you may empower us for the living of that word in the world. Amen.*

Thursday, January 17   Read Psalm 63; Phil. 4:4-7.

The power of centeredness

Paul and the psalmist have two things in common: both find themselves in life-threatening situations. The psalmist is facing those who seek to destroy his life (Ps. 63:9), and Paul is imprisoned not knowing whether he will get out alive (Phil. 1:20-21; 2:17). Both have found a centeredness in God, which empowers them in their situations. The psalmist affirms, "Thy steadfast love is better than life"; and Paul declares, "For to me to live is Christ, and to die is gain."

At first glance the psalmist and Paul appear to be either fools or fanatic fatalists. After all, when faced with similar situations isn't our tendency to fight, to struggle, to do everything in our power to manipulate the situation for our defense and vindication? But Paul and the psalmist are neither fools nor fatalists. Obviously they entered into a level of relationship with God that is so deeply centered in God's presence, purpose, and power that they are able to entrust themselves completely to God in the face of the deepest adversity and remain at peace in their own spirits.

How does such centeredness come? Paul tells us, "I have learned, in whatever state I am, to be content" (Phil. 4:11). The psalmist says, "I think of thee upon my bed, and meditate on thee in the watches of the night; . . . my soul clings to thee." Such a life of centeredness comes from the discipline of daily devotion of our lives to God. We can grow daily into that centeredness in God from which power for effective ministry flows, even in the midst of numbing adversity.

Prayer: *O God, free me from obsessive care for myself; help me to have you as the sole content of my life today. Amen.*

Friday, January 18   Read 1 Corinthians 6:12-18.

The power of discipline

Does it take discipline to refrain from chocolate when there is not a piece within a thousand miles and the culture in which you live abhors the very idea? Hardly! The kinds of discipline that empower lives are those that move against the flow of our surroundings, disciplines that are maintained in the face of multiple opportunities and pressures toward indulgence.

In our culture of gluttonous consumption and unrestricted sexual license, the disciplines of simplicity and purity seem ludicrous and unrealistic, much as they must have in Corinth with its profligate lifestyle. There was also the added element of the Jewish Christian's freedom from legalistic "works-righteousness" as the basis of relationships with God, even as our culture has been liberated from the "Do and Don't" idea of Christian discipleship in an earlier era. In such settings, self-indulgence becomes the means of self-fulfillment, and disciplines are viewed as unnatural restrictions to self-fulfillment.

However, Paul realized that disciplines liberate us from the bondage of indulgence and help us toward wholeness in Christ. Paul also realized that Christian disciplines involve more than abstaining from certain activities; they mean living in the world on the basis of a different order of being than that which shapes normal human life. We are members of Christ, and that reality sets our lives in a frame of reference radically different from that of the culture around us. In such a perspective, Christian disciplines of simplicity and purity become the means of grace by which God shapes our lives in the image of Christ and through which the power of God's presence is manifested in our lives.

Prayer: *O God, may we so live today in the disciplines of simplicity and purity that we may be formed in Christ and your presence released in our lives. Amen.*

Saturday, January 19   Read 1 Corinthians 6:19-20.

The power of possession

Thomas Kelly, the Quaker saint, has a beautiful description of a life completely possessed by God.

> The life that intends to be wholly obedient, wholly submissive, wholly listening, is astonishing in its completeness. Its joys are ravishing, its peace profound, its humility the deepest, its power world-shaking, its love enveloping, its simplicity that of a trusting child. . . . it is a life and power that can break forth in this tottering Western culture and return the Church to its rightful life as a fellowship of creative, heaven-led souls.*

This must be something of what Paul had in mind when he wrote, "You are not your own; . . . glorify God in your body."

What does it mean to glorify God? Glory has to do with the very nature of the being who is described. This can be seen in Paul's claim, "We all, with unveiled face, beholding the glory of the Lord, are being changed into his likeness" (2 Cor. 3:18). The glory of God is the very essence of God's being. Thus, to glorify God is to allow the very essence of God's nature to be manifest. Only those who are no longer their own, only those who have abandoned themselves to God, can glorify God in their lives. Glorifying God is the power of incarnational lives and ministries in the world. As Paul says, "It is no longer I who live, but Christ who lives in me" (Gal. 2:20).

We must continually ask ourselves: Who is in possession of my life and ministry?

Prayer: *O God, you are always ready to reveal yourself in those who are willing to let you take possession of their lives. Help us let you lay hold of us today. Amen.*

---

*Thomas R. Kelly, *A Testament of Devotion*, (New York: Harper and Row, 1941), p. 55.

Sunday, January 20   Read John 1:35-42.

The power of releasing

One of the greatest temptations for us who are clergy is to hold people to ourselves. It is so easy to fall into the habit of developing a circle of disciples who look to us for leadership and guidance in their spiritual pilgrimage. Having such a circle provides evidence of "success." It feeds our sense of identity, value, and purpose. Within such a group, we find affirmations that authenticate our ministry. When our ministry is questioned or attacked, such a group can easily become the "power base" for our defense and for attacks upon our opponents.

John the Baptist gives us a different model of ministry by pointing his disciples to Jesus. When his disciples leave him for Jesus, John does not attempt to keep them. Even when some of his disciples become concerned that Jesus is gaining more disciples than John, John remarks, "He must increase, but I must decrease" (John 3:30).

The two disciples in today's passage aso provide a model of discipleship. Rather than clinging to their spiritual mentor, they are willing to release the security of that relationship for the insecurity of following one of whom they know little. They have no idea where he will lead them. In our own spiritual journey, no matter how rigorous the demands of our spiritual guide, the security of that relationship often seems preferable to the seeming insecurity of following Jesus into the unknown.

The power of our pilgrimage will depend on our willingness to release all lesser securities to follow Jesus. And the power of our own ministry will depend on our willingness to point others to Jesus and release them to follow him wherever he takes them.

Prayer: *O God, help us to release others to follow you and release ourselves from others that we may follow you. Amen.*

THE ATTITUDES OF POWER

January 21-27, 1991   **Fred L. Beck†**
Monday, January 21   Read Psalm 62:5-12.

In the text for today the psalmist sets his priorities. Do not trust in riches or extortion or stolen goods—trust God, who is both strength and love.

What a great combination these attributes of God make! We admire one who is strong. We may even envy the person who seems to take everything in stride, who continues to bear up under the stress and strain of life. We appreciate those who stand firm in the face of temptation and testing, keeping their lives in the path of truth and righteousness.

We admire these persons especially if, coupled with their strength, we see an equal amount of love. Strength alone can be bullish in nature. Strength without love may take upon itself an attitude of pride that looks upon the weak with disdain. Righteous strength often becomes pious superiority. Strength alone may be demanding, but strength coupled with love is unbeatable. That is what the psalmist saw as God's nature, and he found hope and solace in that combination.

We must strive for the combination of those attitudes in our own lives. An emphasis on power alone hinders most relationships, but power and love unite to build each other up. These two forces in tandem produce persons like Abraham Lincoln, Mother Teresa, Martin Luther King Jr., and others. And for those of us who are not as well known, our strength and love together contribute to the good of society in the world we call our own.

Prayer: *Help us, O Lord of power and love, to exercise these attributes in our lives so that we may be a positive influence for good. Amen.*

---

†United Methodist chaplain, Alton Memorial Hospital, Alton, Illinois.

Tuesday, January 22   Read Jonah 3:1-5, 10.

The power of God is often revealed in the Old Testament in the form of destructive judgment. In our reading today, Jonah's message from God to the people of Nineveh is a threat of judgment for their evil ways. They had forty days to change their ways which they immediately chose to do with penitent spirit. This act of contrition caused God to issue compassion and to withhold destructive judgment.

God looks upon judgment from more than one perspective, it seems. In this passage, one kind of judgment was made by God: "You are a wicked people and unless you change, destruction will come upon you." We sometimes use this form as verbal threat, but God used it as a firm warning of things to come unless the people changed their ways. So judgment from God was not always punishment; at times it was a warning to bring about repentance and change.

Thus, God's judgment was sometimes coupled with compassion. God's might and power could destroy. But God's compassion also allowed time for change—forty days in Nineveh's case—and was further expressed in complete pardon at the people's repentance. Again, the combination of power and compassion, like power and love, speaks most meaningfully.

Is there a place for well-intentioned judgment today? Is this what we see in boycotts, withholding of trade or investments, or picketing for our favorite causes? If these judgments are warnings, then they should also be coupled with compassion to bring about the desired change. We are called to remember that it is God's judgment that is final, not ours. Our judgment should be like that of God, full of compassion and love.

Prayer: *O God of compassionate judgment, grant us the ability to judge with compassion and wisdom. Amen.*

Wednesday, January 23   Read Mark 1:14-20.

The psalmist encouraged those who heard him to believe in a God of love and strength. Jonah's message revealed to Nineveh a God of judgment and compassion. Jesus came proclaiming, "The time is fulfilled, and the kingdom of God is at hand; repent, and believe in the gospel."

No timeline was given by the psalmist as he offered his instructions, though he seemed to imply a present tense to his plea. Jonah's message included a forty-day trial period. But with Jesus we have an even greater sense of urgency: "The time is fulfilled, and the kingdom of God is at hand."

I recall the evangelists of my childhood and youth who told what seemed to me to be horror stories. They implied that we should not leave the service without making a commitment to Christ, because "you may not have another chance." Jesus' sense of urgency was as great as his twentieth-century evangelists, but for a different reason. Jesus invited people to enter the kingdom for its worth. Enter now, so you will not miss out on the kingdom values that are held in store for you. Those values were couched in terms of love, as Jesus would later indicate in his answer to the teacher who questioned him (see Mark 12:28-34).

Since the kingdom Jesus spoke about was a kingdom based on love, it was therefore all the more important that they enter it. In that kingdom was acceptance, not rejection. The kingdom was characterized by renewal rather than by condemnation and punishment. Inclusiveness among all was the emphasis; no one was rejected because of race, sex, class, or creed. O that we might enter the kingdom and share its spirit in daily living!

Prayer: *Thy kingdom come, O Lord. Thy kingdom come. Amen.*

Thursday, January 24   Read Mark 1:14;
                                             Acts 20:17-21.

"Repent, and believe in the gospel." This was Jesus' invitation to all who would hear. It was first of all an invitation to change their minds. Traditionally, repentance was connected to sin. Repentance would cause a person to turn away from sin to follow a better way, the way of the righteousness of God. This idea may have been a part of Jesus' thinking also. He saw a need among the people to change their thinking about the kingdom of God that he announced, and to change their thinking about the announcer of the kingdom.

Both the news of the kingdom and the one who proclaimed it are "good news." The kingdom, or rule of God, is one of love and mercy, justice, and peace. It is present and active among us even as Jesus was present and active among the people. In the past much emphasis has been placed on the "building of the kingdom." More recently we have focused more on entering the kingdom revealed through Jesus and being active in that new relationship. In so doing, we have discovered that the kingdom is not *built* so much as it is *revealed* to and through us.

Entering and participating in the good news is the fruit of believing. Believing, like repenting, is a word of positive action. It is mental assent, but it is more. To believe motivates us to be a new person, to do a new thing, to live in and with a new spirit. To believe in Jesus is to follow him and to take of his spirit for our lives.

The call of our Lord is ever before us. Jesus calls us to receive his love and power that transforms our lives and opens the kingdom of God to us.

Prayer: *Gracious God, give us the openness to receive that which you have prepared for us, and to repent and believe the good news. Amen.*

Friday, January 25   Read Mark 1:16-18.

Even the most powerful person needs friends. The most astute leader needs followers. The greatest teacher is unfulfilled without students. Our leadership falls short if we have no followers to continue the good thing we began.

So Jesus proclaimed the kingdom of God as being at hand. It was opening day. Immediately after his public proclamation concerning the kingdom of God, Jesus calls these fishermen to discipleship by the Sea of Galilee. We may find it hard to believe that this was the first time Jesus had seen these four men of the sea. But even so, this experience reveals to us the great charisma of Jesus. He was a person of power that was compelling.

Like some who were offered this invitation, these fishermen might have laughed or cursed. Many leaders were seeking a following. But Jesus was different. His invitation had a drawing power that these men, and others after them, could not resist. So they left their nets and followed Jesus into a new adventure. Not knowing what it would mean, they accepted the challenge of following a new leader.

Are we different from these fishermen? We can never fully know what the Spirit of Christ will cause us to become. We cannot understand clearly what becoming a "fisher of men" will mean. But in hearing the good news and declaring our desire to follow Jesus in the kingdom of God, we open our lives to the adventures of discipleship. And it truly is an adventure as we deliberately apply the spirit of our Leader to our daily living.

Prayer: *Call us to discipleship, O Master, and teach us how to reach others for you. Amen.*

Saturday, January 26   Read Mark 4:19-20.

In our text for today we encounter the second set of fishermen Jesus called to be among the twelve to whom he entrusted himself and the cause for which he came. Besides these four fishermen he chose others who seemed incompatible: a zealot, a tax collector, and several other seemingly nondescript men. Evidently Jesus knew something about these persons that no one else recognized. Their capabilities were visible only to the one who saw beneath the surface.

When I was a teenager, I informed my parents one evening that I felt God had called me into ministry. I had been raised in the church. I had become a Christian at a young age. But I was also very timid. Dad could not see me as a preacher or pastor, but he kept those feelings to himself. Some twenty years into my ministry, Dad revealed his secret to me. He had gone into his private place of prayer after my announcement and said, "Lord, I know that you usually know what you're doing. But this time I think you may have made a mistake." Later, Dad was able to admit that it was he that was mistaken.

We would do well to be as insightful as Jesus was. What persons of leadership do we fail to call because they fail to meet our standards at the moment? Jesus' standard was: "Give me the person and let my Spirit mold him or her into that which I know he or she can be."

Hidden in each of us is a potential that will never be brought to its fullest capability unless it is under the control of our Lord. Let us hear him say, "Follow me" and respond to full discipleship.

Prayer: *Here I am, Lord. Make me truly your disciple. Amen.*

Sunday, January 27   Read 1 Corinthians 7:29-35.

If we really believed that the end of our age was relatively near, what would our teaching be? Paul saw the end of the age from a perspective that caused him to encourage the Corinthian Christians not to marry if they were single, and not to remarry if life situations had left them without a spouse. Paul thought that because it was such a short time until Christ's second coming, it would be best for all to give their undivided attention and time to the cause of Christ. To marry would divide their time and effort and distract them from the higher calling of God.

Later on Paul revised his thinking about this subject. When the end did not come as he anticipated, he gave greater emphasis to the family. He encouraged a spirit of love and respect between husbands and wives that parallels the relationship between Christ and the church (see Eph. 5:22-33).

Now that centuries have come and gone, each with its predictions of "the end," what is our word to the people of the last decade of the twentieth century? For me there is no better answer than the words Jesus left with the disciples as he prepared them for his own death: "Love one another." There is no greater need and no greater power to solve the world's ills than genuine selfless love.

Love feeds the hungry and clothes the poor. Love heals the ills that lead families to self-destruction. At its very best love causes enemies to become friends, wars to cease, and peace to reign. Love reaches out, lifts up, strengthens the weakened spirit, and fills life with joy. Love never loses its power, for the more it is applied to life the more effective it becomes. I do not know when Christ shall return, but until he does, let us love one another.

Prayer: *Teach us the power of your love, O Lord. Help us love more, for the days of loving are so good. Amen.*

THE WORD OF TRUTH

January 28–February 3, 1991　　**Sr. Barbara Jean, S.H.N.**†
Monday, January 28　　　　　　Read Psalm 111:7-8.

The lessons this week focus on *truth* and *trust*. Each reading points, in some manner, to an aspect of truth as it relates to God's handiwork and our participation in it. Also, it directs our attention to the need to trust in that truth. Trust comes from a recognition that God and God's word are reliable and constant. Our foundational faith is endorsed by the conviction that we can believe the revelation of the God of Abraham, Isaac, and Jacob.

Psalm 111 is one of the acrostic poems of scripture, in which each line, from the beginning to the end, is set in alphabetical order according to the Hebrew alphabet. In this psalm the past mercies of Yahweh are displayed and assurance is given that God fulfills his promises. God's actions are sound and God's commands are stable and profitable directions for living. One of the poet's techniques to make this point is not only to enumerate all of God's wonderful works but also to draw the picture from "A" to "Z." Nothing is left hanging in the balance.

Certainly trust rests not only on the mercies of God but upon the assurance that punishment will be rendered against those who persistently refuse to follow God's directions. This punishment, rather than being a malicious act of retribution, will come as a logical consequence of unrighteous living, of going contrary to God's intent for humanity.

Suggestion for meditation: *Think about how trust manifests itself in your own life. Where has trust broken down, and in what circumstances has it been strengthened? Which attributes or actions of God have you personally experienced as trustworthy and true?*

---

†Anglican Religious of the Sisterhood of the Holy Nativity, Fond du Lac, Wisconsin.

Tuesday, January 29   Read Deuteronomy 18:15-20.

As one of God's clearest promises of the sending of a messiah, this passage was used by the early church to substantiate its claim of Jesus as the final voice, through whom God chose to reveal himself. The weight of this claim carried profound responsibility, not only on the part of the prophet himself but also on those who accepted the prophet's word as God's word.

Any prophet was subject to skepticism. The prophet's messages bore their truth usually only after the test of time. But if a prophet was discovered to have pronounced a false word or prophesied under false pretenses, he was immediately denounced and most often put to death. Who would dare misrepresent the word of the Lord? To do so was not only to dishonor the prophet's profession but to malign the God he served and to discount the reality of truth itself. Such was a blasphemy unthinkable to the devout Jew. Truth and God were inseparable.

Just as people today seek to know their future, so too did the people of Israel. The writer of Deuteronomy sought to dispel the clamoring after the disgusting practices of some in favor of following instead the One whose directives could be trusted. Since oracles of God were not merely arbitrary pronouncements, only God could choose the instrument fit to carry the divine messages. The import of God's self-revelation could not be left to the common soothsayer.

The prime consideration of this passage was that God would not leave his people without a mediator between himself and them. The mediator was to point out the divine life as it touched human history. Therefore God promised a prophet of the same sort as Moses, from among ordinary folk. That prophet could be trusted because the prophet's words would be God's own.

Prayer: *Grant, Almighty God, that we may receive your word into our hearts. Inspire in us truth to the glory of your name. Amen.*

Wednesday, January 30   Read 1 Corinthians 8:1-3.

"Knowledge puffs up, but love builds up." An important aspect of trust is the love upon which it is built and in which it abides. We have often heard the phrase "a little knowledge is a dangerous thing." A little knowledge, in this context, is an accumulation of facts which dangle loosely in one's mind instead of being anchored firmly in love. Who can trust in bits of information not grounded in the heart of God, who is love? Being anchored in God's heart suggests that knowledge acquires a sense of reliability associated with truth.

In Paul's theology, a primary thesis revolves around our being known to God or by God. According to Paul, it is only from this stance that the Christian is able to make any claim for true knowledge. This thesis resonates with the same discernment as that which is stated in First John 4:19: "We love, because [God] first loved us." All that we know, all that we think, and all that we do must be rooted and grounded in this understanding. For the Christian, the insight which comes with love works to transform knowledge into wisdom. And we know that the pinnacle of wisdom is the *mysterium tremendum* (fear) of the Lord.

Paul told another group of Christians to speak the truth in love (see Eph. 4:15). We must strive to develop the sensitivity to know how much of the truth to speak and when to speak it. We might look upon today's passage as a premise of Paul's instruction to the church at Ephesus. We might conceive of Paul speaking this way: "Since mere knowledge fosters conceit and love edifies, always speak what you know with loving concern." To use our knowledge in the manner befitting our covenant relationship with God, we must cultivate a spirit of charity.

Suggestion for meditation: *Consider how you may have used information to promote your own cause without considering the larger picture. How would charity have spoken to that circumstance?*

Thursday, January 31   Read 1 Corinthians 8:4-6.

In examining the controversy concerning whether or not a Christian could consciously partake of food consecrated to idols, we are presented with an illustration of how knowledge and love must work in mutuality. Paul assented to the fact that idols had no true existence, so in reality there were no occasions in which eating such foods constituted sinful action. We may be rather confident of Paul's legalistic mentality, that he would have left no circumstance in question on this matter. He went on to conclude, however, that to act only in accord with such enlightened intelligence was a grave mistake. A person must be motivated by charity, not merely knowledge, having consideration for those who had not benefited by enlightened thinking. To act contrary to charity might do spiritual harm to those others.

For Paul, truth reached its culmination in Christ. In this letter, he suggested that our knowledge of truth is enhanced within us as we become able to discern Christ's presence in all of creation. Once it is discerned, homage and obedience are rendered by the Christian toward God, whose lordship is disclosed in the Son. As the Christian then cooperates with the message of the gospel, the laws of charity take precedence and are lived out in the daily struggles of humanity. The question of food offered to idols was one such struggle, certainly not to be minimized by the church. The work of the people of God, according to Paul, was to lead people into truth, by the path of love, using means as were made available to them. One of those means was the consideration of another's conscience. This can be no less important for us today.

Prayer: *God, grant that I may know you to be the way, the truth, and the life. Open my eyes and my heart to the love you desire for those whose knowledge of you is dim, that I may offer them stepping stones instead of stumbling blocks on their way. Amen.*

Friday, February 1   Read Psalm 111:2-3.

The concept of "truth," in Hebrew, was not concerned as often with "falsehood" as it was with "fickleness." As a noun, truth (*emeth*) held a close connection with the verb "to sustain" or "to support" (*aman*). Contained within this view resided an understanding of truth as the manifestation of God's life, particularly in the world. The most important word in Hebrew sentences is most often the verb, rather than the noun. Action takes precedence over object.

The gods of pagan cultures were always characterized by their various behaviors, and the same could be said of the God of the Hebrews. A major expression of God's behavior was faithfulness. *Emeth*, translated "truth," could just as easily have been translated "fidelity." God, by his own expressed nature, would not prove fickle. God would not act in a manner opposed to that which he had revealed about himself.

The pagan gods, on the other hand, left considerable room for doubt and conjecture in their worshipers. Their behavior could not be relied upon and left their followers anxious or apprehensive about future theophanies. Just what would the gods do next? But God, while being outside the realm of human control or predictability, could be completely trusted to act, to behave, as promised. Was God merciful? Then God would act with mercy. Was God vengeful? Then God would wreak vengeance. God's commands were clearly revealed and God's word clearly spoken. What we all are ultimately left with is an ineffable mystery which transcends earthly concepts of divine being and purpose. Come what may, God is God, and God can be trusted.

Suggestion for meditation: *Consider the various qualities or behaviors you know about God from scripture. Choose one of them and remember the times in your own life that particular behavior was made evident to you.*

Saturday, February 2   Read Mark 1:21-22.

"And they were astonished at his teaching. . . ." The first recorded miracle and "official" teaching, according to the Gospels of Mark and Luke, were done on the sabbath, in a small Galilean town. The people in the synagogue were accustomed to itinerant preachers, but on this particular occasion something strange and different reached their ears. A note of authority, the like of which they had never heard, met them and challenged them from the "pulpit" of their own congregation.

Jesus did not teach as the scribes did. Their teaching was nothing more than the recitation of others' opinions, others' scholarship. Their religious jurisdiction was derived from previous scholars. If their personal opinions were stated at all, they were given without confidence or conviction at the end of their instruction. Jesus astounded his hearers. He spoke from the depths of his own wisdom, from his own personal resources.

The people were "astonished." In Greek, the word *astonished* (*exeplaysonto*) is a compound word which brings together three words whose meanings are "to strike," "out of" and "at." Possible interpretations might then be rendered in two ways: It meant either that the people vehemently pushed away from themselves the teaching of Jesus or that they were so excited they came out of their self-possessed attitudes to accept what they heard with joy.

Jesus not only refrained from using other sources to substantiate his teaching, he also went beyond the injunction of the prophets, who usually began their testimony with "thus saith the Lord." Jesus spoke out of his own authority. Who but the Son of God could take such prerogatives? Again, we are compelled to focus on the truth, which in this amazing instance dwelt bodily in the life of the itinerant preacher from Nazareth.

Prayer: *Come down, O Love Divine, and astonish me with the power of your word. Amen.*

Sunday, February 3   Read Mark 1:26-27.

"A new teaching!" With authority Jesus commanded the demon, the unclean spirit, to come out of the possessed man, and then silenced it. The idea conveyed in the word *new* projected a meaning of "freshness of quality." The exorcisms which people were used to hearing were trite formulas which had become worn-out and ineffectual. When Jesus spoke, however, so much power and authority went forth from him that people could not but respond in amazement.

Jesus backed his teaching with a demonstration of his divine right to speak in this way. If his authority were not from God, how was it that evil spirits cowered in obeisance? The spirit world needed no proofs of Jesus' true identity. It recognized him immediately and spoke vocatively when confronted by him.

Amazing as this situation was, it did not establish solidarity among the witnesses. As suggested in yesterday's meditation, it possibly sharpened the division between people. Most often a new doctrine splits people into camps: those opposed and those in favor. Problems can then arise on either side of an issue because of the propensity people have for taking a "hard party line" stance. Once that happens, communication breaks down and truth is suppressed. Who will hear the truth in its pureness when the "body politic" begins to vocalize?

It is a problem still unsolved, still plaguing the church. Each doctrine, each issue brought before the Body of Christ becomes a controversy which clouds the truth. Controversy juggles opinions, pro and con, and in such instability it becomes difficult to know whom or what to trust. Only as we strip away the vestige of popular opinions and center ourselves in the Word, in Christ, will we come to a deeper understanding of the truth.

Prayer: *Free us, Lord, from the tendency to follow every wind of doctrine. Establish in us your truth and your love. Amen.*

TRANSFIGURATION

February 4-10, 1991   **Gary Chamberlain†**
Monday, February 4   Read 2 Corinthians 4:3-6.

What is it that Christians know, that is unknown to those who are perishing and unfaithful? Despite the claims of this passage, many people (including many church people) would not agree that there is anything special about Christian faith. It seems arrogant and old-fashioned even to think of "unfaithful" and "perishing" as the same thing. Don't we all know unchurched people, people of other religions, perhaps even people with no religion, who are as upright, generous, and wise as the best Christians? Such people as Mahatma Gandhi come to mind. And on the other side, do we not hear of people who claim Christian faith, yet their conduct, insight, and emotional stability are far below our expectations? Haven't we all read about serial killers who claimed to be acting on orders from God?

Paul, in his letters to the Corinthians, is trying to undo some false ideas of Christian wisdom and superiority, by which he himself is judged inadequate by his own church. But Paul is not even trying to answer the questions as we have posed them. There is no "what" that only Christians know. There is only Jesus Christ, "the likeness of God," a *person* and not an idea. Faith is neither a concept nor a rule of conduct, but a relationship, within which Paul found that his whole previous life seemed like death. Christ's cross **manifests** who God is, and who we are intended to be.

Prayer: *God, we seek from the scripture, today and every day, not rules or ideas, but you yourself. Do not hide your face from us. Give us life in your presence, through Jesus our Lord. Amen.*

---

†Pastor, Trinity United Methodist Church, Waverly, Iowa.

Tuesday, February 5   Read 2 Kings 2:1-7.

When we tell a story that has three parts, especially when the second part is a repetition of the first, there are two possible outcomes. The third part of the story can repeat the first and second. When that happens, we know that nothing is going to change, and the pattern is set. For example, three times Balaam is sent out to curse the Israelites, and three times he blesses them instead, so Balak knows that Balaam will never do what Balak hired him to do (Numbers 22–24). In the second possible outcome, the third part of the story can differ from the other two. For example: Jesus' parable of the good Samaritan (Luke 10:29-37).

In Second Kings, both things happen. Three times Elijah tells Elisha to stay behind while Elijah goes to another place, and three times Elisha swears never to leave his master. "So the two went on." So we know that Elisha is bound to Elijah, and will keep his oath. Twice the "sons of the prophets" (that is, apprentices who are learning to be prophets) come out to meet Elisha, to tell him that Elijah will leave him on that day. The third time, a large group comes and stands at a distance. These people are not going to inform Elisha of anything (especially something he already knows); they have a different function. As they stand back, that function can only be that they will be observers, witnesses to the departure of Elijah.

This story is not simply about Elijah's departure. The whole structure builds our suspense about what will happen *to his companion,* to Elisha. Will God be **manifest** through him? So far we know only one thing, but it is crucial. God will deal with Elisha, as with us, *in community*—in relation to Elisha's faithful love for Elijah, and in relation to their faithful witnesses.

Prayer: *Lord, keep me faithful to others, and keep others faithful to me, that together we may see how your love will be given to us. Amen.*

Wednesday, February 6   Read 2 Kings 2:8-15.

Now we see how God deals with Elisha. His faithfulness to his master Elijah, and the faithfulness of his own followers to him, led to the vision of Elijah's departure, and to the manifestation of God's faithfulness to Elisha who is left behind. Now we see for the first time who Elijah really is—he is someone who is so close to God that he does not die, but is taken directly into God's presence. Only to one other person—Enoch—does such a thing happen (see Gen. 5:18-24).

Elisha is no different from Elijah! Elisha is also acknowledged by God as a man not only of faithfulness but of power, fit to wear Elijah's mantle, able to do Elijah's deeds. He has a double portion of Elijah's spirit. This was the gift that Elijah could not give, though he could name the sign by which the gift would be known.

Because he did not die, Elijah becomes an important figure in Jewish hope and expectation. We will see how he figures in the transfiguration of Jesus. He is also central to the celebration of Passover. During this festival, an extra place is set for him in every home, and the youngest person at the feast is sent to the door to see if Elijah has come. If he has, then the Age of the Messiah is here! If not, then the family will close the feast with the hope and prayer, "Next year in Jerusalem!"

But even without Elijah, God has not abandoned us. We have seen God's power in Elijah's disciple. We have seen it in our own faithful communities. We have seen it in one another, for *you* are, in the power of *your* prayer, like Elijah (see James 5:16-18). When our prayer and hope arise out of faithful community, then like Elisha we see God **manifested** in our own experience.

Prayer: *Lord, make us faithful friends and witnesses, seeing your power in each other. Through Christ our Lord. Amen.*

Thursday, February 7   Read Mark 9:1-5.

This is the moment when the primary apostles see Jesus as he will appear after his resurrection. They see him clothed in light, his garments radiant with a whiteness unattainable by earthly means. They see him in relation to the two greatest men of ancient Israel, and in relation to the traditions of the Torah and the prophets for which they stand. In short, they see Jesus as God sees him, as the true Messiah.

From time to time, for all of us, come those revelatory moments, when we *see* someone for the first time. It may be our spouse, or a friend, or a stranger. Some crucial aspect of that person's identity and purpose, how he or she fits into God's plan, breaks through, and we wonder how we could have missed seeing how deeply God is **manifested** in him or her. In short, we catch a glimpse of how God sees the other person. And then we face a choice. We can surrender our own desires and wishes about this person, surrender our claims that he or she should meet our needs as we define them, and let him or her delight in God's way of meeting our true needs. Or we can keep our own egos at the center, try to direct the divine drama in accord with *our* version of reality, assume that this "breakthrough" or "insight" marks us as superior spiritual beings, and treasure the experience for the good feelings we can draw from it.

Peter wanted to memorialize the experience, to make monuments to the wonderful moment. He didn't know what he was saying, because he was afraid to surrender his false ideas of the Messiah who would be triumphant on *his* terms. James and John continued to nurture false hopes for their own glory aiming to sit at Jesus' right and left on splendid thrones (see Mark 10:37).

Prayer: *Lord, claim us with your vision, and let us set each other free. Let us see ourselves and you more truly. Amen.*

Friday, February 8   Read Mark 9:6-9.

Here the vision finds clarification through the Word of God. What is God's purpose for this experience, that contradicts Peter's intention to build a memorial of it? The voice from the cloud declares: "This is my dear Son; listen to him." God's command is that the insight of the disciples should result in obedience and trust. And that is Mark's aim in telling the story.

Already in Mark, Jesus has tried to teach the disciples about his coming suffering and death, and he will try twice more (see 8:31, 9:31, 10:33-34). The third attempt is followed at once with the request of James and John that they should sit at Christ's right and left in his glory. The disciples never do understand, and in Mark, they flee at Jesus' arrest. The only exception is Peter, who stays around long enough to deny his Lord three times over— once for each time he refused to hear that Jesus would suffer and die and wanted his disciples to take up their own cross.

But we are in a different position. We have the word of Mark's Gospel and Christ's vindication in being raised from the dead. Mark does not want us to make the same mistakes as Peter, James, John, and the others did. We, too, have had "transfiguration" insights, knowing Christ as God's Son, as the **manifestation** of God's will for us. We have seen one another, from time to time, as God's children and as instruments of the gospel. We have had our own "mountaintop" experiences. And Mark does not want them wasted! Every time we fail to translate vision into obedience, everytime we flee suffering and surrender, we have missed the point. The transfiguration shows us who Jesus is, but it *tells* us who we are—God's needy people.

Prayer: *Dear Lord, fulfill our visions through your clarifying word, that every high moment may deepen our obedience and trust, and that we may truly be yours. In Christ we pray. Amen.*

Saturday, February 9   Read Psalm 50:1-6.

The Psalms are different from the rest of scripture. They are not generally to be used as texts for preaching but as the prayerful *response* to the word of God we hear in the other texts. That is why we read them responsively, and why it is even better if we learn to sing them. They were, from the beginning, songs and hymns, intended as prayers to be chanted by the whole congregation. This means that they are not only God's word to us but the word intended for our use in addressing our Lord.

Despite so much in the Psalms that seems "wrong," the complaints and prayers for vengeance and protestations of innocence, we need to learn that our idea of prayer may not be God's idea. The Psalms teach us to pray with forthright honesty, even when such honesty is childish, fearful, or even spiteful. Apparently, when we have to choose between being mature and being truthful, God would rather we were truthful. So we *hear* God's word to us in all of scripture, but we *speak* God's word, the words God teaches us for prayer, in the Psalms.

How then is this psalm a prayerful response to the readings for this week? It is most directly a response to the Old Testament reading, in which Elijah is taken up and Elisha becomes his successor. We are reminded of the promise in Deuteronomy 18:15-18, that God will always raise up a prophet, so that no generation will be without someone to speak God's living word.

So the psalm declares that when God is **manifested** in perfect beauty, in fire, in the witness of creation, in judgment, the purpose is always the same—God is claiming an obedient people and will vindicate and sustain them against all the powers of death, evil, and despair.

Prayer: *God, let us hear your word to us, and let us dare to live in the confidence of your sustaining power. Amen.*

Sunday, February 10   Read Mark 9:1-9.

With the story of Christ's transfiguration, we close the season of Epiphany and are ready for Lent. As an Epiphany story, the transfiguration is a **manifestation** (Greek: *epiphaneia*) of Christ's identity. The season opens with the coming of the Wise Men, to whom Christ is manifest as the Savior of the nations. The season closes with the transfiguration, when the disciples catch a glimpse of the glory that will mark the risen Lord. So transfiguration prepares us for Lent, for the suffering and death of Jesus. Since we know Christ as the true manifestation of God, his cross must not be seen as an accident or a failure; it is the chosen and fitting way of manifesting God's love and power.

Transfiguration is also a revelation of who *we* are, for "when he appears we shall be like him, for we shall see him as he is" (1 John 3:2). In other words, this story is not simply about the revelation of Jesus as a manifestation of God; it is also a manifestation of our true humanity. Other stories—Elijah, Moses on Sinai, Moses' shining face—are Old Testament precedents for this story. The appearance of Moses and Elijah with Jesus reminds us that God's reign in Christ means a transformed *humanity*.

Hence the story of Christ's transfiguration, and the other readings this week, invite us to test our experience by the word in scripture and by Christ, the Word incarnate. Our visions are to issue in deeper obedience and trust. Epiphany is to be disciplined by Lent, so that the nature of God may be **manifest** not only *to* us, but also *through* us. God has saved us through Christ, so that we may be an invitation to salvation for the world.

Prayer: *Dear God, at this intersection of vision and suffering, of empowerment and surrender, make us manifestations of your love, through Jesus Christ our Lord. Amen.*

LIVING A HOLY LENT

February 11-17, 1991   **Elizabeth Canham, Obl. O.H.C.†**
Monday, February 11   Read Mark 1:9-15.

Mark leaves us almost breathless as he begins to tell the good news of Jesus Christ. Right after the advent of John the Baptist, Jesus appears on the scene, is baptized, and hears the divine voice proclaiming him God's beloved Son. Then Jesus is driven into the wilderness by the Spirit. The Greek word *ekballei* indicates a forceful expelling or casting forth into that desolate place where temptation abounds.

The desert is an important image for us as we begin our journey through Lent. Traditionally it has been a place of profound encounter with the living God, a place of revelation and call to action. Moses experienced the numinous presence of God at the bush that burned in the desert. The long wanderings of God's people through the wilderness under his leadership enabled them to discover the faithfulness of God through hunger, weariness, and waiting. Amos heard God's call in the desert of Tekoa, and John the Baptist's compelling message was forged in the barren wilderness around the Dead Sea.

God's invitation to us at this season is to follow Christ into a desert place where we can be still enough to know who we are. In the quiet emptiness, fearful though it may seem, there is a gift we can receive. The Spirit who drives us out also speaks into the silence, telling us we are beloved children and strengthening us to withstand the demons of fear that try to haunt us.

Suggestion for meditation: *Take some time each day to be silent in God's presence, listening for the Word who tells you who you are.*

---

†Episcopal priest, program director, Holy Savior Priory, Pineville, South Carolina.

Tuesday, February 12   Read Psalm 25:1-10.

This psalm, attributed to David, begins with a plea that God will grant victory over enemies. The human enemies David encountered were real and many. But like us, David also had to deal with fear, lust, infidelity, pride, and selfishness. In this psalm he prays for understanding of God's way, God's truth, and asks for mercy as he recalls youthful unfaithfulness. In these verses David sets a pattern for our own prayers.

In the silence of the desert we know, as Jesus knew, the good news about ourselves. We are created in God's image, we are designated children, and we are loved. But we also encounter our shadow in the desert. When the usual distractions and busyness are left behind, we remember the moments when we turned from God's way. The times of denial, half-truth, lack of discipline and faithfulness reenter our consciousness. At those moments the demon of despair is ready to attack us, telling us we are worthless and encouraging us to give up the struggle to be the people God created us to be. This is when we need to wait humbly in God's presence (Ps. 25:5), owning our infidelity, and trusting in the steadfast love and faithfulness of our God who restores us to life.

One of the surest ways to dispel our enemies is to name them. In Hebrew thought, to name persons (or demons) meant to have power over them. As we recognize who our attackers are and speak their names, recognizing the temptations they place before us, we rob them of their power over us. In that powerful desert wrestling, God gives us courage, victory, and strength to go on.

Prayer: *Make me know your ways, O God. Teach me your paths and give me victory over all that would deflect me from your will. Amen.*

February 13 (Ash Wednesday)
Read Joel 2:1-2, 12-17*a*.

In Israel and Judah the prophetic voice was frequently raised against complacency and trust in the externals of religious duty. The prophets called for a continuous, inner conversion of life that manifested itself in compassion, justice, and concern for the poor. Joel judges feasts and elaborate worship to be worthless and predicts that the "day of the LORD" will be one of gloom and darkness for those who refuse to fashion their lives after the commandments of a righteous God. Joel sees that it is time for God's people to acknowledge publicly their sin, call to the Lord for mercy, and change their lives.

Today many of us will wear the ashes that remind us of our mortality and of our call to live as God's people. We receive them as a sign of our willingness to amend our lives as we experience the loving acceptance and forgiveness of God. But beyond our personal sins, we hear a call to recognize our corporate responsibility for all that is amiss in church and society. The prophet Joel invites us to return to God, who is gracious and merciful. In that returning we rediscover our mission.

When God created the world and humankind in the divine image, God thought everything that was made "was very good." Our task, as the community of the New Covenant, is to so live our lives that God can go on pronouncing the goodness of all that is. As we reach out to poor, marginalized people, as we work together for peace and justice, God says, "It is good!" As we recognize our responsibility for the environment and our call to inclusiveness, and as we give ourselves to the needs of those who are abused and exploited, God says, "It is good!"

Prayer: *Living God, reveal our carelessness, show us where we must act to bring hope, and strengthen our resolve to work for justice and peace. Amen.*

Thursday, February 14   Read Psalm 51.

"Whoever wishes to repent should scrutinize the deeds of David."* David was not perfect, but he was willing to hear God's judgment on his shortcomings, own his sin, and seek forgiveness. Psalm 51 is traditionally associated with David's repentance following his adultery with Bathsheba and the death of her husband, after the prophet Nathan confronted him with his sin. The psalm reveals David at his best and at his worst.

True repentance comes only when we know ourselves and are willing to deal with the mixture of good and bad that makes up our lives. Like David, we are a composite of integrity, honesty, and desire for God and of fearful yielding to self-interest and greed. God does not invite a groveling, breast-beating confession of our worthlessness that fails to recognize that we bear the divine image. Rather, God calls us to celebrate who we are—children of a loving Creator—and to come home with open-hearted sorrow when we violate the trust God places in us.

Living a holy Lent means living with a sense of wonder. We wonder at the imagination of God who made us, loves us, and trusts us with the joyful responsibility of sharing this good news. We wonder at our own capacity for life, for being agents of compassion, and for manifesting the divine love in the world. Each time we catch ourselves being pulled into a prideful, selfish response to life, we turn again to the One who loves, forgives, and empowers us to go on with hope.

Suggestion for prayer: *For centuries the Christian mantra known as the "Jesus prayer" has helped people to be mindful of God's love for sinners. Try using it as part of your own prayer, repeating the words over and over until you establish a prayer rhythm. "Lord Jesus Christ, Son of God, have mercy on me, a sinner."*

---

*From the *Midrash*.

Friday, February 15   Read 2 Corinthians 5:20–6:2.

Paul is the only New Testament writer who uses the word *reconciliation* to describe the work of Jesus Christ in bringing about a new relationship between God and humankind. We all know the need for reconciliation between nations, churches, and in human relationships where conversation has broken down. Here Paul appeals to us to be reconciled to God—to deal with the things that have caused a breakdown in our relationship with the Creator—and to become agents of reconciliation in a hurting world.

There is a major difference, however, between many of the attempts at reconciliation in society and the kind of relationships between God and persons that Paul envisions. Much negotiation is required in international relationships, litigation, and even in the interface between Christian denominations. Our reconciliation to God is non-negotiable: Christ has done all that is necessary to effect the new relationship. We come simply with the words "I am sorry," not pleading mitigating circumstances or asking for concessions but owning the painful truth of our unfaithfulness. The honest naming of our denial of God's love is met with the embrace of forgiveness and acceptance on the part of the Creator who gave us life and made us children.

As Christian believers we are also ambassadors, sent in Christ's name to draw others, now distant from God, into intimacy. We joyfully proclaim the reconciliation made possible through Christ, announcing that *now* is the moment when life can be transformed through forgiveness and grace.

Devotional exercise: *Take time to recall one person who needs to hear the good news of God's love and healing. Consider how you may be an agent of reconciliation in that person's life.*

Saturday, February 16 Read Matthew 6:1-6, 16.

> Things are seldom what they seem,
> Skim milk masquerades as cream.*

Jesus paints an outrageous caricature in Matthew 6 in order to expose the "skim milk" of a piety practiced to attract notice by others. This kind of piety may look like the real thing, may appear to be rich in self-denial, but it is a tasteless version of religion. This kind of prayer and fasting has more to do with self-interest than with honoring God and growing in faith.

The power of caricature lies in the grain of truth it magnifies. Few of us would literally hire a trumpet player to announce our generosity to the world. But there are more subtle ways of letting others know how good we are, and we might be tempted to use these ways. Telling the story of some "needy" person may be done in such a way that it becomes an advertisement for our giving of help. Saying someone "needs our prayers" because he or she is involved in some morally unacceptable activity may give us feelings of great moral uprightness and show others where we stand on such issues. Whether there is any real prayer offered, on our part or by others, is questionable.

Jesus calls us to be real. Give anonymously, because as you receive from the fullness of God's grace, you realize how much you have that can enrich others. Pray, because in the secret place where you are alone with the Creator, you can bring to God all concerns about others without embarrassing them or getting caught up in impressing people. Fast, because in those moments of self-denal you give space for the love of God to take hold of you and to sharpen your vision of a world that needs your care.

Prayer: *Loving God, help us root out the bits of unreality that choke our discipleship, and live lives rich in blessing for the world. Amen.*

---

*William Schwenck Gilbert, *H.M.S. Pinafore*, act II.

Sunday, February 17   Read 1 Peter 3:18-22.

Our baptism as Christian believers signifies our incorporation into the covenant community established through the death and resurrection of Jesus Christ. The promises we make—or which are made for us as infants and confirmed later—call us to discipleship and new life. We have been brought to God and, as members of Christ, we share his victory over death and all evil powers.

In the early church during the season of Lent, converts to the faith were prepared for baptism. At that time, believers who had been excluded from the fellowship because of notorious sin were made ready for restoration following penitence and forgiveness. For many, this time in the liturgical year served as a reminder of the part confession and forgiveness play in the life of discipleship. We continue to observe this time in the church's calendar because it reminds us of the costliness of our redemption, it inspires our gratitude, and it moves us to more holy living.

The Episcopal *Book of Common Prayer* contains this invitation in the Liturgy for Ash Wednesday:

I invite you . . . in the name of the Church, to the observance of a holy Lent, by self-examination and repentance; by prayer, fasting, and self-denial; and by reading and meditating on God's holy Word. . . .

Lent is God's gift to us. We approach it not as a burden but as an opportunity to enter more deeply into the richness of our inheritance as children of the New Covenant.

Prayer: *Gracious God, open our eyes to see the truth about ourselves; open our ears to hear your word; open our hearts to repent of our sin and love you; and open our lips that we may share your joy with all people. Amen.*

GOING DEEPER

February 18-24, 1991   **William Moremen†**
Monday, February 18   Read Genesis 17:1-4.

Going more deeply into our vocation

Our Bible passage makes it humorously clear that age is not a barrier to going more deeply into an awareness of our vocation. Abram, we are told, was ninety-nine and his wife Sarai ninety when deeper intimations of God's call came to them.

Whatever our age, whatever our occupation, we have the possibility of opening our hearts to a more penetrating sense of vocation. Vocation means an intimation of a call, a lure, a beckoning from the deeper currents of life: our own life and the time of history in which we live.

Our scripture makes it sound as if the call to Abram and Sarai was clear and decisive. We know, however, that this passage was written long after the experience. Perhaps at first, Abram and Sarai felt the need simply to go more deeply into the question: to listen, to ponder, to discern, to risk. According to our scripture, the central part of this experience was the sense of God's presence. In the experience of God's presence, lives are changed and the future unfolds.

As we live into God's presence a covenant takes form. A covenant is a dialogue of wills in which God's loving intention is offered, and in our own heart a willingness emerges to follow the deeper current.

Suggestion for meditation: *Sit quietly and gradually relax. Ponder the question: To what is God inviting me at this time in my life?*

---

†Minister, Eden United Church of Christ; staff member, Pacific Center for Spiritual Formation, Hayward, California.

Tuesday, February 19   Read Genesis 17:5, 15-16.

Going more deeply into our self-identity

According to the biblical storyteller, Abram's and Sarai's names got changed to Abraham and Sarah. Scholars tell us that there is not a significant difference in meaning in the two forms of the names. Perhaps the storyteller felt that as Abram and Sarai understood more deeply their vocation, new names were called for. Perhaps it is an echo of the practice of naming a child at circumcision—a ritual sign of entering into covenant.

When we ponder the meaning of our own lives at greater depth, or when we see a change in direction, there is often a shift in self-identity. We are not the same persons we were. Sometimes we feel that a new name or a new version of our name would better express the new person coming into being. Someone might say, "Don't call me 'Bill' anymore, call me 'Will' or 'William.'" Or someone might say, "Don't call me 'Debbi' anymore, call me 'Deborah.'" Sometimes we may discover an even more obscure name that might go along with our new self-identity—a name known only deep within the soul, or known only to God.

At times we are not clear about our self-identity; we question and wait for a more profound level of understanding. But, as our self-identity comes to be grounded in God, we may be able to voice a new name, or it may remain silent within.

Suggestion for meditation: *Sit quietly and listen within. Turn your attention to your heart and ask, "What is my true name?" Don't be afraid if you hear only silence. Know that your name is hidden in the love of God.*

Prayer: *God of Abraham and Sarah, keep my mind open to the changes you bring me. May I not be afraid but rather learn to embrace the new me that your ever-exciting creative power can bring. Amen.*

Wednesday, February 20   Read Genesis 17:6-8.

Going more deeply into our generativity

Abraham and Sarah were called not only to a more profound understanding of their vocation and self-identity, they were called also to let their deepened life expand so that it might have an effect on many others, including later generations.

Being true to one's own self-identity as it deepens in God is like planting a seed in rich soil. The seed grows and becomes fruitful for others. The lives of Abraham and Sarah had enormous influence on countless generations. Their lives are having an impact on us today as we read their story.

Our own influence will likely not be as far-reaching as that of Abraham and Sarah. But if we are true to our own vocation and identity in God, we will have an influence. Like the sound of your voice, which generates sound waves that spread out through time and space, so your life in God sounds its authenticity to others and makes a difference.

At times we may wonder whether our lives count for anything or will ever count for anything. At other times we feel more confident and hopeful. Whatever our mood, there is only one essential thing to do: go ever more deeply into God's life as it moves in our life. If we do, in some way, known or unknown to us, God's generativity will move through us to others.

Suggestion for meditation: *Sit quietly and relax. Have the awareness that God is planting a seed of divine purpose and intention deep within you. Contemplate the mystery of how that seed may have an influence on others. Conclude your meditation with the speaking or chanting of a single word. Sense the sound waves of that word going out beyond you.*

Prayer: *Loving God, keep me honest with myself and my true beliefs. Give me courage to stand with integrity as I live out my faith among those others with whom I share this life. Bless the relationships I have with other people, that they may reflect your image and will. Amen.*

Thursday, February 21   Read Genesis 17:15-19.

Going more deeply into our sense of humor

Abraham laughed heartily. He laughed so hard he fell on his face laughing. At other places in the story we read that Sarah also laughed (see Genesis 18:12 and 21:6). As we become more clear about our vocation, identity, and generativity in God, we are bound to be struck at times with the humor of it all. Abraham and Sarah laughed at the preposterousness of their having off-spring at their advanced ages. The storyteller probably exaggerated to make a point. We get the point. Some of the intimations of God's purposes in our own lives seem preposterous. We look at our own limitations and wonder how God could possibly fulfill an important intention with us. Sometimes we shake our heads and smile. Sometimes we laugh out loud.

Laughter has its value. For one thing it feels a great deal better than worry, doubt, or resistance. Laughter lightens things up. Laughter is healing. In laughter there is a seed of belief. You have to entertain the possibility that you are God's instrument in order to see the humor of that proposition. "What?" I say. "You want to use me with all my weaknesses and limitations to advance your purpose? That is laughable!" But laughter that is a response to God echoes out into the universe and returns with an affirmation. "Yes, this is what I have in mind for you—trust!"

Suggestion for meditation: *Sit quietly and get in touch with an intimation of God's purpose in your life. Explore possibilities and potential outcomes. Knowing your limitations, feel the humor of that consideration. Smile! Laugh!*

Prayer: *Laughing God, help me learn to laugh with you and not to take myself so seriously that I miss out on the great power you put within me, even amidst the weaknesses that are a part of my human nature. Teach me that you can use me for your purposes regardless of how laughable it may seem to me at the time. Amen.*

Friday, February 22   Read Psalm 105:1-11.

Going more deeply into our heritage

As we try to live into God's purposes for our lives, we can benefit by being part of a community that has a rich heritage of faith. Psalm 105, written many centuries after the time of Abraham and Sarah, is a hymn of praise sung by a worshiping congregation. As people met together, they were encouraged by their faith tradition to seek God's help and strength and to worship God continually. They were encouraged by the psalm to remember their faith history, to remember how God had acted in their lives in the past, not only in their own personal past but in the collective past of the community of faith. The people who joined in worship were encouraged by the words of the psalm to remember that they were offspring of Abraham and Sarah, and part of an ongoing covenant with God and one another.

As we go more deeply into our life with God, solitude is essential, but that does not mean we are alone. Ironically, the more we discover God's life within our own individual lives, the more we will know that we are part of a community and a great heritage of faith. We will find that we can draw inspiration from the story of such people as Abraham and Sarah, and that we are the living extension of God's intent that was generated through them. We belong to the family.

Suggestion for meditation: *Read Psalm 105 again. Read slowly and reflectively. Sense that you are part of a community that goes back in time and exists today. Spend time with words or phrases that speak especially to you, and join in spirit with the larger chorus that speaks and sings them.*

Prayer: *God of the ages, help me never forget that I am a part of the family of humankind. When I feel lost, remind me of my heritage—as a part of the church, as a part of the lives of those who love me, as a part of your family. Amen.*

Saturday, February 23   Read Romans 4:16-25.

Going more deeply into trust

In our deepening life with God we may experience times of doubt and distrust. Since God's life with us is a mystery, we may wonder sometimes if the mystery is truly God or simply emptiness. Further, we may wonder, *if* the mystery *is* God, does this God actually care, and does God care about each of us? And even if God cares about us, are we included in the creativity and purpose of God's work in the world?

We may experience doubt and distrust not only about God; we may experience these feelings about ourselves. Given my weaknesses and shortcomings, can God actually use me in any significant way?

The apostle Paul points to Abraham and Sarah to show us the kind of faith that is strengthened and not weakened by distrust and doubt (see Romans 4:20). Our scripture doesn't say that Abraham didn't experience doubt, just that it didn't cause him to waver and that he grew stronger in faith. If we have the courage to go deeply enough into our questions about self and God, we will find a level of faith that is deeper still. We will find the faith that God is present and the trust that God is able to do what is promised even through people like you and me.

Suggestion for meditation: *Sit quietly and relax. Ponder your vocation, your work, your purpose in life. Allow doubts and distrust to arise, if they are there in some corner of your mind or heart. Without trying to erase those feelings, quietly look more deeply to see whether there is another level of faith and trust.*

Prayer: *Faithful God, you know there are times when my faith weakens and my doubts become overwhelming. Help me remember that I need not be afraid of my doubts, that they can be a part of greater growth and maturity in my faith. Amen.*

Sunday, February 24 Read Mark 8:31-38.

Going more deeply into loss and the gift of new life

Abraham and Sarah stood to lose a great deal. They would give up their homeland, their old ways of belief, their old identities. They would let go of all this to follow an open road offered to them by God. Jesus taught his disciples that loss is an important principle for the discovery of new life (see Mark 8:35).

As we go more deeply into our awareness of God we find that we grow by letting go. We find much about ourselves that, from a new perspective, seems obsolete: habits, behaviors, ways of thinking. We must let these things go, lose them, in order to let the new life within us come more fully into being.

Hardest of all is to let go of what seems to be at the very center. We feel that at the center of our being is something solid, something we would call our self. But suppose I let go of that solid sense of self. At first it feels like a loss. Who am I, what am I, if not that self? At first this loss feels like emptiness. But if I go more deeply into that emptiness it begins to feel like an open-ness, a spaciousness that welcomes me into the presence of God. In losing self I find myself as a much more open being.

Suggestion for meditation: *In quiet reflection ask, Of what do I need to let go to be more open, more spacious, more able to welcome the presence of God? What is at the very center of my being? Is there a way I can let that go in order to be more open to new life?*

Prayer: *Dear God, I want you at the center of my life. When other powers push in to try to claim my allegiance, give me the courage to recognize them, the strength to fight them, and the wisdom to seek you at last. Amen.*

67

THE TWO COVENANTS

February 25–March 3, 1991   **Rosalind Marshall†**
Monday, February 25   Read Exodus 20:1-12.

The Israelites were terrified. Three months to the day after they left Egypt, they had entered the Desert of Sinai. And God had instructed Moses to tell them, "Now if you obey me fully and keep my covenant, then . . . you will be for me a kingdom of priests and a holy nation" (Exod. 19:5-6, NIV).

So for two days Moses had consecrated the people in preparation, and now it was the third day. Thunder and lightning split the air, smoke billowed up from the mountain, and a trumpet blasted louder and louder. The people watched, trembling.

Then this consuming fire who was God called Moses up the mountain into the dense cloud and gave him the covenant for the chosen people—the Ten Commandments. Moses wrote down everything the Lord told him, and read it to the Israelites. Then he took the blood from sacrificed bulls and sprinkled it on the altar and the people, saying, "This is the blood of the covenant that the LORD has made with you in accordance with all these words" (Exod. 24:8, NIV).

And God called Moses up again and said to him, "I will give you the tablets of stone, with the law and commands I have written for their instruction" (Exod. 24:12, NIV). These two tablets of stone were inscribed by the finger of God!

What a favored people! To no other nation had Yahweh made such a commitment. All he asked was the obedience of faith. They had experienced the miracles of Passover and of manna in the desert; surely they would continue to trust God.

Prayer: *God of Israel, call your chosen people back to yourself, and bless your holy land. Amen.*

---

†Writer, teacher of poetry workshops, Joseph, Oregon.

Tuesday, February 26   Read Exodus 20:13-17.

Moses stayed on the mountain forty days and forty nights. But while God was giving Moses detailed instructions for the tabernacle to be built, the people lost their attention span.

"Come," they pestered Aaron, "make us gods who will go before us. This fellow Moses has disappeared" (Exod. 32:1, NIV, AP). Apparently Aaron thought so, too; he took their gold earrings and made a calf idol of them. He even built an altar before it and proclaimed a festival to the Lord. Israel had a bacchanal, and it reached the ears of God. But when Moses saw the calf and the dancing, in a fury of despair he dashed the stone tablets to the rocks and broke them.

Only forty days had passed, and already these Hebrews had broken the covenant. They always would. This law, given to be a way of life, brought condemnation. The people were incapable of keeping it, being, as they were, without the Holy Spirit. So there must always be the blood sacrifices to bring forgiveness. There must always be the priesthood to administer the sacrifices. And there was always the sense of guilt. Like Esau, God's people were forever giving away their birthright.

How could God love them—a faithless, betraying, often evil people? As he loves us, through his Son. They looked ahead to Christ: "He [Moses] regarded disgrace for the sake of Christ as of greater value than the treasures of Egypt, because he was looking ahead to his reward" (Heb. 11:26, NIV).

We look back to the Incarnation, knowing (don't we?) that we are redeemed from the curse of the law (Gal. 3:13). Yet, too, we often walk in guilt, self-condemned because we insist on trying to live by laws and not by God's grace.

Prayer: *Jesus, do you get tired of our trying to earn your love, when you have already opened the sea for us? Help us trust your grace. Amen.*

Wednesday, February 27   Read Psalm 19:7-14.

What joy David found in the law! The law was the revealed word and will of God for the nation, and King David walked in the grace of its true intent. But he knew he was capable of great sin (vv. 12-13) and begged God to keep him from falling into it.

When his lust proved louder than the voice of conscience and he brought disaster upon his posterity through his marriage to Bathsheba, still David's intimate relationship with God enabled him to believe God could forgive him. "Have mercy on me, O God, according to your unfailing love," he cried in Psalm 51. "Create in me a pure heart, O God, and renew a steadfast spirit within me. Do not cast me from your presence or take your Holy Spirit from me. Restore to me the joy of your salvation and grant me a willing spirit, to sustain me" (vv. 1, 10-12, NIV).

The man God had brought from tending sheep to be the shepherd of Israel knew God loved him. And he knew the law was precious and perfect, even if he could not keep it. So in the fullness of time God sent his Son, David's descendant, to keep the law perfectly on our behalf, and then to become our sacrificial lamb. By his one sacrifice we were set free forever from law-keeping, and given a new covenant: " 'This is the covenant I will make with the house of Israel after that time,' declares the LORD. 'I will put my laws in their minds and write it on their hearts'" (Jer. 31:33, NIV).

God's grace invites us to accept what his Son did for us. God wants us to become righteous by faith—as did Abraham, who was "fully persuaded that God had power to do what he had promised" (Rom. 4:21, NIV).

Prayer: *Dear Lord Jesus, I give myself to you—as I am. Thank you for doing what I cannot, for washing away all my sins and making me wholly new. Amen.*

Thursday, February 28   Read John 2:13-21.

Jesus had just performed his first miracle, at the wedding in Cana. John says, "He thus revealed his glory, and his disciples put their faith in him" (2:11, NIV).

The Jews knew about miracles. Yahweh had brought Israel out of Egypt with great signs and wonders. At Joshua's command his power had flattened the walls of Jericho, and he had caused the sun to stop in the middle of the sky. Elijah's word had given the widow a perpetual supply of flour and oil and raised her son from the dead. His prayer had called down fire from heaven to consume the sacrifice and defeat Baal. And Elisha, with double Elijah's anointing, had performed twice as many miracles.

Indeed, the Jews expected supernatural works from a prophet of God. But it had been hundreds of years since God had so favored them. Now they were cynical. Here was this Jesus (could anything good come from Nazareth?), acting like he owned the temple. He actually had the presumption to scourge the merchants and money changers, shouting them out of the temple area. He even implied that he was God's Son!

So they decided to test him. "What miraculous sign can you show us to prove your authority to do all this?" they demanded (NIV). Jesus gave them an honest answer. "Destroy this temple, and I will raise it again in three days" (NIV).

But their hatred had blinded them to his emphasis: the temple he meant was his body. He was predicting the greatest miracle of all history, past or future—his own resurrection from the dead. He knew they would murder him, and obliquely informed them. They chose to practice denial.

Prayer: *Father, give us the humility to accept the miracles you still offer us. In the name of Jesus, the miracle worker. Amen.*

Friday, March 1   Read John 2:22.

Even the disciples did not understand what Jesus meant when he said he would raise the temple again in three days. Though Isaiah had prophesied a suffering messiah, who would bear the iniquities and the diseases of those who believed in him, they longed for a temporal leader. "Lord, is it at this time you will restore the kingdom to Israel?" pleaded one. To be under the domination of Rome was a bitter thing.

Just before his crucifixion Jesus told his followers plainly what was about to take place. "Now you are speaking clearly and without figures of speech," they exclaimed. "Now we can see that you know all things and that you do not even need to have anyone ask you questions. This makes us believe that you came from God." "You believe at last!" Jesus answered (John 16:29-31, NIV). Yet not until he had demonstrated his absolute power by rising from the dead and visibly ascending to the Father did they fully understand.

Jesus had declared in the Nazareth synagogue that he was, himself, the fulfillment of the prophecy in Isaiah 61. The Jewish leaders knew well what he was saying. Yet when he told them they would reject his miracles, they drove him out of town and tried to kill him (see Luke 4:16-30). Like some in the present-day, they considered him mainly a great teacher. Yet all of the Old Testament pointed to him as the promised Redeemer. Not until the risen Christ appeared to them and "opened their minds so they could understand the Scriptures" (Luke 24:45, NIV) could they accept Jesus for who he was: "Everything must be fulfilled that is written about me in the Law of Moses, the Prophets and the Psalms" (Luke 24:44, NIV).

Prayer: *Risen Christ, open our minds to receive your word, and deliver us from crippling unbelief. Amen.*

Saturday, March 2   Read 1 Corinthians 1:22-24.

While the Jews demanded authentication by signs, Paul found the Greeks in Athens to be enamored of theories. "All the Athenians and the foreigners who lived there spent their time doing nothing but talking about and listening to the latest ideas" (Acts 17:21, NIV).

As Paul reasoned in the synagogue and the marketplace with the Jews and God-fearing Greeks, some philosophers challenged him. They thought because he was preaching the good news of Jesus and the resurrection that he was advocating foreign gods. Here was yet another new idea to debate! So they hurried Paul to a meeting of the Areopagus, and asked him to explain: "You are bringing some strange ideas to our ears, and we want to know what they mean" (Acts 17:20, NIV).

Paul, trained as a rabbi by the great Gamaliel, was quite as intellectual as they were. He was also a student of human nature ("I have become all things to all men so that by all possible means I might save some"—1 Cor. 9:22, NIV), and knew how to appeal to their egos.

"Men of Athens!" he smiled. "I see that in every way you are very religious. For as I walked around and observed your objects of worship, I even found an altar with this inscription: TO AN UNKNOWN GOD. Now what you worship as something unknown I am going to proclaim to you" (Acts 17:23, NIV).

Paul went on to introduce the Creator to them, in contrast to their pantheon of idols, and he proclaimed the resurrected Christ. Some sneered; Paul's words were foolishness to them.

With every kind of listener, Paul's message was always the same: the cross and the miraculous resurrection of Jesus.

Prayer: *Lord, give us minds uncluttered by the world to focus on the lovely simplicity of what you alone did for us. Amen.*

Sunday, March 3   Read 1 Corinthians 1:25.

For many years our family lived in the "Athens of the Midwest," so-called because it was the home of the state university. There were many cultural advantages in that town, yet not once in the metropolitan church we attended did we hear the message of salvation.

At last we found a "Paul," a pastor who was studying for his Ph.D. at that university. Through the "foolishness of preaching" he had created an island of believers in Christ crucified.

Among the multitudes of lost intellects, still searching in the classical antiquities of Greece and Rome for meaning to life, walked the Life himself—unseen, unknown. About this Life, Paul wrote: "The foolishness of God is wiser than man's wisdom, and the weakness of God is stronger than man's strength."

Paul told the Corinthians also: "I resolved to know nothing while I was with you except Jesus Christ and him crucified. I came to you in weakness and fear, and with much trembling. My message and my preaching were not with wise and persuasive words, but with a demonstration of the Spirit's power, so that your faith might not rest on men's wisdom, but on God's power" (1 Cor. 2:2-5, NIV).

The miracles attested to the reality of the Messiah. John wrote that "Jesus did many other miraculous signs . . . which are not recorded in this book. But these are written that you may believe that Jesus is the Christ, the Son of God, and that by believing you may have life in his name" (John 20:30-31, NIV).

Suggestion for meditation: *"You are a chosen people, a royal priesthood, a holy nation, a people belonging to God, that you may declare the praises of him who called you out of darkness into his wonderful light" (1 Pet. 2:9).*

Choosing Eternal Life

March 4-10, 1991   **Judith Freeman Clark**†
Monday, March 4   Read 2 Chronicles 36:14-18.

In Old Testament descriptions of God's wrath, often God appears harsh or unyielding. Those who continually refuse to obey God's laws do, finally, evoke God's anger—as the Israelites learned. For even when God reminded them of his laws many times, the Israelites ignored them.

Today, God gives us many gifts and, in return, wants us to honor his blessings and follow his commandments. God intends that we should benefit from his love, but leaves the ultimate choice up to us. If through ignorance, deceit, or anger we deny God's love, we run into trouble as the Israelites did. Their grief was the inevitable result of a very human choice.

As he did with the Israelites, God gives us options and permits us to make choices. God offers us the chance to live fully, in the comfort and protection of his love. God provides us with everything we need and offers us the opportunity to accept his many gifts. But he reminds us that there is a price to be paid if we reject him. The cost of that rejection is counted not ony in a spiritual way but often also in real human suffering on earth.

God does not cause this suffering. We create it by our inability to live according to God's commandments. In perfect love, God offers life. Our task is to accept it.

Prayer: *God, help us remember the many choices you offer and the many opportunities we have to end suffering. Give us the wisdom and strength to choose wisely and to accept your love. Amen.*

---

†Writer; Episcopal laywoman, Northampton, Massachusetts.

Tuesday, March 5   Read 2 Chronicles 36:19-23.

We can see clearly the devastating changes brought about in the Israelites' lives because they ignored God's commands. In the midst of abundance, the people sinned. They polluted God's house and misused the creation. The cost was high—exile and slavery. This scene is all too easily repeated in our time.

In mercy and love, God places richness all around us. He blesses all nations of the world with different resources, enabling the most powerful to thrive in wealth and comfort. He gives each of us the ability to determine how we will use our planet's abundance, and how to employ our human capabilities to honor creation and acknowledge his love.

Like the Israelites, however, we are tempted to disregard God's will concerning our use of his blessings. Like the Israelites, we are in danger of suffering the consequences of ignoring God's will. And, most tragically, like them we appear blind to the danger in which we place ourselves.

We make decisions daily that damage the environment beyond repair. We refuse to support medical research due to its cost or implications. We walk blindly past the homeless who crowd our sidewalks. Our ears are deaf to the cries of abused children and the appeals of oppressed people.

God sorrows at our reluctance in the face of such critical need. Long ago, the Israelites suffered for their apathy and willful ignorance. Today, God provides us with the time, tools, and talent needed to turn our twentieth-century indifference into loving action. What nature of exile and enslavement could be ours if we continue to refuse God?

Prayer: *Dear God, keep us mindful of how individual choices affect our entire world. And provide us with the strength to seize each opportunity that you offer. Amen.*

Wednesday, March 6   Read Psalm 137:1-3.

Often God's love is revealed to us under difficult circumstances. These unpleasant, confusing, or painful times may leave us feeling so empty and alone that we panic. In our fear, we may believe that God has abandoned us—just when we need him the most. In our desperation, we may forget just how enduring God's love can be.

God promises to be with us always. But then, when we suffer, we wonder whether God might be playing a cruel trick on us. Is God deliberately ignoring our misery? We may even believe that God is too far away to hear us when we call out for help.

Sometimes God seems to remain silent when we crave reassurance. But actually, if we pause and listen, we may be able to hear God most clearly at these difficult times. God's voice is often more audible to us when we are vulnerable than when we are strong.

In exile, the Israelites learned about themselves and their own vulnerability. They also learned about God's constancy. Their trials opened them up to God's love. When they cried, "By the rivers of Babylon, there we sat down and wept, when we remembered Zion," they were acknowledging great loss. But their pain became a door through which God walked and healed them.

Alienation, exile, and suffering brought the Israelites to their knees. But these experiences also brought the Israelites to a deeper realization of God. In their great despair, they finally heard God's voice. Pain enabled the people to recognize, understand, and accept God's love.

Prayer: *God, help us remember that there can be release and salvation in pain and despair. Help us to listen for your voice at those times when all we can hear is silence. Amen.*

Thursday, March 7   Read Ephesians 2:8-10.

No matter how thoroughly we believe in God's mercy, we are surprised when we confront the extent of God's love. For although we try to live according to God's teachings, we are human and bound to slip once in a while. However, in our concept of human failings we sometimes forget that God has no such human limitations. We do not always remember that God's love is constant, steadfast, and true.

Paul's letter explains that, despite our efforts, we will fail because we are human. Our weakness inevitably surfaces when we try to put our good intentions to work.

These good intentions come in many shapes and sizes. We may promise to spend more time with our family, or we may vow to take time to help a friend. But we become self-absorbed and self-important, forgetting others' needs. We are short-tempered with children, parents, or partners. We ignore spoken and silent appeals for understanding, compassion, or love. We may understand these shortcomings and we may feel ashamed of them. And we may also despair, because no matter how hard we try, we cannot seem to conquer human weakness.

We are surprised to learn that God loves us despite our failings. We find it difficult to accept God's caring and understanding—which are endless.

Paul says that, even though we are weak and our human errors are inevitable, we are saved through grace. We may be beset by sin, but God will always give us another chance. God loves our humanity, even as he offers us the hope of improving. Each day, we awake to the opportunity that God extends: the potential of living fully, in grace and harmony, according to his love.

Prayer: *Help us bear in our hearts, O God, the remembrance that your love knows no boundaries and will never fail us. Amen.*

Friday, March 8   Read Ephesians 2:4-7.

The phrase "even when we were dead through our trespasses" contains powerful imagery. Few of us would deny that we think about death reluctantly. And most of us do not contemplate willingly the times when we have sinned, when we have been faithless or selfish or careless of others. We do not summon up images of sin or death with good cheer; to be "dead in sins" sounds perilous, frightening, and repulsive.

Because we understand our mortal limitations, we cherish a keen appreciation of the finite. Death signals the end, a loss of the familiar, the negation of love. Sin means the denial of good, a destruction of all that is meaningful, precious, or sacred.

In his letter to the church at Ephesus, Paul chose his words carefully to be sure that they would have maximum impact. He understood that people recoil from images of death and sin.

God loves each of us, no matter how we have lived, what terrible acts we have committed, or to whom we have lied. In trying to convey this certainty, Paul underscored how completely God's mercy enfolds us, how significant is God's love in each of our lives. In powerful terms, Paul described the utter poverty in which we all are doomed to live—unless we accept the salvation that God's love can bring to us.

Death, sin, darkness, exile, sorrow, pain, despair—God resurrects us from these circumstances. God's infinite love waits for us at the end of each day and at the completion of each imperfect, human act. God's gentle blessing is a benediction bestowed on us simply for being human. Because God loves us, we are saved—for eternity—from death in sin.

Prayer: *Stay with us, Lord, when we are drowning in sin and selfishness. Resurrect us from these deaths of the spirit through your merciful and eternal love. Amen.*

Saturday, March 9   Read John 3:14-18.

The Gospel of John explains that God comprehends our human frailty and accepts the inevitability of our failure. John affirms that through divine understanding, God created the covenant of grace—the forgiveness clause in his contract with humanity.

Through this forgiveness, God honors human nature. He does not prevent us from making mistakes, and he does not make our decisions for us. Rather, God allows us to succeed or fail on our own merit. But he readies a safety net of perpetual forgiveness if, through human error, we fall from grace.

Because we are only mortal, we find such an all-forgiving, divine love hard to comprehend. Since we are often unable to forgive each other—or ourselves—it is a challenge to believe that God will always forgive us, no matter what we do or say. But in a love utterly complete and perfect, God forgave, redeemed, and saved us through the birth, death, and resurrection of Jesus Christ.

God knows that, being human, we will fail. But because he is divine, God anticipates our imperfection and loves us anyway. Each time we fall from grace, God picks up the pieces of our shattered lives, shoulders our failures, and shelters us with his love.

God's great gift to us cannot be altered through anything we do or think or say. God loves us unconditionally, and through Jesus Christ he provided for our redemption to eternal life.

Prayer: *Dear God, be with us each day and assist us as we seek the way of truth. And if, through human weakness, we fall from grace, uplift us and keep us mindful of your everlasting love. Amen.*

Sunday, March 10   Read John 3:19-21.

While they were exiled, the Israelites were filled with despair. They wept, lamenting their enslavement and their loss. Such images of sorrow are often used in the Old Testament. On the other hand, images of light, discovery, and joy are used frequently in the New Testament. In the Gospels, we learn of the healing grace that comes when we accept Jesus Christ into our lives.

Knowing Jesus is an opportunity to know peace, truth, and goodness. New Testament stories tell how Jesus brought joy to those who believed in him, how he quieted the fretful, calmed the grief-stricken, and encouraged laughter and celebration among his followers. The New Testament stories of Jesus' life present us with multiple images of love, nurturance, and respect.

The lessons Jesus taught are simple to learn; the choices he offered are easy to comprehend. In trusting God, we allow ourselves the opportunity to know light rather then darkness. Jesus promised that God's tender mercy will illuminate our every waking moment if only we will allow him to enter our lives. Over and over again, Jesus assured us that as we accept God's great love for humankind, we experience our salvation.

The rewards for accepting salvation and eternal life are innumerable. By contrast, without God we have only an empty existence full of painful limitations. God wants us to accept love and to live joyful lives. So we learn, in the New Testament accounts of Jesus' life, how to live in simplicity and serenity. We learn that if we live according to the pattern that Jesus showed us, salvation is ours.

Prayer: *Dear God, enlighten our lives through the example of your Son, Jesus Christ. Help us accept him as the one, perfect example of your divine love. Amen.*

THE RECREATED HEART

March 11-17, 1991 **Joseph Ray Kutter†**
Monday, March 11 Read Psalm 51:10-17.

Lent is for the heart, the center of the self—that mysterious place where feeling, thought, and intuition converge to declare, "This is who I am and this is what I shall do." Lent is the season for an examination of the heart, an honest acknowledgement of weakness and dysfunction and an inspired hope for healing and more. Re-creation! "Create in me a clean heart, O God, and put a new and right spirit within me." This is the season for the recreated heart!

We have been created in the image of God. The mark of the eternal has been stamped upon us. We were conceived to grow into God-like characters who rejoice in fellowship with our Maker and reflect that fellowship in our behavior with our neighbors. To be in the image of God is to have the power of choice between good and evil and to make the right choices.

The choices are real. Some are important; some seem insignificant. But in the choosing, the heart will either be true to the nature of its creation in God's image or it won't.

Sometimes we make good choices. Sometimes, bad! Unkind, unfaithful, unloving, immoral, stupid choices—choices that tarnish the mark of the eternal God on the human heart.

"Create in me a clean heart, O God." Some would say that forgiveness follows confession. I supect that we are able to confess because we have been forgiven.

Prayer: *Create me again, O God, in your image as revealed in Jesus Christ. Amen.*

---

†Pastor, First Baptist Church, Royal Oak, Michigan.

Tuesday, March 12   Read Psalm 51:14-17.

Surgery makes sense only when there is some possibility for success. The risk is real, and only a fool would refuse to consider the danger.

Lent is a season to consider spiritual surgery. In his exaggerated way, no doubt designed to catch our attention, Jesus once said, "If your right eye causes you to sin, pluck it out and throw it away. . . . And if your right hand causes you to sin, cut it off and throw it away; it is better that you lose one of your members than that your whole body go into hell" (Matt. 5:29-30).

Before we consider the surgery, we must consider the possibility for success. Is wholeness, salvation, a genuine possibility? Can broken hearts be mended? Is the procedure worth risking a change of heart?

The provisions for God's wholeness are already in place. Before we confess our sin, indeed even before we realize the fact of our sin, God provides for the pardon of sin and the restoration to abundant living. Hearts broken on the anvils of bad decisions can be mended. The heart can be recreated!

The procedure? We will invite the Holy Spirit of Christ to examine our heart. Under the Spirit's guidance, each of us will be led to honestly confront the realities of life. If sin exists, it will be exposed. We will experience honest guilt. We will receive strength for the hard work of transformation. We will suffer some spiritual discomfort, quite probably the pain of remorse. But we will receive God's pardon. The Holy Spirit of Christ will become our abiding companion. And we will experience the joy of salvation and wholesome living.

Prayer: *Merciful God, grant us wisdom and courage to accept the cleansing of our heart that you offer in Jesus Christ. Amen.*

Wednesday, March 13   Read Jeremiah 31:31-34.

At the center of every life is a place designed for making decisions. There our deepest emotions, our best thoughts and ideas, our feelings and drives, our loyalties and commitments, and our relationships all connect to inform the decisions that direct our life. The Bible calls this command center the *heart*.

God created the human life to be directed from the center. All the parts are connected to this center. No single part has autonomous control. We are not just emotional creatures; nor are we merely intellects. We are not just flesh; nor are we just spirit. We are more than all of the above, and each part has a contribution to make. It is the heart that decides. It is the heart that experiences both thought and feeling, both the uniqueness of the self and the connections of loving relationships. It is the heart that says, "Be this and not that and do this and not that."

To live abundantly, we must have a balancing, organizing, directing center. Like the planets around the sun, the parts of life must find their places in orbit around the center. Otherwise, life becomes an internal tug of war with each part demanding to be the whole. Chaos reigns. Life goes nowhere, and either boredom or futility becomes the dominant emotion.

But who guides the heart? How does the heart decide?

The heart was created to be both a distinct self and a self in relationship. The heart was created for communion with God.

"I will put my law within them, and I will write it upon their hearts; and I will be their God, and they shall be my people."

The heart is at the center of life; at the center of the heart there is a place for God alone, who loves us more than we love ourselves.

Prayer: *Eternal God of Jesus Christ, shape our hearts from the inside. Inform us by your Holy Spirit. Amen.*

Thursday, March 14   Read Hebrews 5:7-10.

The hope of the Lenten season is nothing less than a re-created heart—a renewed life centered in a new person.

"New person," "new heart"; phrases like this have no content! So we must ask, "Like what or whom does the recreated heart look? Is there a picture, a model, a design somewhere?"

The answer is no and yes. On the one hand, there has never been nor will there ever be another heart created to be just like yours or mine. Every human heart is a once-in-a-universe creation; therefore, no picture or model exists by which we can absolutely and minutely shape our hearts.

On the other hand, while each of us is unique in some way, no human heart is unique in every way. The Christian witness is that every heart bears the imprint of God's personhood. There is a humanity that is common to us all. Our commonalities far outnumber our unique traits.

So, is there somewhere a flesh-and-blood human being who lives, or has lived, in such a perfect way that we can say, "That is the kind of heart that I would like to have"? Is there somewhere a human heart that has not sullied the imprint of God? Is there somewhere a heart that is truly, purely, cleanly human?

This is the Christian claim: Jesus the Christ was the perfect human. His life was directed from the perfect human heart. From the center of his life, all the parts of life were properly ordered. His heart had its own center, that place made for communion with God. Jesus is the picture, the model, the design we need for the recreated heart.

Prayer: *You have not left us alone, O God. In Jesus we have the picture we need of the human heart. And you have given us more than a picture. You have offered to live at the center of our lives. We accept your offer. Amen.*

Friday, March 15   Read Hebrews 5:7-10.

The human heart is a mortal heart, even when it is a perfect heart. Jesus died! The inescapable and uncompromising fact of death is critical as the heart seeks to set the direction of life.

The psalmist wrote, "Teach us to number our days that we may get a heart of wisdom" (Ps. 90:12). Life in this world has a definite end. The limits are severe. No one can be everything. No one can do everything. Within the limits imposed by death, every heart must choose both that which will be and that which will not be. The fact of death forces a focus, and that focus determines the character and quality of the life of the heart.

Death is a hard fact—a fact that the human heart cannot readily accept. Even Jesus wrestled mightily with this unwelcome reality. "Jesus offered up prayers and supplications, with loud cries and tears, to him who was able to save him from death." Jesus did not want to die. Even the perfect man with the perfect heart living in perfect relationship with God did not want to die.

The night before his death he prayed, "Father, if thou art willing, remove this cup from me; nevertheless not my will, but thine, be done" (Luke 22:42). His meaning was clear: "God, I do not want to suffer and die; nevertheless, I'll do what you want." Jesus had both a will to live and an honest acceptance of the fact of death.

Jesus' death has a special meaning and power, and there will never be another like him. But in some ways, he is like us all. His death gave a focus to the decisions of life. His death gave definition to the meaning of life. Knowing that he was going to die, he fully lived.

Prayer: *God in heaven, give us courage to face the unwelcome fact of death so that we may number our days fully alive. Amen.*

Saturday, March 16   Read Jeremiah 31:31-34.

The recreated heart is a loving heart. Jeremiah proclaimed the word of the Lord: "I will put my law within them, and I will write it upon their hearts."

What is the law for the heart? Jesus was once asked about the law. "One of them, a lawyer, asked him a question to test him. 'Teacher, which is the great commandment in the law?' And he said to him, 'You shall love the Lord your God with all your heart, and with all your soul, and with all your mind. This is the great and first commandment. And a second is like it, You shall love your neighbor as yourself. On these two commandments depend all the law and the prophets'" (Matt. 22:35-40).

The recreated heart has been reshaped by the spirit of love. The love of God, given and received, informs this heart's being and doing. Loyalty to the mission of God, gratitude for the grace of God, sensitivity to the will of God, confidence in the faithfulness of God, enjoyment in the presence of God, commitment to the justice of God: these are the traits of the heart reshaped by the love of God.

A love for neighbors, nearby and around the world, shapes the life of the recreated heart. Deciding that this life (my life) will contribute to the well-being of the human community: this is the hallmark of the loving heart.

The loving heart cannot neglect the first gift of God, the gift of life itself. The requirements for the spiritual and physical well-being of the self cannot be ignored. If God lives at the center of this heart, then even this life is worthy of care.

I can neither despise nor ignore that which God has created, even if the creation is me.

Prayer: *God of powerful love, I entrust my heart to you with the confidence that you will reshape it with the power of your love. Amen.*

Sunday, March 17   Read John 12:20-33.

The recreated heart is a suffering heart. Suffering is the dark side of love.

Love is nothing less than deciding that my life will contribute to the well-being of my neighbors, nearby and around the world. To love is to want, to will from the center of myself, that my neighbor will be whole. To love is to invest my time, my energy, my talents, and myself in the life of someone else.

Sometimes this kind of investment does not yield the desired results. Sometimes love is rebuked. Sometimes our best is rejected, and the neighbor chooses to self-destruct. Sometimes our love is accepted and the evil contingencies of life damage our neighbor. When that happens there is nothing we can do to prevent the suffering. When we love and those whom we love suffer, their suffering becomes our suffering.

But this suffering is not like any other, for the spirit of love transforms suffering from mere pain into purposeful life. By the power of God's Spirit, the joy in love transcends the suffering imposed by evil. Broken hearts are made whole in spite of evil.

Experiences of purpose, power, and joy in the midst of genuine suffering are the testimonies of the Holy Spirit to the ultimate hope of resurrection unto eternal life. "Although [Jesus] was a Son, he learned obedience through what he suffered; and being made perfect he became the source of eternal salvation to all who obey him" (Heb. 5:8-9).

Jesus loved, and because he loved, he suffered. In his suffering, his heart was perfected. And the perfected heart was resurrected to reveal the God who loves enough to accept suffering.

Prayer: *Creating and recreating God, teach me to love. By the power of your Holy Spirit, grant me courage to accept the suffering that love brings so that I may know joy, now and forever more. Amen.*

THE JUSTICE PARADE

March 18-24, 1991   **George Donigian†**
Monday, March 18   Read Mark 11:1-6.

Dress rehearsal

Jesus sent two of his disciples to pick up an unknown colt—an animal used by conquering kings to symbolize peace—that Jesus might ride into Jerusalem. Jesus helped the disciples by giving them a response should anyone ask what they were doing. He probably thought that given this strange command to walk to an unknown place, to find a colt tied up on the street, and to bring that colt to Jesus, the disciples would need some help. The two went about this business, and bystanders asked what they were doing. The disciples responded as coached. Satisfied with the answer, the bystanders let the disciples take the animal.

I walk to work in Nashville and pass a number of homeless people. Sometimes we walk together. It is not a triumphant procession into the city; it is a walk that sometimes does not inspire confidence because of the nature of life on the streets. Some of the regulars have gone beyond the first impression they had of me as a lawyer and know me as an ordained person. Steeped in conservative theology, they ask questions such as "What's God going to do with the world?" "What's the good of being a Christian?" "What does God have to do with me?"

Some days I can answer their questions, and some days I cannot. At times I wish God would rehearse the answers with me, as Jesus did with those two disciples, so I could claim the colt of peace and justice for people on the street.

Suggestion for meditation: *How do I walk with the Christ for justice and peace? What can I do today to serve God?*

---

†United Methodist minister serving as editor of children's curriculum, The United Methodist Publishing House, Nashville, Tennessee.

Tuesday, March 19   Read Psalm 118:19-20.

Renewed righteousness

Psalm 118, the last of the Hallel psalms, sets before us a doxology following the psalmist's deliverance by God. Earlier in the psalm the speaker tells of the enemies around the army or perhaps around the individual psalmist. Out of the midst of the oppression came the salvation of the Lord. Hence the cry, "Open to me the gates of the Temple; I will go in and give thanks to the LORD!" (TEV)

A royal psalm of thanksgiving for military victory, Psalm 118 was probably used to remember and celebrate God's victories in past years. Take time now in your mind's eye to imagine the rich pageantry of this psalm being enacted. Outside the temple walls see the priest intoning the first verses of the psalm. Then see the company of prophets, servants, and kings walking behind the priest and entering the gate of the Lord to receive the blessing of righteousness.

Righteousness cannot be considered as military victory today. Our world needs renewed understandings of the meaning of a righteousness that grows from the spirit of humility. We find ourselves receiving the blessing in the midst of other victories that come while giving and receiving, serving and being served. The blessing happens in the midst of our ministries with God for justice for all people.

How will the gate be opened for you today? How will you serve God to proclaim the blessing of righteousness? How will you help the oppressed find justice outside the gates of the temple?

Prayer: *O God, righteousness sometimes becomes prostituted into smugness. Help us enter the gate by our service of love. Amen.*

Wednesday, March 20   Read Psalm 31:9-16.

Collecting discards

Grappling with the contentiousness of life, the psalmist laments his condition before God. Rather than offering a prayer of one afraid that emotion might hurt God, the psalmist displays feelings ranging from sorrow and loneliness to confidence and hope. He asks for God's mercy because he feels discarded.

> All my enemies, and especially my neighbors,
>   treat me with contempt. . . .
> Everyone has forgotten me, as though I were dead;
>   I am like something thrown away. (TEV)

The world has a "discard" problem. Our growing production and consumption of material goods have created a garbage problem around the world because we do not have the capacity to deal with the waste. Some places in the United States have martialed forces to deal with the problem of garbage and landfills, but only because there was a crisis.

We also discard people who no longer seem useful. We discount the contributions of persons with handicapping conditions, of the aging, and of children. As English-speaking people we discount the contributions of persons whose native language is not English and who therefore have an accent when they speak English. We think of homeless persons as problems. We forget that they are God's people and that God may speak to us in the guise of a homeless person.

The great commandment was to love God and to love one's neighbors as oneself. Walking as a disciple of Christ calls us to stand in love and with mercy beside all our neighbors.

Prayer: *God, you have collected all people into the folds of your love. You discard no one. Thank you. Let thanksgiving overflow my heart to reach all the people I encounter today. Amen.*

Thursday, March 21　　　　　　　　Read Isaiah 50:4-8.

The suffering community

When you read Isaiah 50, think of the suffering servant as the covenant community. The interpretation of Israel as the suffering servant may be a modern one, and yet it is more in keeping with the biblical understanding of community. See Israel made new each morning in obedience to God's teachings. Understand the community as one that bares itself to insult for the sake of obedience to a vision of God's justice. How may a community become a suffering servant?

I am reminded of my Armenian ancestors. My people were converted to Christianity around A.D. 300, and our alphabet was invented in the fourth century in order to translate the Bible. Despite a rich history, Armenia is much unknown because other nations ruled Armenia, and victors write official histories that differ from histories passed on by the oppressed. But the history of the Armenian nation cannot be written apart from the Armenian church. The church continues to proclaim and serve the gospel despite oppression and, indeed, a genocide in which over one million Armenians died in April of 1915. Our suffering has happened because of our obedience to God.

Let all our communities incarnate the suffering servant. Let us be open to God in ministry with others so justice may ensure the end of oppression and genocide.

Prayer: *O Christ, the eternal flame, inflame my soul by the fire of your love, that the stains of my soul be burned, my conscience purified, and the sins of my body purged. With your love kindle in me the light of your knowledge.*

Have mercy upon all your creatures and upon me, a sinner.*

---

*A prayer of the Armenian Saint Nerses Schnorhali (the gracious one).

Friday, March 22   Read Psalm 118:21-25.

What price success?

Tsalach is the root word translated in verse 25 as "prosperity" in the KJV and as "success" in TEV and RSV. The new RSV also translates the word as "success." *Tsalach* is a rare word in Hebrew that derives from an original meaning of "to break out, to come mightily, and to cause prosperity." Many in the United States would equate success and prosperity with individual financial gain and reward. What does success mean to the psalmist celebrating the victory of Yahweh?

For Israel the issue was not financial independence or fame. The importance of the individual was not a prime factor in the attainment of success. *Tsalach* was rooted in the covenant community, and the well-being of the entire community was at stake. The word *tsalach* is used in Joshua 1:8: "Be sure that the book of the Law is always read in your worship. Study it day and night, and make sure that you obey everything written in it. Then you will be prosperous and successful" (TEV). Success may be an offspring of covenantal faithfulness; however, one's faithfulness to the covenant was primary and grew out of a love for God, not material things.

Such success is not meant simply for individuals, but for all those within the community. The question posed by the psalmist's use of *tsalach* concerns the borders and boundaries of the community: how far does prosperity extend? If prosperity is to break out as in the day of the Lord, then prosperity becomes like justice, and God is concerned that the oppressed and the poor share in *tsalach*. We sing Psalm 118 only as we strive for justice for all people.

Devotional exercise: *Today open yourself to* tsalach. *Who are the oppressed around you, and how can you seek prosperity with them?*

Saturday, March 23   Read Mark 11:7-11.

On the road

Too many times I have heard sermons about the people who were lining the road into Jerusalem. These sermons focused on messianic history and how Jesus reversed those messianic expectations. The kingdom was *of*, but not a part of, this world. Jesus' kingship was quite unlike the norm of royalty. You have heard those sermons, and they are safe given our vantage point from this side of the crucifixion.

I remain fascinated by the response of the people. The people could not have been the merchant class. They would not have been the establishment. These people were outside and beyond the establishment because messiahs always upset the system. These people were outcasts who, recognizing the love of Jesus, put down branches and clothes that he might ride on. The Gospel writers agree that words from the Hallel were shouted to celebrate the entry of Jesus. We move quickly to the praise, "Blessed is he who comes in the name of the Lord!"

Before going into the temple, stay with the people on the road a little longer. They are walking with Jesus to bring in God's new day. All they may know about messianic theology is that Jesus is one sent from God and that God is about to do something new. So for the messiah, these people spread their clothes on the road.

Focus on this scene and become part of that crowd. Who is on the road with you? What marks your brotherhood and your sisterhood with others in the crowd? What do you expect from these brothers and sisters? What do you give them? What would you strip from your life to spread before Jesus?

Prayer: *O God, help me remove my mask. Lead me to examine my own life and my own motivations. Help me find what it truly means to say "Blessed is he who comes in the name of the Lord!" Amen.*

March 24 (Passion/Palm Sunday)
Read Psalm 118:26-29.

The big day

I served as pastor in a town with churches representing the whole theological spectrum. Each year we held a Palm Sunday parade. After a brief litany we marched down the main street, singing the few hymns we had in common and waving flowering branches. Our litany included words from Psalm 118: "May God bless the one who comes in the name of the LORD!" (TEV)

These words do not come out of satisfied isolation, but from the thanksgiving of a fulfilled and expectant community. Victory has been achieved by God. And God's victory is yet to come.

God's victory has been achieved throughout the history of Israel. We can trace God's victory through the stories of Abraham, Ruth, and Amos, and through the stories of Jesus. The church has witnessed to this victory many times.

Yet, God's victory is still to come. The word of the prophet remains before us: "Let justice roll down like waters, and righteousness like an ever-flowing stream" (Amos 5:24). God's victory will happen when justice flows down the hill and takes care of the baby whose picture is in all the guilt-inducing magazine advertisements for this or that "love ministry." God's victory will be celebrated when skin color, ethnic background, and cultural heritage are no longer barriers, and when women and children all over the earth can be the free creations God intended all to be. God's victory will be fulfilled when God's people are no longer homeless or exploited and God's earth is no longer poisoned.

Until that time, we pray and work in expectant hope, and we bless the one who comes in the name of the Lord.

Suggestion for prayer: *Pray Psalm 118:19-29 today, and consider where the spirit of justice is leading you in the parade.*

March 25-31, 1991   **Walter Wink**†
Monday, March 25   Read Isaiah 52:13–53:12.

The first transformation: the scapegoat

Society is a war of each against the other, in which intragroup rivalry is regulated by the scapegoat mechanism. Revenge would destroy the social fabric if allowed to run unchecked. But if a victim can be found, someone on the fringes, perhaps deformed, with no family or clan able to avenge his death, this victim can be offered as a sacrifice to restore order. The servant of Yahweh is one such victim. He is marginal, sickly, painful to behold. He is expendable. It is God who has blighted him; surely it is God's intent then that we load on him our sins, our violence, and our hatreds and kill him as our surrogate.

Indeed, God has acted in all this. But not the way they thought. No one wants to take responsibility for the killing. The crowd speaks in the passive voice, as helpless bystanders, as if they had not hurled the rock, or pulled the trigger, or thrown the switch. All rulers, all mobs have acted thus. They say it is God's will.

But God's will is different. This is the beginning of the great transformation. They carry out their violence, as always. But here is something new: the scapegoating mechanism is unmasked! The guilt of the murderers is revealed! God takes the side not of the powerful but of the victim. God vindicates the true innocent: the scapegoat. This presents the authorities with a crisis: without the scapegoat mechanism, how will they siphon off the passions of violence before they explode?

Prayer: *Subverting God, how have I made you the God of the oppressors? Who have I been willing to sacrifice? Amen.*

---

†Professor of Biblical Interpretation, Auburn Theological Seminary, New York, New York.

Tuesday, March 26   Read Mark 14:12-16.

The preparation

On first glance this looks like a miracle, or perhaps a feat of psychic power: Jesus foresees the future. On closer examination, it looks more like a carefully prearranged plan, perhaps to prevent Judas from learning in advance where Jesus would eat the Passover, thus buying a bit more time. Jesus has apparently made all these arrangements beforehand (the upper room is already "furnished and ready").

The church's concentration on the miraculous has blinded it to the man with the water pitcher. In Palestine water was stored in large jars, containing fifteen to twenty-five gallons, which were permanently embedded in the ground. Girls usually had the responsibility of keeping these jars filled, but if a man happened to be near the well, he was expected to draw the water.

What are we to make of this signal? Any number of other signs could have been devised. Men simply did not carry water jars in first-century Palestine, not even male servants. Such an act would have been considered humiliating. Even a widower would have found a girl to carry water for him.

With what droll humor did Jesus prearrange this scene? Where did he find a male willing to carry it out? This event is in preparation for a Passover meal in which Jesus will reverse all the meanings, in anticipation of a death in which God will overturn the world. What is Jesus saying about patriarchy, sex-role stereotyping, "women's work"? What kind of modeling is this? This Aquarian figure, carrying his own unconscious consciously, rather than swimming in it, as the Piscean fish—what kind of future does it auger? And why have we resisted it so?

Prayer: *Subverting God, am I prepared to betray you rather than let you change my ways? Amen.*

Wednesday, March 27   Read Mark 14:17-21.

The first betrayal

Treachery can come from anywhere, but betrayal arises from the inner circle. Three times Mark emphasizes that Judas is one of the twelve (14:10, 20, 43). Theories have been spun to account for his perfidy. Some believe he was a Zealot, disillusioned when Jesus refused to fight. Others suggest that Judas, still expecting God's violent kingdom, hoped to provoke Jesus to battle, or even to trigger divine intervention by heavily armed heavenly hosts. John's Gospel has the earliest surviving theory: Judas was simply addicted to money (John 12:4-6). The other Gospels offer no explanation whatever. They are correct. There is never an explanation for betrayal. Reasons are merely after-the-fact rationalizations. We can be sure of that here, because of the kiss.

The horror of that kiss: to betray, not by pointing—"There he is, seize him!"—but by a kiss! Judas had seen so much of God displayed through this person, had himself been caught up in the inrush of God's reign. As one of the twelve he had healed and cast out demons (Mark 6:7-13). As a member of the inner circle of disciples he had had, as his spiritual mentor, the world's greatest teacher. He must have loved Jesus, loved him deeply, owed him his very life. Why then does he do it? Why do we?

According to Matthew, he repents, but too late (Matt. 27:3). If he had come back to the group and asked forgiveness, would they have granted it? Perhaps not. But he too, at the Last Supper, had eaten the bread and drunk the cup of salvation "for the forgiveness of sins" (Matt. 26:28). Is he not also saved? And if he is not, is anyone?

Devotional exercise: *Make a list: How have I been betrayed? How have I been a betrayer? Do I know the Judas in me that betrays with a kiss what I know is truest and best?*

Thursday, March 28   Read Mark 14:22-26;
                                          Luke 22:15-18.

Jesus' last fast

Entertain, for a moment, this hypothesis:

Luke, who has a special source for the passion narrative that he tends to prefer to Mark, depicts Jesus in 22:15-18 as earnestly desiring to eat the Passover with them before he suffers. But, he says, "I shall not eat it until it is fulfilled in the kingdom of God." The same with the cup: "Divide it among yourselves; for I tell you that from now on I shall not drink of the fruit of the vine until the kingdom of God comes." In this account, he *abstains* from the meal. How can he eat it? He is the firstborn son, and the angel of death will not pass over him this night (see Exod. 11:4-7). How can he eat it, when he has declared the bread his own body, the wine his own blood? It is for them to drink, to take his life into themselves. For him to partake would be symbolic self-cannibalization.

So he fasts. He identifies with the Egyptian elder sons. He crosses over and identifies with the enemy. He takes Israel's oldest, founding myth and breathes a whole new meaning into it. He does not ignore tradition, he transforms it. He interprets Israel's collective myth in the light of his own, emergent myth. He reaches out to include the Gentiles, the enemies, the oppressors, the excluded.

What if we were to exercise the same creative fidelity to his tradition that Jesus showed by both observing Passover and reshaping it to fit the circumstances of his own death? How would we change the way we celebrate the Eucharist?

Suggestion for meditation: *What is it that is moving within and among us, that wants to be ingested, incorporated, incarnated, become one with our flesh? Will we let it?*

99

March 29 (Good Friday)

Read John 19:17-30.

The scapegoat revisited

The scapegoat is back, only this time not in poetry but in person. What Isaiah had pictured, Jesus now incarnates: a surrogate victim, dying for the people, "that the whole nation should not perish" (John 11:50). This victim, however, is voluntary. He chooses to play the scapegoat in order to put to death the scapegoating mechanism. He offers himself as sacrifice in order to end sacrificing. He is counted with the transgressors, crucified between two criminals. His status is satirized; Pilate acidly hails him "King of the Jews," as if to say, "Is this the best you Jews can do?" Jesus is left naked; even his clothes are confiscated by soldiers. He drinks, then dies.

Every other scapegoat ended thus. Finished. But Isaiah had predicted something more: vindication through death. God vindicates Jesus by raising him from the dead. What is that to us, who may have no idea what "raising from the dead" means?

God's action means that the murder of this man could not be covered up as "the will of God" (though theologians would later attempt that very thing). That the scapegoating mechanism was revealed for what it is: murder. That the veil of religion cast over the sacrifice of human life (or even animals) is a lie intended to keep society complicit in its murders. That the life crushed by the System leaps from the grave to trouble the course of injustice. That expectation of miracle is the only reasonable stance in a world where God is loose. That joy is possible in suffering, that life rises from death, that hope is grounded in reality, that God's victory over evil is certain.

Prayer: *Subverting God, free me from the powers of death, that your light might flash through me. Amen.*

March 30 (Holy Saturday)

Read John 20:2-10.

The second betrayal

What an odd narrative John 20:1-18 is! Mary Magdalene alone goes to the tomb (20:1), yet says "we" in verse 2. (In the other Gospels she is with other women.) She sees the stone rolled away and runs and tells Peter that Jesus' body has been stolen; yet she hasn't even looked inside. Peter and the beloved disciple then engage in a footrace, which John easily wins; but he waits at the tomb and allows Peter to enter the tomb first. They see only linen cloths and a napkin (Mary will see two angels). Then they go home, without even telling the other disciples (vv. 2-10)!

Nothing was said about Mary returning, but here she is again, outside the tomb (v. 11). No doubt she could have tagged along. But try this possibility: Read verse 1, and then skip to verse 11. You have a story that is internally consistent, that corresponds to the assertion in Matthew 28:9-10 and Mark 16:9 that Jesus appeared first to the women, and, in the latter case, specifically "first to Mary Magdalene."

Whence John 20:2-10 then? Perhaps because God, some male decided, had botched the job, having Jesus appear first to women, whose witness meant nothing in Jewish society. So we have to insert some men—at least two witnesses were required.

So the men take preeminence away from women. When Paul reports on the witnesses to the resurrection (1 Cor. 15:3-8), he mentions not a single woman. Peter is the first witness he mentions, but significantly, he does not say Peter was the first. Mary was. Was it a fair trade-off—providing the resurrection with credible witnesses, at the cost of what God meant us to learn when he had Jesus appear first to a woman?

Prayer: *Subverting God, what did you mean for us to learn when you had Jesus first appear to a woman? Lead us to greater understanding of your will for us. Amen.*

Sunday, March 31 (Easter)
Read John 20:1, 11-18.

The second transformation: the witnesses

The struggle over the status of women in the early church was fought out over the question, Who is a valid witness to the Resurrection? In the earliest tradition, Jesus first appeared to Mary Magdalene (Matt. 28:9-10; Mark 16:9; John 20:1, 11). In Mark, the women are so terrified that they violate the angel's instructions and tell no one (Mark 16:8). In Luke, the women do tell the disciples but they receive it as "an idle tale" (24:11). Even in Mark 16:9-11, where Mary tells the disciples, they reject her authority as a witness to the risen Lord.

In John 20:1, 11-18, however, Mary is not only the first witness but also the first apostle. Jesus will not allow her to cling to him, but sends her forth: "Go to my brethren and say to them, I am ascending" (v. 17). If a woman could be an apostle (Rom. 16:7—the Greek text reads *Junia,* who would be a woman), or a disciple on equal footing with men (Acts 9:36-42), could lead house churches (Acts 12:12; 16:14-15), open new fields for evangelism (Phil. 4:2-3), endure persecution and jail just as men did (Acts 8:3; 9:1-2), be Paul's co-workers (Rom. 16:3, 6, 12), lead congregations (Philem. 1-2), and even, in one case, have authority over Paul himself (Rom. 16:1-2—not "helper" but "ruler"!)—then a truly profound transformation has taken place: the equality of the sexes is honored in the household of God.

The resurrection of Jesus Christ brought new life to a world that was dying. And part of that new life, that new order, was the recognition by Christ that men and women are to be equal in their place in society and in the family of God.

Prayer: *Subverting God, how am I resisting your new order? Break down my resistance, and free me for joyful service to you. Amen.*

LIVING TOGETHER AFTER THE RESURRECTION

April 1-7, 1991 **Phyllis R. Pleasants**†
Monday, April 1 Read Psalm 133.

"How good it is and how pleasant for brothers [and sisters] to live together!" (NEB) How can this be? we ask. We know from scripture that there was conflict among the people of God, both in ancient Israel and within the early Christian communities where the Psalms were their hymnbook. We know the conflict in our faith traditions.

The psalmist takes what was probably a wisdom saying about the family and applies it to the people of God. The living together to which the psalmist refers is something more than a collection of individuals who come together periodically for a special purpose. The psalmist is testifying to life where people are joined by their common identity as the people of God. This is not dormitory living where the lives of those who occupy the same physical space may or may not ever connect. The fragrant, abundant, overflowing life in the presence of God to which the psalmist refers occurs only when people are united by the God who gives them their identity as God's own people—when their responsiveness to God joins them in responding to one another. When our identity as the people of God transcends the human differences that separate us, then living together is the place where the Lord bestows life for evermore.

Suggestion for meditation: *Our lists can be our prayers. List every-thing that prevents you from experiencing living together as being the people of God. Then list everything that allows you, or would allow you, to experience life this way. How do you move from one list to the other? Let this question be the focus of your prayer.*

---

†Doctoral candidate in church history at Southern Baptist Theological Seminary, Louisville, Kentucky.

Tuesday, April 2   Read John 20:19-23.

With the arrest of Jesus in the garden of Gethsemane, the disciples fled, scattered to the wind in terror. Then slowly they reassembled—for reassurance, justification, protection. Fear settled in to stay for a while. If this is what they did to Jesus, what will they do to us, his followers? When will they come looking for us? Not even the reports of an empty tomb and Jesus appearing to Mary Magdalene dissipated the fear.

The witness of scripture is not that fear is not a part of the people of God; on the contrary, the risen Christ comes to us in the midst of our fear. Christ did not wait until the disciples were no longer afraid before revealing himself to them. They were hiding behind locked doors, terrified of what might happen to them, when Christ stood in the midst of them and said, "Peace be with you." Christ did not castigate them for their fear. He came to assure them he was who he claimed to be, and that he was with them. He came to them silently, without their knowing anything about it, in the midst of their fear.

As disciples today, we, too, experience fear. We are afraid to believe, or to stand firm in what we do believe. We are afraid of what others will do to us, or of what we will do to them. We are fearful for our comfort, safety, and protection. We are fearful of pain, loss, and suffering. In the midst of our fear the risen Christ comes to us. The disciples responded with joy when they recognized their Lord. How do we respond? Only as we recognize the Christ standing in our midst can our fear turn into joy.

Prayer: *Forgive us our arrogance, O God, when we try to conquer our fear on our own and fail to recognize you in the midst of it, waiting to quell our storms. In the name of the risen Christ, we pray. Amen.*

Wednesday, April 3   Read John 20:24-27.

The Gospel of John testifies that doubt also is part of living together. Throughout history Thomas has been labeled "Doubting Thomas," as if he were the only one of those first disciples to doubt. Chapter 20 reveals that *all* of the disciples had a hard time coming to faith in the risen Christ.

At the beginning of the chapter, Peter and the beloved disciple saw the empty tomb. Verses 8 and 9 record that they believed, even though they still did not understand the scriptures that revealed how Jesus must rise from the dead. Verse 18 has Mary Magdalene coming to the disciples with her news that she has seen the Lord and that he has given her a message for them. However, in verse 19 the disciples, including Peter and the beloved disciple, are together behind locked doors fearing for their safety.

Thomas is not the only disciple to doubt. He is not the only one who had to see in order to believe. None of the others believed until Christ appeared to them. Thomas's story represents the coming through doubt to faith of all disciples.

Doubt is part of living together. No one can believe for another. The disciples could believe neither on the basis of an empty tomb nor on the basis of Mary's testimony. Thomas could not believe on the basis of a majority report. Nor can we. Only as we experience the risen Christ in the midst of our doubt do we come to faith. As Thomas doubted, Jesus appeared to him inviting him from unbelief to belief. And now it is so for us. Doubt is a sign not of unbelief but of receptivity to the invitation to belief, when we recognize the Christ who comes to us.

Suggestion for meditation: *What do you doubt? Doctrines? Yourself? God? Others? Name your doubts. Listen. In the silence of this moment, in the midst of these doubts, how is Christ inviting you to belief?*

Thursday, April 4   Read John 20:28-31.

While living together after the resurrection includes doubt and fear, it also includes faith. Through recognizing the risen Christ in our midst, we are brought through fear and doubt to faith in the One who accompanies us.

Thomas had insisted he would not only have to see the Lord but he would also have to touch him. Touching him just any- where would not suffice, either. Thomas would have to stick his finger into the place where the nails were and his hand into the place where the sword pierced Jesus' side. How often are we, also, this insistent on proof? If you do such and such, Lord, then I will believe and surrender my whole life: let me get married, make my marriage work, help me through this class, get me that promotion, make me successful, let me win, and I will give you all the glory. We, like Thomas, often insist on exactly what has to happen for us to believe.

All of Thomas's insistence vanished in the presence of the risen Christ. There is no record he ever touched Christ anywhere. Recognizing he was in the presence of his Lord, all Thomas could do was confess his faith. "My Lord and my God!" (NEB) So it is for us. Experiencing the risen Christ reveals how trivial our insistence on proof is. This experience is a mystery no proof can ever comprehend.

Like the first disciples, our living together is possible only by the risen Christ bringing us to faith. All we can do is confess, "My Lord and my God!" We do not read the Gospel stories in order to duplicate their experiences. Instead, these stories pre- pare us to expect, anticipate, and recognize the risen Christ who has come to lead us through fear and doubt to faith.

Prayer: *Our Lord and our God, we pray as did the father of the epileptic child, "I believe; help my unbelief!" By your grace we follow you through to faith. Amen.*

Friday, April 5   Read Acts 4:32-35.

After experiencing the risen Christ and receiving the Holy Spirit, the believers in Jerusalem experienced unity. The account in Acts is reminiscent of Psalm 133. Wherever Christians were throughout the city, they experienced a bonding of caring, a common vision of how to live a Christian life. The risen Christ is never just for us to receive; we must also do our part by sharing with others out of the foundation of that experience.

Sharing is a community phenomenon with external and internal components. The external manifestation of sharing God's grace in the Jerusalem community was the sharing of property. Those who had property sold it when needed for the benefit of the entire community, because their identity was found in the community rather than in individual property. The community was held in high esteem because its members were never needy.

The internal component that motivated the sharing of property was the sharing of themselves. When individuals gather with their identities based on individual achievements and possessions, the result is people hiding their needs or pretending to be something they are not. When a community gathers with its identity found in the well-being of the entire group, then people are more willing to share themselves, to be vulnerable, and to express their needs.

Communities form around a variety of shared interests or causes. Christian communities are drawn together in the experience of the risen Christ. The risen Christ unites us heart and soul, enabling us to overcome our isolation as individuals and become the people of God.

Suggestion for meditation: *Is the congregation where you worship a collection of individuals or a community? What does the image of your congregation in the community reveal about what unites the congregation?*

Saturday, April 6   Read 1 John 1:1-4.

Christian communities may form on the basis of shared experiences with the risen Christ, but they also focus on specific affirmations about Jesus prior to the crucifixion. In this prologue the author states quite plainly, "Our theme is the word of life. This life was made visible . . ." (NEB). I know this word of life was made visible, he writes, on the basis of what I have heard, seen, and felt. I share it with you so that you may know it, too, for yourself, and so that all of us will experience completed joy.

The unity shared by the experience of the risen Christ is not a permanent condition. For example, the story of Ananias and Sapphira immediately follows the passage in Acts where the Christians are holding all property in common. And, in John's community there is conflict between those affirming the tradition of the Incarnation as the focal point of faith and those insisting on continuing revelation and new understanding. The writer would not have to insist so fervently on the belief in the Incarnation as that which determines sharing life with God if those denying this idea did not exist.

Christian communities exist in the tension between the already and the not-yet. There are moments of significant insight into the life with God that is intended for all creation. Living together after the resurrection, though, also includes incompleteness, the not-yet. Experience has a surplus of meaning. There is tension between what is experienced and what is believed about the experience. The claim of faith is that the living God is in the tension continually working to bring God's creation to completeness.

Prayer: *Grant us humility, O God, to recognize that our most profound understanding of you is not you. May we hold to the essence of our affirmations of faith and still be open to you as you lead us to more complete understanding. Amen.*

Sunday, April 7   Read 1 John 1:5–2:2.

The incompleteness of living together after the resurrection is not a hopeless situation. Our hope is in the one who is the remedy for sin, and our advocate before God. Christian community is not based on our goodwill—that is always flawed. Yet we do our part when we live according to the light we have received from God in Christ and are open to continually receive more.

One danger in living together is self-deception. We deceive ourselves, both individually and as a community, when we say, "Okay, this is all there is to truth, and we've already got it." Or, "We've never done such and such, therefore we are perfect." Or, "We accept this doctrine and will shout it from the rooftops as the only way truth can be expressed." The darkness of self-deception is like being shut in a closet, or shut in a room with heavy drapes pulled tight across the windows. Neither shutting the door nor closing the drapes puts out the light. The light still shines, but we are not open to receive it.

We are walking in the light of God rather than the darkness of self-deception when there is integrity and coherence between our words and our actions. Knowing the truth is not intellectual knowledge alone. It is not knowing something *about* the truth. Knowing the truth means *doing* the truth—participating in God's communication of truth. We are able to do that when we recognize we are always in need of insight, understanding, and direction from God.

Suggestion for meditation: *Today the Christian community gathers. Where is the community locked in to self-deception? Pray that we will risk being open to new life in God as revealed through the Holy Spirit, rather than remaining in the bondage of self-deception. Listen to what God is leading you to do to begin being more open in your own life.*

A CALL TO HIGHER LIVING

April 8-14, 1991   **Emmanuel L. McCall†**
Monday, April 8   Read Acts 3:1-5.

Getting the attention of persons in need

"Peter looked straight at him, as did John. Then Peter said, 'Look at us!' So the man gave them his attention, expecting to get something from them" (NIV).

People in need want their needs to be met. Their perceived needs may not be their most important or only needs. Those who can focus the attention of persons in need on their real needs are blessed indeed.

The upper room prayer experience that preceded Pentecost was kept alive daily by Peter and John. They understood the power of an active prayer life. Equipped with a holy boldness, they went about fulfilling the command of our Lord. They remained open to whatever God wanted to do through them.

One afternoon, entering the temple for daily prayer, they encountered a man whom they often saw begging at one of the temple gates. His perceived need was charity to sustain his life. But the disciples perceived his need to be a sense of wholeness, a release from all that crippled him.

Peter's holy boldness allowed him to take charge of the encounter. Once he had the man's attention, the Holy Spirit's power could address all the man's needs for healing, mobility, self-determination, self-esteem, and independence.

Suggestion for meditation: *What needs do others have that God wants you to meet? How can you direct the attention of needy persons to the Holy Spirit that can bring them wholeness?*

---

†Director, Black Church Extension Division, Home Mission Board, Southern Baptist Convention; adjunct faculty, Southern Baptist Theological Seminary and New Orleans Baptist Seminary, Atlanta, Georgia.

Tuesday, April 9   Read Acts 3:12-19.

Giving credit where credit is due

"When Peter saw this, he said to them: 'Men of Israel, why does this surprise you? Why do you stare at us as if by our own power or godliness we had made this man walk? The God of Abraham, Isaac and Jacob, the God of our fathers, has glorified his servant Jesus'" (NIV).

It must have been awesome to see one known to be an invalid jumping, leaping, walking, and running. Gratitude for the miracle caused the man to embrace Peter and John. Those witnessing the deed concluded that these men possessed miraculous powers. In view of their conclusion, Peter had three options: (1) take full credit for the miracle, (2) emphasize his role in the miracle, or (3) use it as an opportunity to preach about Jesus.

Option one would make Peter a liar. What if the Holy Spirit withdrew power when other miracles were needed? Peter would have proven to be a phony. Option two would also have been a lie, for Peter was only an instrument God used. The power was not in the vehicle, but in the Holy Spirit. Peter did not hesitate to choose option three. Since his hearers had been participants in the crucifixion, Peter went to the heart of the matter. He proclaimed the resurrected Christ, triumphant over life, death, evil, and potentates. Peter announced Christ as the fulfillment of prophetic oracles. Peter preached Christ as the hope of their redemption, the object of their repentance, and the judge of their destinies.

Peter had no false piety; he was empowered by the Holy Spirit. He boldly preached Jesus as Lord, and he gave God the glory for what God had done.

Suggestion for reflection: *What have you recently taken credit for that you did not deserve? What will you do about it?*

Wednesday, April 10 Read Psalm 4.

Now I lay me down to sleep

"I will lie down and sleep in peace, for you alone, O LORD, make me dwell in safety" (NIV).

The problems of insomnia sometimes rage like flood waters. Often we have trouble getting a good night's sleep. However, the psalmist seems to have found the key: peaceful sleep is a by-product of complete trust in the righteousness of God and a right relationship with God. Here are the psalmist's suggestions:

(1) Appeal to God when you feel life has not been fair. God is righteous, merciful, gracious, and selective (vv. 1, 3).

(2) Don't become awed by detractors. Their words are based on fairy tales and fantasies (v. 2).

(3) When you prepare for bed, have pleasant thoughts. Don't waste time plotting retaliation and vengeance. Vengeance belongs to the Lord. God's payback is complete, exact, and just.

(4) Don't neglect spiritual disciplines (v. 5). They reinforce divine perspectives and help us focus on God.

(5) When others cry out in despair, be ready to witness to your faith (v. 6).

(6) Give thanks for God's goodness. Meditate on your blessings rather than your hurts and losses (v. 7).

(7) Then go to sleep confident that our righteous, merciful, just, and powerful God has complete charge of the personal and global destinies of all creatures (v. 8).

Prayer: *Gracious God, help us recapture the simple trust found in the child's prayer:*

>*Now I lay me down to sleep,*
>*I pray the Lord my soul to keep.*
>*If I should die before I wake,*
>*I pray the Lord my soul to take. Amen.*

Thursday, April 11   Read 1 John 3:1-2.

Becoming

"Dear friends, now we are children of God, and what we will be has not yet been made known. But we know that when he appears, we shall be like him, for we shall see him as he is" (NIV).

"Please be patient with me. God is not through with me yet" was one of the popular clichés of the early 1980s. The same idea appears in First John 3:1-7.

Through infinite mercy, God has drawn us into a new relationship. We are no longer aliens, but children—God's children, divine offspring, new creations. We have not earned this status; it is strictly a gift of God's grace.

Just as we expect there to be a resemblance between biological parent and child, so there should be a resemblance in this divine-human relationship. We are moving toward our true identity. We are becoming. To forecast what we shall be like, we look at Jesus. He is not only the key to our changed nature; his Spirit is at work in our becoming. As the firstfruits of the new creation, Jesus abides in a resurrected body—a body truimphant over sin, glorified, and capable of transcending space and time. We shall be like him.

As a child I thrilled to the adventures of Superman. "Faster than a speeding bullet, more powerful than a locomotive, able to leap tall buildings in a single bound." But Superman pales in comparison to what the redeemed of the Lord are becoming. Our becoming is not complete in this life; it will be completed only when Jesus comes again. Then we shall be just like him.

Suggestion for meditation: *"Everyone who has this hope in him purifies himself, just as he is pure" (NIV).*

Friday, April 12   Read 1 John 3:3-7.

A call to higher living

"Everyone who has this hope in him purifies himself, just as he is pure" (NIV).

Popular usage sometimes hinders our understanding of the language in scripture. "Pure" and "purity" are a case in point. We take these words to mean "without flaw"—"with no defects."

"Pure" appears more than 20 times in the New Testament. In about ten of those instances, the reference is to being "clean." In the other instances, "pure" refers to single-minded, non-manipulative attitudes. Purity is not an ethereal state to be reached; it is an attitude to be lived.

Purity calls for a heart, mind, and will that are single, devoted to only one loyalty. Purity calls for honesty about oneself. It avoids attempts to be impressive, to flatter oneself or others.

In a society that awards manipulators and manipulative relationships, purity often goes unrewarded. Some "pure ones" are heralded only after their deaths, reminding us of Jesus' words in Matthew 23:29-30. Fortunate are the "pure ones" who live long enough to see their dishonor become honor.

What gives evidence of our purity? Verses 4-7 of today's passage are very specific. The "pure ones" do not keep on sinning. They abhor anything that detracts from the divine image restored in and through Jesus Christ. A righteous person produces righteous deeds. To claim purity while continuing to sin is a contradiction.

Until the Lord returns, we must consciously guard against low-level living. We are sons and daughters of God. We must live like we belong to God.

Prayer: *Father, forgive us for sloshing in the bogs of life when we have been set free to glide like eagles. Amen.*

Saturday, April 13 Read Luke 24:35-39.

Touch me and see

"He said to them, 'Why are you troubled, and why do doubts rise in your minds? Look at my hands and my feet. It is I myself! Touch me and see; a ghost does not have flesh and bones, as you see I have" (NIV).

What will our resurrected bodies be like? This question has been in the minds of believers since the resurrection of our Lord. The apostle Paul made this a key item of his first letter to the church in Corinth (see 1 Cor. 15).

Our question is answered in this experience of Jesus' disciples in Jerusalem. Two of them had just encountered the risen Lord as they trudged from Jerusalem to Emmaus. Jesus had been walking and talking with them, but they did not know who he was. They even invited him in to dinner and rest. Not until he broke the loaf did they recognize him to be the risen Lord.

Even after running the several miles back to Jerusalem, the two disciples could not convince the others that their experience was real. Even when the risen Lord reappeared behind locked doors, they still didn't believe it was Jesus. They assumed it was a ghost, since myth informed them that ghosts could move through solid substances. But Jesus took the initiative in helping them see past myth to a new reality. First, Jesus invited them to *look* at the imprint of nail holes in his hands and feet. Then, if they thought their eyes were deceiving them, they were invited to *touch*. What they felt was a complete body, not a shadow or image. To prove he was not an insubstantial spirit, Jesus asked for food. They responded by giving him fish and bread.

What will our resurrected bodies be like? Just like the resurrected Jesus.

Prayer: *Thank you, Lord, for a foretaste of eternity. Amen.*

Sunday, April 14   Read Luke 24:40-48.

History in the making

"You are witnesses of these things" (NIV).

Picture the scene. Jesus had just confirmed his resurrected state. The disciples had not only looked at him but had also touched him. He was not a ghost. But other misunderstandings remained to be corrected.

One such misunderstanding concerned the nature of the kingdom of God. The disciples thought the kingdom was banners, flags, kings, queens, positions, armies, and power. Jesus had to displace these notions so that his followers could begin to understand his teachings on the kingdom. A second area of misunderstanding concerned the teachings of the prophets. The disciples did not understand what the prophets were trying to say until Jesus reinterpreted Israelite history with himself as center. Suddenly it all made sense. They were now to interpret history as *his story*. "The Christ will suffer and rise from the dead on the third day, and repentance and forgiveness of sins will be preached in his name to all nations, beginning at Jerusalem" (NIV; see Hos. 6:2). Now life took on a new purpose and meaning. Henceforth, they were to be Jesus' witnesses. They were to tell "his story" to the ends of the earth, a story they knew because they had experienced it.

Since the story seemed so ludicrous, how would they convince anyone of their sincerity and the story's truth? They were to wait in that upper room, behind locked doors, until the Spirit came. Then, clothed with the Spirit's power, they told the story. We are heirs of the promise because of their faithfulness.

Prayer: *Lord, thank you for the faithful witness of those who followed you. Help us be powerful witnesses of your truth not because of what we have heard but because of what we know. Amen.*

TRUST AND LOVE IN TRUTH AND DEED

April 15-21, 1991   **Georgine Lomell Buckwalter†**
Monday, April 15   Read Psalm 23:1-4.

"The LORD is my Shepherd, I shall want nothing" (NEB). *My* Shepherd. *No* thing. If a believer can sincerely assert that, then come what may, the rest of life can be managed.

Early in Israel's history, the covenant faithfulness of God was exclusively seen in relation to the nation as a whole. Imagine the joy as believers began to appropriate God's loyal concern for them as individual sheep! Can you remember the first time you truly grasped the reality that God knew even the hairs on your head? Such knowledge makes us feel cherished, looked after, protected. The promise that we shall be *personally* led gives us the courage to move forward as pilgrims into the unknown.

Yet it can be frightening. The psalmist knew all about inadequate pasturage, scarce and sour water. He knew all about rocky precipices and the predators that lurked. In our own days and ways, so do we. If not a desert, it's at least a jungle out there!

But *my* shepherd, the psalmist says, leads me through it all to it all. Can we declare that? Through dark, death-filled places and experiences, through lean pickings and polluted waters and wrong ways of living and being . . . to what is green and still and righteous, to what restores us to God. Can we declare that by the rod and staff which guides and goads we are led forward— lacking no thing, fearing no thing—not even evil?

Prayer: *Lord, you know our needs and you provide. When we stray, you nudge us back. When death shadows and evils loom, you see us through. We count on that. Amen.*

---

†Chaplain, Westminster Health Care Center; assistant at St. Thomas Episcopal Church, Louisville, Kentucky.

117

Tuesday, April 16   Read Psalm 23:5-6.

God as Shepherd, tenderly and wisely leading us to what restores, is familiar. The Shepherd as hospitable host is less so. Yet the reality of the laden table and the ever-open tent flap must stand beside the rod and staff in our declaration of trust. The nomads of Israel very much counted on this aspect of God's character.

Hospitality to the sojourner was not a matter of entertainment but of covenantal gratitude to God for past deliverance. Israel knew well that when the night was dark and enemies circled, there was safety and surfeit to be found in God's tent. Not leftovers but plentitude and abundance!

Perhaps the psalmist was an aged shepherd looking back in wonder on his life in relationship with God. Life review is a critical spiritual task for the elderly and one which searches for and celebrates God's providing presence from birth to death. With a grateful heart as overflowing as that cup, the psalmist pens his praises as one who knows. That's what encourages me. How about you? He's been there and knows the Shepherd was there. He remembers the Exodus and the desert: the leading and feeding, the water and manna. Do we?

The back-lit eyes of the faithful elderly I work with as they tell of being downright pursued by God's mercy and goodness is a sight to see. It anoints the answering soul with the oil of gladness. The life testimonies of those who have struggled against financial, physical, and emotional enemies and yet say they were protected, of those who have suffered deprivation and yet say they lacked nothing have much to teach us about trust.

Suggestion for meditation: *Review your own personal salvation history. Prayerfully remember times of deliverance. Recognize the purposeful pattern and celebrate times of abundance. Renew your trust.*

118

Wednesday, April 17   Read John 10:11-13.

The audience who listened to Jesus knew about shepherds from daily experience. Their prophet Ezekiel had railed against the shepherd-kings of old who had fed themselves at the expense of the sheep, ruled with harshness and scattered the flock through neglect. Do we know any religious leaders today who exploit believers for personal gain? Headines say yes. Ezekiel promised a time when God would come as shepherd to gather the lost and tend to Israel. In the face of the hostile Pharisees, possibly represented here as hirelings, Jesus announces that he is that Good Shepherd. The one that can be trusted. "Hirelings take heed" the world over, for the flock belongs to God, not those charged with keeping watch!

What distinguishes Jesus from the other shepherds? The Good Shepherd loves the flock enough to die for them. In John's Gospel, Jesus knows all. He recognizes the wolf of death that circles. He knows all and is willing to give his all for the salvation of the sheep. Do we sometimes forget the enormous price he was willing to pay to lead us, feed us, save us?

A meditation on the Passion of our Lord in the context of this passage juxtaposes the images of shepherd and paschal lamb in powerful ways. Rod, staff, and cross intersect. Truly, he is a shepherd like no other.

In our own time we appreciate those leaders who are willing to make sacrifices in the exercise of their responsibilities. But there are so many hirelings and thieves, so many who exploit, deceive, and desert! Only one Shepherd willingly gave his life. Only one didn't flee so we could be both saved and free.

Prayer: *Like a shepherd lead us, Lord. We remember the price you paid. Though wolves encircle, we know you will not desert us. With trusting hearts we follow, fearing nothing, lacking nothing. Amen.*

Thursday, April 18   Read John 10:14-16.

Have you ever been in a large lecture class and realized that despite your faithful attendance, you remained a nameless entity to the professor? Did it affect your participation? Being part of God's flock is not the same as being lost in a crowd. Being named and known makes all the difference. The Good Shepherd not only lays down his life, "he knows as he is known."

Knowing names means a lot in John's Gospel. Jesus comes as the heavenly revealer of God's name, and God's children are those who believe in the name of God's only Son. Jesus' use of the "I am" formula intentionally calls forth the divine name. So not only are we known, we know God's name in a special covenantal way.

Jesus' listeners would have understood the deep intimacy in "I know my own and my own know me." Loyalty, trust, and intimacy are all interconnected. Our readings are irradiated with the steadfastness and love of God, and all our trust and intimacy are grounded in this reality. Leaving cold anonymity behind, can we warm our hearts today around that steady blaze?

Intimate relationships have a way of becoming exclusive. Some are supposed to be. But Israel had difficulty sharing God's closeness and chosenness with the Gentiles. The Shepherd has other sheep and knows other names! Sometimes we need to be reminded that our special relationship with God is not threatened by another's. Being one with God necessarily includes being one with others.

Suggestion for meditation: *Think of Jesus' words of invitation or promise in the Gospels and hear your own name at the end. Example: "Come, follow me, Kristin"; "I will be with you, Hank, until the close of the age." Feel chosen and cherished today.*

Friday, April 19   Read 1 John 3:21-23.

To know and be known by God is to love and be loved. Intimacy is like that. But the vertical always includes the horizontal in the Christian faith. Knowing and believing in the name of God's Son involves loving others. According to the Johannine community's love ethic, you can't have one without the other. The author tells us that if we obey these twin commandments we may have confidence before God. Sound good?

At first glance, we may be relieved. Only two? Perhaps the Jewish converts in the early church, accustomed as they were to many do's and don'ts, also thought this simplified matters. But does it? Believing in Jesus' name is much more than intellectual assent. It means full acceptance of his revelation of God and the salvation tucked therein. This gift comes with demand! The indicative comes with an imperative.

Believing in the name of God's Son means doing as he did, loving as he loved. Suddenly it's not so simple. Our confidence before God waivers. We can love others enough to converse at coffee hour, bake a casserole now and then, and even attend their funerals. But to love enough, as Jesus did, to really lay down one's life for our brothers and sisters? If not given this maximum holy opportunity, are there ways we can be creative about how to live out the spirit of this love command in community?

Jesus' love ethic was radical as evidenced in his ministry to the outcasts and in his sacrificial death. God's "greater love" for us in Jesus (John 3:16) is radical and demands our responding "greater love" for others. (John 15:13). It's that simple. It's that hard.

Suggestion for meditation: *Several years ago a plane crashed into the Potomac River. A man in the water helped many to safety before he went under. Explore ways to practice that "greater love" every day.*

Saturday, April 20   Read 1 John 3:24.

That we shall dwell in him and he in us is both the promise and the hope of covenantal intimacy. Believers everywhere both yearn for this mutual indwelling and existentially experience it in amazing ways. The term for abiding in the Johannine community did not just mean to stay awhile. It described an in-the-middle-of-it-all tenting and tabernacling that was to be conditional. One was not to presume upon covenantal intimacy!

The passage promises that only if we keep the twin commands will God pitch his tent with us for keeps. Again our confidence before God waivers! To share in the life of the unending fellowship with God that we so desire depends upon our manifesting a radical love ethic which seems beyond our abilities. The good news is that it's not all up to us.

As ever, it is the power of the Holy Spirit that enables us to keep the commands just as it is the presence of the Holy Spirit that witnesses to the mutual indwelling. There is a way in which we can only have confidence before God because we first have confidence in God's gifting greatness. How very much we need the gifts of the Holy Spirit, which make possible true fellowship with God and with one another. Scripture tells us that with humanity alone little is possible, but with God much is. Don't you find that reassuring?

Prayer: *Lord, we long to believe enough and love enough. We want you to pitch your tent in our hearts and souls. Grant that the fruits of your Spirit's indwelling (love, patience, joy, kindness) may be manifested in our lives. To your honor and glory. Amen.*

Sunday, April 21   Read 1 John 3:17-19.

The litmus test for the indwelling of God in the believer is *acts* of love. Loving one's brother and sister in Christ is more than feelings or words. Loving *works* convince. After all, isn't that how we know that God is love? (1 John 4:8) We know by God's saving, just, and merciful acts of love. What God does grows out of who God is.

As the Truth, Jesus did the works of truth. As Love Incarnate, Jesus did the works of love. When the Spirit of Truth and Love dwells within the believer, doing the works of love and truth becomes possible. So when a sister or brother is in need, we are able to respond with loving deed. Not to do so would belie the absolute claim of Love and Truth in our lives! What we do grows out of who we are!

The overall theme this week has been "Trust and Love in Truth and Deed." Surely in the Christian pilgrimage, square one is trusting in the Good Shepherd and believing in Jesus as God's Son. Such trust gives us the courage to respond to the imperative to love radically. In addition to the courage to risk we are given the means of obedience as well as the proof—the presence and power of the Holy Spirit. We are flock-folk. We are never alone. The Shepherd ever feeds and leads and protects. We are never lost, for we know God and are known by God. And we are doers of love and truth.

Suggestion for meditation: *Using the first person singular, reword and repeat the last five sentences above as affirmations. Bathe yourself in them throughout the day. Close each declaration session with thanksgiving and praise.*

April 22-28, 1991   **Michael J. O'Donnell†**
Monday, April 22   Read Psalm 22:25-31.

Why do we worship?

First, God deserves our worship. God has given us every good thing we have; therefore, it is right to give God praise and thanksgiving. We would be ungrateful indeed if we did not acknowledge God's graciousness to us.

Second, worship puts us in our proper place. God is first in all things; we are not. However, that idea goes against all that we learn during our lifetime. When we are taught to look out for Number One, that means we really should be worshipping God!

Worship is sacrificial. It is not easy to put another before ourselves, even if that other is God. We want to be in charge of our lives. But worship forces us to admit that there is someone else in charge. And I thank God there is. I cannot imagine what my life would be like if all I had to work with was my own strength, my own wits, and my own sense of direction. Without God quietly nudging me along toward the right path, bailing me out of situations I get myself into, and providing moments of grace when it is most needed, I would be a sad case indeed.

When I put aside my ego long enough to admit that God has been helping me, I find that I must go before God in worship. My worship may be private or it may be public—there are times when each is appropriate. But both are important. We need to do both in order to be faithful to the One we worship and the community of faith in which we gather in Jesus' name.

Prayer: *O God, our help in ages past, our hope for years to come; be thou our guide while life shall last, and our eternal home! Amen.*

---

†Pastor, Christ United Methodist Church; editor, *Sacramental Life;* abbot of the Order of St. Luke, Akron, Ohio.

Tuesday, April 23   Read Acts 8:26-35.

Many Christians today are timid, afraid to talk about their faith and their church. Being religious is no longer the "in" thing. When we become afraid of expressing our religious beliefs and values, we open ourselves to forces that are not of God.

Our problem is not that we have nothing to share. We *do* have something to share: the good news of Jesus Christ. It is not that we lack the desire to share this good news. But matters of faith are often not readily expressible. In the church we talk in code, in a language that separates us from non-church people: "Jesus is my Lord and Savior," "I believe in God the Father, Son, and Holy Spirit," "Jesus died for my sin," "Jesus is the Lamb who is my Shepherd," and so forth. Those within the church know what is meant by these phrases, even if we can't explain them very well. But when we take these words outside the church, people look at us strangely because we are not speaking their language. They do not understand, and therefore feel left out even as we are attempting to draw them in.

Faith defies logic—that is what makes it faith. When we try to share our faith with a friend who respects us, we don't want to sound illogical or strange. So talking about our faith is difficult. Our timidity emerges especially when we want to invite this friend into a relationship with Jesus Christ, but we lack the words. "Then Philip opened his mouth, and beginning with this scripture he told him the good news of Jesus." What an easy way to evangelize. Let us trust God enough to supply the words that will tell the story to our friend. The Holy Spirit will give us both the words and the courage to utter them.

Suggestion for prayer: *Instead of using words to pray today, close your eyes and imagine your friend sitting at Jesus' feet and hearing the good news that Jesus taught and demonstrated with his life.*

Wednesday, April 24   Read Acts 8:36-40.

God called Philip to a peculiar task: he was to help an outcast. But he was not to follow our normal procedures for helping outcasts. The eunuch did not need clothing or food or water; he had all those things. He needed something greater. Philip gave him baptismal water and, therefore, Jesus Christ.

We are not called to share our faith only with those with whom we are most comfortable. If we are to challenge the world with the good news of Jesus Christ, we must challenge ourselves first.

Not very often, not often enough, but on occasion, when someone raises my suspicion or fear, I try to remember that Jesus died for that person as well as for me. That thought gives us a kinship that is deeper than blood. When one child in a family is threatened by someone outside the family, all the other brothers and sisters rally around to protect and support the one threatened. That love between brothers and sisters is wonderful. Our kinship with even our least lovable neighbor is based on our unity in Jesus' blood shed for all humanity. That person is indeed our brother or our sister.

Whom do you most fear? Whom would you be most comfortable sharing a hymnal with in church this Sunday? Who would be a stranger in your pew? This is the beginning of the next step in your spiritual journey—seeing the outsider as an insider. Jesus has brought us inside: inside the family of God, inside the realm of life eternal, inside the arena of forgiven sins. Yet we often forget that. When you feel like you are the outsider, remember that Jesus' death and resurrection were not in vain. They are for you—because God loves you.

Prayer: *Help us, O Lord, to recognize those people we dislike or even hate as persons who have been redeemed by your blood. Let them be for us our as our own kind. Amen.*

Thursday, April 25   Read 1 John 4:7-8.

"Beloved, let us love one another." Love is the most basic of human emotions. Without love our lives are never complete. Love is also the most difficult of human emotions because we allow so much to get in the way—a cross word, a strange look, an offending remark, an unfulfilled expectation.

Yet "love is of God." There is more to love than just human emotions. Many of us live beyond our means, spending more money than we earn. Through Jesus we are called to live beyond our emotions. We are to be guided by God's loving Spirit, not by our emotional state at the moment. That is why Jesus said that we are to love our enemies. Loving our enemies is possible if we live beyond our emotions. It takes discipline. It doesn't just happen because we want it to happen; it happens because God wants it to, makes it possible, and empowers us to live it out.

Sometimes I try to imagine what Jesus thought and felt about his persecutors. They must have angered him immensely. How disappointed he must have been when he was not heard, when God was not heard through him. Had Jesus relied on his emotions of anger, fear, and disappointment, he would not have subjected himself to the cross.

Yet he did. He died because his love was deeper than his feelings. His love was of the Spirit. By separating our emotions from our spiritual abilities, we can reach beyond the limits of our humanity. We are made in God's image, which means there is more to us than we know.

Spiritual discipline helps us know God—beyond and within us. "He who does not love does not know God." God is sufficient to supply our needs when we live beyond our emotions.

Prayer: *Help me love, O God, so that in loving others, I might know you more fully. Amen.*

127

Friday, April 26   Read 1 John 4:9-12.

We find it hard to love when we have been hurt or offended by another. Yet God has shown us that being offended is not an excuse not to love. Humanity has offended God seven million times seven million. Yet God keeps coming back to us, inviting us, loving us. Either God is foolish, or I am missing something. Since a foolish god is no god at all, I must not understand.

God's persistence tells me there is more to love than some emotional state we talk ourselves into or out of. Love is a spiritual gift. This gift is independent of our worthiness to receive it.

Since God's love is not based on our worth, it can bless us two ways. First, it means that we can be loved. Many of us feel unloved at times. Sometimes we have alienated others; sometimes we are cut off because of health or distance or hatred. Yet God has demonstrated that love is not always something we *feel*. It is something we *experience* through God's abiding presence within us. How can we hate ourselves when God loves us?

Second, God's love blesses us by making it possible for us to love others. Imagine for a moment Jesus dying for your sins. Imagine him on the cross, suffering for what you have done in your life. Imagine him pouring out his life that you might have new life. That abiding love makes it possible for us to love others—even our enemies. We can move beyond what others have done to us to what God has done for them. Imagine Jesus on the cross again. This time see him dying for the sins of your enemy. We say that Jesus died for the sins of all. Does that not make all persons loved in God's eyes? "If God so loved us, we also ought to love one another."

Suggestion for meditation: *Visualize yourself at the foot of the cross. Ask Jesus to forgive you of your sins. Then ask him to forgive the sins of your enemy.*

Saturday, April 27   Read John 15:1-4.

Whenever I read this passage I ask myself which branch of the vine I am. Do I bear fruit? Or am I just sapping nourishment from the vine and thus being more of a hindrance than a help?

Sometimes we nourish others; sometimes we are nourished by others. It varies at different times in our lives. During some seasons we are fruitful; during some seasons we are barren. Barrenness can give way to despondency, to spiritual emptiness. We feel that if there is a God, God doesn't care about us at all. We might as well be cut off from the vine because we already feel alienated from it.

On the other hand, the more fruitful times can lead to spiritual arrogance. "Gee, I managed to read my Bible every day this week—I'm a good Christian."

The difficulty with both these seasons is our emphasis on ourselves. Our most fruitful times are when we are totally open to Jesus Christ to use us or set us aside for his purposes.

John Wesley's Covenant Prayer puts this idea into perspective:

> I am no longer my own, but thine.
> Put me to what thou wilt, rank me with whom thou wilt;
> put me to doing, put me to suffering;
> let me be employed for thee or laid aside for thee. . . .

Being laid aside is not a time for spiritual laziness. Rather, God may be telling us to rest awhile, to reflect on what we have been busy doing and on why we have been doing it. Being set aside does not mean a vacation from God or the church. Rather, it is a resting place on a spiritual plateau before we venture up the next cliff. The important thing is not that we are always busy but that we are always faithful.

Prayer: *Help us, O Christ, not to measure our own worth in terms of busyness but rather through obedience. Amen.*

Sunday, April 28   Read John 15:5-8.

I heard this line of dialogue one day on television. The main character was facing an impossible situation, and his friend said to him: "Only God has the answer to that question." Then the friend said, "Only you have the answer; it lies within you."

When I heard the first statement I was encouraged. But after hearing the second part of the friend's response, I was grievously disappointed. The friend had come so close to the mark, missed it, and then sort of hit it unknowingly. "He who abides in me, and I in him, he it is that bears much fruit, for apart from me you can do nothing."

For the friend in the television drama that answer inside was called "character." It was the sum total of everything the main character had learned and been influenced by in his life. According to his friend, he could do no better than that. What he thought of himself was all he was allowed to be. With this analysis, self-imposed limits were placed on the character's ability to deal with his problems. His friend sold him short.

Imagine if the friend had said, "The answer lies within you, in Christ Jesus who dwells within!" It is an entirely different story when Christ dwells within, for Christ is from beyond and chooses to dwell within us. When we allow Christ in, we are no longer limited by our own mortal, expendable being. We have power beyond. We have grace.

Yes, the answer is God. The answer does lie within us. But it is far more majestic than anything we can imagine. "If you abide in me, and my words abide in you, ask whatever you will, and it shall be done for you." What a promise! What words of hope for the dark days of the soul when all appears to be lost!

Prayer: *Come Lord Jesus, and dwell within me. Let me be your instrument of love, justice, and peace. Amen.*

PENTECOST POWER

April 29–May 5, 1991   **Rita Anne Houlihan†**
Monday, April 29   Read Acts 10:44-46.

"While Peter was still speaking . . ." (JB). The parallel between the events described in Acts 10 and the Pentecost event as described in Acts 2 is self-evident. "They were all filled with the Holy Spirit, and began to speak foreign languages as the Spirit gave them the gift of speech" (Acts 2:4, JB).

"While Peter was still speaking. . . ." Here and in previous verses (see Acts 10:24-25) we see demonstrated Jesus' promise in Acts 1:8: "You shall be my witnesses in Jerusalem and in all Judea and Samaria and to the end of the earth."

"While Peter was still speaking. . . ." God's grace runs ahead of the preaching of the gospel. God's grace, God's love, God's yearning for us is all around us. We live in it. We do not cause it. We do not earn it. We cannot work toward it, nor do we deserve it. We are invited to use it, to grow by and through it, and to celebrate it.

Suggestion for meditation:
1. Sit quietly in faith in God's presence.

2. Recall an experience in the past that demonstrated God's grace, God's love, in your life.

3. Spend time being "in" the experience, using your dynamic memory (imagination plus memory) to make this experience as vivid as you can in the present moment.

4. "Sit" in the experience in the presence of the all-loving One, and allow yourself to relive the experience as deeply as you can. When you have finished, express in your own words whatever thoughts and feelings come to you.

---

†A sister of the Cenacle (Roman Catholic); retreat and spiritual director, Cenacle Retreat House, Highland Park, New Jersey.

Tuesday, April 30   Read Acts 10:44-48.

"The Holy Spirit fell on all who heard the word. . . . The circumcised . . . were amazed, because the gift of the Holy Spirit had been poured out even on the Gentiles." Again we see the parallel with the first Pentecost, when witnesses of that event are described as "amazed and astonished" (Acts 2:7, JB). The Holy Spirit consistently works in weakness, emptiness, and need, and triumphs through weakness, emptiness, and need.

What a challenge to the faith and love of those first followers of Christ! How in touch they must have been with the Spirit's action in their own lives, to be able to recognize the action of the Holy Spirit in such unlikely subjects as the Gentiles!

How much trust they must have had in Peter as a leader to agree with his observation that these people "received the Holy Spirit just as we have" (v. 47). How much trust and faith they must have had in Peter as leader and in the way Jesus' promises were being lived out (see Acts 1:8) to follow Peter's directive that these people "be baptized in the name of Jesus Christ" (v. 48).

Have you been surprised to see God's action in unlikely persons? Have you been challenged to be more open, more broad-minded, in accepting that God can and does love and work through others even when they seem unacceptable? Perhaps God is even trying to teach you through those persons!

How in touch are you with God's love and grace working in your life in the here and now?

Suggestion for meditation: *Sit quietly in faith in God's presence. Recall an experience today or in recent days when God's love and grace invited you into a greater inner freedom. Relive the experience as vividly as you can. Notice how it began, what feelings it released, and where it led you. Let your heart speak whatever comes to it—its yearnings, its gratitudes, its anxieties.*

Wednesday, May 1   Read Psalm 98.

This psalm echoes the closing chapters of the Book of Isaiah, which celebrate the mystery of God's action in the whole of creation.

The psalmist leads us to pray over God's universal salvation and God's steadfastness as seen by the whole world. He then encourages us, along with all the nations, to sing joyfully to the Lord and give the Lord praise. All creation is invited to enter into this celebration. This psalm is surely a good reminder to us of the close bond among all God's creatures.

Words of selfless joy and praise permeate the psalm, until we are presented with a more playful image of the floods clapping their hands and the hills singing for joy before the Lord (see v. 8). Finally the psalmist gives us the assurance, which we need to hear again and again, "He will judge the world with righteousness, and the peoples with equity."

Suggestion for meditation:
1. Sit quietly in faith in God's presence.

2. Ask the all-loving One to help you set aside any personal or global anxieties and lead you deeply into the spirit of celebration, joy, praise, and playfulness in this psalm.

3. Take one image of the psalm: The Lord proclaiming salvation to all the nations, the triumphant procession, the sea and its inhabitants, or the floods and the hills. Play with your chosen image. See how it might look and sound and feel to you. Draw the image if you wish. Allow your feeling to become as involved with your image as you can.

Thursday, May 2   Read 1 John 5:1-3.

The pentecost event described in Acts 10:44-48 is a paradigm of our own entry into the life of the church, of our own baptism as children of God, and of our own ongoing experience of the Holy Spirit acting in our lives.

In today's scripture, John leaves us in no doubt about what we need to enter into this pentecost: we need the belief that Jesus is the Christ. This faith in Jesus Christ is the sure sign that we are children of God. From this faith flows the love of others, because those who are children of God love God's children just as they love God (v. 2).

We know we love God and God's children when we keep God's commandments (see Rom 13:10). And, according to John, these commandments are not "burdensome" (v. 3). Here we are reminded of the great truth enunciated in Deuteronomy 30:11-14: "For this commandment . . . is not too hard for you, neither is it far off. It is not in heaven. . . . Neither is it beyond the sea. . . . But the word is very near you; it is in your mouth and in your heart, so that you can do it."

In the rush of daily living, how easily we forget that this faith and love is God's gift to us. It is not something we earn, or work toward, or achieve. God is eager, ready, and anxious to give us this gift. Our faith becomes burdensome when we try to rely on our own efforts to believe and to love, forgetting to ask God to increase these powers in us.

Suggestion for meditation:
1. Sit quietly in faith in God's presence.
2. Ask God to deepen your faith in Jesus who is the Christ. Choose a word or phrase that spoke to you in today's scripture. Say this word slowly again and again as your word of petition, indicating your need and your desire for this special grace.

Friday, May 3   Read 1 John 5:3-6.

In today's scripture passage John tells us clearly that everyone who is a child of God has conquered the world. The power that conquers is faith in Jesus who is the Christ. This faith in Jesus, believing that he is the Son of God, is inseparable from the love of God and of others.

This kind of practical faith, closely intertwined with love of God and others, gives us a power that overcomes the world. This faith changes us so that we have the power to conquer the world, just as Jesus has "overcome the world" (John 16:33). We conquer the world by accepting our need and our emptiness. We conquer the world by recognizing that without God we are nothing. But we must remember that we will not necessarily feel the Spirit's action. Often we will know the Spirit's presence more in retrospect, in reflection on the events in our lives. Part of the experience of our poverty and our need is not having the certainty that we have overcome the world.

When we accept God's gift of faith and open ourselves to growing in this gift, it becomes *our* faith. Our faith is not just a passive acceptance of this great gift; it is an active moving toward, reaching out, making our own, living in and through God's wondrous gift.

Prayer: *Dear God, thank you for this precious gift of faith. Forgive me for all the times I have failed to give the ready response of the true believer, all the times I have fought the experience of emptiness and inner poverty, all the times I have failed to rely in faith on you. Lord, deepen this great gift in me. Help me grow in a realistic, practical faith. Give me a vibrant spontaneity, and eager generosity of response. Help me be truly liberated in my going out to others, especially those in need, those from whom I think I could not receive anything profitable. Fill me with joy and love in your service and the service of others. Amen.*

Saturday, May 4   Read John 15:9-12.

Today's scripture passage is from the last discourse of Jesus in John's Gospel, that section of the fourth Gospel sometimes referred to as John's version of the Pentecost event. This passage is located within a longer section comprised of chapters 15–17.

For many of us these familiar verses are difficult to penetrate because we have heard them and read them and used them for prayer so often. We stop at favorite sections, reflect on one verse or another, and fail to experience them as part of the whole. The familiar becomes a barrier. As a result the richness of the context in which the tightly interwoven truths are expressed can be lost. We fail to penetrate the whole more fully because we are caught up in the parts.

Jesus asserts that he loves us as the Father loves him; that he wants us to remain, to live on in that love (v. 9); that we do live on in it if we keep his commandments, just as he has kept the Father's commandments (v. 10); that he wants us to follow his pattern so we will know the joy out of which he lives (v. 11); and that his commandment requires simply that we love one another (v. 12). All he says seems so obvious, yet it is so deeply mysterious.

Suggestion for meditation:
1. Sit quietly in faith in the presence of God. Spend as much time as necessary to become quiet and centered.

2. One way to break through the barrier of the familiar is to read Chapters 15–17 slowly, prayerfully, but without stopping at favorite passages. If possible, read these chapters aloud.

3. When you have finished reading, close the Bible, and then jot down phrases, images, and feelings that come to mind at that moment.

Sunday, May 5   Read John 15:13-17.

The ongoing tradition of the church has always understood the words of John 15–17 as addressed to all believers (see John 17:20), to all who believe that Jesus is the Christ (see 1 John 5:1). So as we pray over these verses and see how they are speaking to us today and also to the church, we can again be caught up in the mystery and marvel and wonder of the gracious dispensation of our loving God!

Jesus proclaims that the greatest sign of love is giving one's life for friends (v. 13), then makes the awesome assertion that we are his friends if we do what he commands (v. 14), which is to love one another (v. 17).

Jesus seems to need to defend and explain why he claims us as friends: not only has he made known to us everything the Father had made known to him (v. 15); he also is the one who picked us. He emphasizes that we did not choose him. And we have been chosen to bear fruit: the fruit of love and service to others (v. 16), living out the commandment of love (v. 17). But since this fruit is to endure, we are not to hesitate to ask the Father for all we need in fulfilling Jesus' commands (v. 16). We can ask with the calm assurance that our request will be granted, because we are asking in Jesus' name. "Whatever you ask the Father in my name, he may give it to you."

Prayer: *Jesus, I believe you have called me and made me one of your friends. I believe you love me and give me all I need, through the gift of the Spirit, to live a life of love and service. Bring me into an ever greater dependence on your leading in my life. Teach me to use all my abilities and gifts for others with courage, venturesomeness, and creativity. Teach me to ask for all things, always trusting that your work will be done through me even when I don't know it's being done. Help me learn to live in deep gratitude, taking nothing for granted. Amen.*

CHOICES TO MAKE—PROMISES TO CLAIM

May 6-12, 1991   **Linda B. Hinton†**
Monday, May 6   Read Psalm 1.

Psalm 1 is an introduction to the Book of Psalms as a whole and to one of the smaller collections of psalms (Psalms 1–41) that make up the book. The psalmist offers here "a word to the wise," or a word to those who want to be wise, about how to approach not only the Book of Psalms but also everyday life. Do you want to get the most out of these "songs of praise" to God? Do you want to thrive and prosper in your personal life? If so, you need to make wise choices. Do not associate with or imitate those who despise God's law and who live outside God's will. Rather, you must dedicate yourself to studying and obeying God's word. This must be your first "delight." Life's greatest blessings will flow from this dedication.

We can find joy in God's word when we carry it in our hearts day and night as an ever-present guide. When we live daily with God's word, we can flourish and bear good fruit. In the psalmist's view, the blessed and happy person is free to enjoy the fullness of life that only righteous living can bring: love, beauty, piety, wisdom, forgiveness, and trust. The psalmist urges us to daily aspire to live among the blessed.

Prayer: *Dear Lord, help us accept and cherish the gracious gift of your word. Guide our meditations on this day and always. Amen.*

---

†Writer; youth minister, First United Methodist Church, Watkinsville, Georgia.

Tuesday, May 7   Read Psalm 1.

In Arlington National Cemetery in Washington, D.C., there is a tomb of a soldier who died fighting for his country but whose name and origin are lost to history. In a large city not long ago, a man was brought to the city hospital because he had been hit by a car and was in a coma. He had no identification, so his picture and description were published in the newspaper for several days in hopes that someone would recognize him and come forward with his name. No one ever did, and he died a few days later, still unnamed. How sad to die unknown. How sad, too, to live alone, at least unknown to anyone in a close, caring way.

However, in the midst of the uncertainties of this world, the psalmist offers the assurance that we are known by God. In a special way, God knows those who seek to live under God's will. In the Old Testament, knowledge does not mean just mental comprehension. Knowledge also involves the will as well as a sense of action toward a goal. Thus, God knows us in order to claim us as his own. If we are rooted and grounded in God's love, God knows our way and blesses it.

The psalmist knows God as judge as well as redeemer. In recognition of this twofold nature of God, we are called to know God's laws, to reject evil, and to live a moral life. Only then can we stand confidently in adversity and not fear the day of judgment (see also Jer. 17:7-8).

In Psalm 1, then, the psalmist offers us this instruction for our journey of faith: if we live day and night with God and under God's will, we will be known, redeemed, and blessed by God.

Prayer: *Our Lord, we offer you thanks and praise that you know us and call us to be your own. Grant us your comfort, strength, and wisdom on our way. Amen.*

Wednesday, May 8   Read John 17:11*b*-19.

Can you imagine where the community of faith might be today without the prayers of the faithful? Communion and communication with God through prayer have sustained and guided us through the ages. Prayer touches all our lives, whether we realize it or not.

A monk living in a secluded religious community has dedicated his life to prayer for the world. He spends his days bringing the world and its people into God's presence through his prayers.

An elderly woman living in a large city goes immediately to the sanctuary when she arrives at church each Sunday morning. She kneels at the altar and offers a prayer on behalf of her ministers that God will guide them in their ministry that day.

A widow in a rural community lives down the road from the county junior high school. As the cars and buses pass her home in the mornings, she prays for the students and teachers that God's will might be done in their lives that day.

Think about the people in your own life who have offered prayers for you and about what their concern meant to you. How wonderful to know that Jesus prayed for us as well! In the last hours of his earthly ministry he prayed for his disciples and for the church of the future. As heirs of the original disciples, we can claim Jesus' petition as our own.

We who now live under God's name continue Jesus' ministry in the world, and we share his perfect joy (v. 13). A full measure of grace, joy, and truth is ours through Jesus' prayer on our behalf. As we offer our own prayers of thanksgiving and petition, may we remember his abiding love, and may we remember the faithful whose prayers have brought us to this day.

Prayer: *Dear Lord, we thank you for all the prayers that bind our lives to you and to one another in an unending chain of love. Amen.*

Thursday, May 9   Read John 17:11*b*-19.

As you reread Jesus' prayer for his disciples, think about your own prayers. What concerns do you bring before God today? How do these petitions fit in with Jesus' concerns for us?

Jesus prays that we may live in oneness with God and with one another (vv. 11*b*-12). Jesus knows that we need a sustaining connection with God and with other believers.

Jesus prays that we will be protected from the evil in the world (vv. 14-16). Even though salvation through Jesus has brought a new dimension to life, in some ways the world has not changed. We still see opposition to God's will and to those who bear God's word.

Jesus also prays that we will be set apart ("sanctified" or "consecrated") for the sacred task of witnessing to God's truth in the world (vv. 17-19). We are sent into the world not just to speak the facts of the gospel but to tell of the divine reality revealed in Jesus.

In our own prayers, we bring very individual, personal concerns before God. However, these concerns are always part of the larger vision that Jesus has for us. We do not pray alone; we are part of the fulfillment of God's will for the world. And in this participation we also find our own fulfillment. Because we are one with God and with one another, because we are shielded from evil, and because we fulfill our calling to witness to God's truth, we find the joy that Jesus seeks for us.

Prayer: *Gracious God, may your will be done in our prayers and in our daily lives. In Jesus' name. Amen.*

Friday, May 10   Read Acts 1:15-17, 21-26.

Most of us probably own at least one "how to" book. Many so-called experts offer to share their wisdom on everything from how to dewrinkle your face to how to build your own house. Many such books focus on decision-making in our personal lives and in the marketplace. In the midst of the flood of advice, the Bible also has something to say about making decisions.

After Jesus' resurrection and ascension, eleven apostles are left to carry on the work of the gospel. The first chapter of Acts tells how they choose a new apostle to keep their ranks at twelve, corresponding to the traditional number of the tribes of Israel. These apostles are commissioned and sent out into the world as witnesses to Jesus. They are believers who can testify to the events of Jesus' life, from his baptism to his resurrection. They are also to proclaim the meaning of these events to the world.

The process the remaining eleven use to choose Matthias to join them offers us a model for our own decision-making. They weigh their decision against the scriptures and against what they have learned from and about Jesus. They share experiences and opinions with one another. They seek God's will through prayer, and they cast lots (or perhaps simply "cast their votes").

We probably would not cast lots as we make our own decisions. However, we can profitably look to scripture and to the experiences of others in the community of faith to guide us. We can turn to God in prayer, and, as the apostles did, we can then wait in confidence for God's will to be made known.

Prayer: *Dear God, help us always seek your will in the decisions we make and accept with open hearts your guidance for our lives. In Jesus' name. Amen.*

Saturday, May 11   Read 1 John 5:9-13.

We live in a world full of conflicting claims. Every day we are bombarded with appeals to give our attention, our loyalty, and, most of all, our money to something or someone. In exchange, we are promised "salvation" of a sort:

"Want love? Get whiter teeth!"

"The good life is just around the corner if you invest your money with us!"

"Come worship this Sunday at the One Church of the Pure Gospel—you'll be blessed!"

These claims, often superficial, appeal to a fundamental human need to find something or someone to make our lives worthwhile. In many different ways we are asking, "Where is true meaning in life to be found?" and "Whom can I trust?"

Early Christians also had questions and choices to make about living out their faith. The First Letter of John seeks to answer some of these questions. This letter apparently circulated among several congregations in Asia Minor around A.D. 100, at a time when Christians had major disagreements about who Jesus was and what it meant to lead a Christian life. John addresses those "who believe in the name of the Son of God" (v. 13) but who are struggling to maintain their faith in the face of competing claims for their loyalty. He wants them to know, beyond a doubt, that they now have eternal life—life at its fullest and most complete. This life originates with the Father, is made manifest in the Son, and is shared by all who live under his name (1 John 1:1-4).

So, where does our true joy lie? In whom do we find ultimate fulfillment? John answers that we have only to claim what is already ours in Christ Jesus.

Prayer: *Gracious God, help us always look to you as the source of true life. Amen.*

Sunday, May 12   Read 1 John 5:9-13.

When you really stop and think about it, making God out to be a liar seems outrageous. Who would not believe God? Yet, the Christians John addresses in this letter were not the first to doubt a divine revelation. Many generations before, Abraham and Sarah laughed at God's word to them (see Gen. 17:15-17; 18:10-12). At first Jesus' own disciples thought Mary Magdalene's news of the risen Christ was "an idle tale" (see Luke 24:10-11).

In John's congregations Christians disagreed over whether Jesus was really human as well as divine. Some people believed that God's Spirit only *appeared* in the flesh for a time, but was not really "in the flesh." For them, knowledge of the true Spirit took the place of strict obedience to God's commandments concerning a life of love and moral purity. However, John rejects these beliefs. He calls all believers to confess that Jesus is God incarnate and to live in obedience to God's laws.

We all have moments of doubt and confusion, and we will fail at times in the life of love because our inner conviction falters. However, John wants us to be clear about one thing: God has given us eternal life through Jesus. As proof, John offers the testimony of Jesus' ministry—his baptism with the coming of the Holy Spirit ("water," v. 6) and his death on the cross ("blood," v. 6). John also offers the testimony of the Spirit (vv. 7-8) as a continuing presence in the community of faith.

If we believe that Jesus is the Christ, we ourselves become witnesses to God's revelation. We have eternal life—a life of love, obedience, and truth—because we have God's Son. Jesus is the proof that God does not lie.

Prayer: *Dear Lord, help us always receive your word for us with open and glad hearts. In Jesus' name. Amen.*

THE SPIRIT OF GOD

May 13-19, 1991   **Anne Broyles†**
Monday, May 13   Read Romans 8:22-25.

The Spirit gives us hope

The daily newspapers, radio, and television bombard us with the bad news around us: natural disasters, murders, airplane crashes, government corruption—the list goes on and on. We can indeed hear creation "groaning in travail." But, as Christians, we know that the bad news surrounding us is only one small part of the story. The daily news rarely tells us of lives transformed by God, of new relationships between people, of possibilities for good and potential for peace.

Because we believe in Christ and live in his Spirit, we live in hopefulness. As Paul says, "Hope that is seen is not hope. For who hopes for what he sees? But if we hope for what we do not see, we wait for it with patience." This does not mean a simple Pollyanna attitude (though there is certainly nothing wrong with playing a "glad game"). Waiting with patience does not mean ignoring the present realities of our world and waiting only for "pie in the sky."

Rather, we live in a hope that tempers our understanding of what we see occurring around us. We see present reality in light of the future that is to come, and we work to help bring God's future into being. We know that God's work is not yet done in the world or in us.

Prayer: *Thank you, God of hope, for all you have done in the past and for all you will still accomplish in the days to come. Help us wait patiently as you unfold your role in the human story. And help us always to live in hope. Amen.*

---

†Co-pastor, Malibu United Methodist Church, Malibu, California.

Tuesday, May 14   Read Romans 8:26-27.

The Spirit comes to help us

Katherine was ill for over a year with a strange virus that attacked her body and her spirit. When she heard of a young woman dying of the same virus, she realized that she, too, might not recover. During the long and difficult illness, Katherine experienced what is best described in classical spirituality as "the dark night of the soul." Even though she herself is a United Methodist minister, Katherine found herself unable to pray in any of the ways that had strengthened her in her earlier life.

During this time of absolute physical and spiritual weakness Katherine discovered the "breath prayer." She did not read about the breath prayer in a book; she created it as the only way she could pray in her debilitated condition. Her breath prayers were part of the healing process that eventually led to her recovery.

We all have times when prayer is difficult, when we are dry or depressed or too beaten down by life to know how to reach out for God. As Paul writes, "The Spirit helps us in our weakness; for we do not know how to pray as we ought, but the Spirit himself intercedes for us with sighs too deep for words."

What a comfort to know when we are too weak to pray, the Spirit comes to help us! When life seems too much to bear, the Spirit of God lifts us up, undergirding us until we are stronger. Although we may not realize it at the time, when we most need God, God's Spirit will be there to give us strength and help.

Suggestion for reflection: *Think back on some of the most difficult times of your life. Did you feel God's Spirit with you at the time? Did you later realize that God had continued to work in your life through the hard moments? Give thanks to God for all the help the Spirit has given and will continue to give you in times to come.*

Wednesday, May 15   Read John 15:26-27;
                                                        16:4*b*-15.

The Spirit will lead us to truth

Although it upsets his family when they hear him say it, Evan affirms that "AIDS is the best thing that ever happened to me." He does not mean that he is glad he must suffer the ravages of a virus that attacks his immune system and leaves him defenseless against other diseases. What Evan means is that if it had not been for his HIV-Positive diagnosis, he might have continued to live in ways that were tearing him apart spiritually and physically.

For Evan, discovering that he had AIDS meant that he made changes in the way he ate, the way he thought, the way he spent his time. It was a time of reckoning: "What is it I really want from life?" Knowing that his time is now limited, Evan is trying to make the most of his life and make a difference in the world.

Just before his death, Jesus gathered his friends around him and tried to prepare them for their life without him. They found his words difficult, but Jesus realized that his leaving them would open up a new perspective which would come to them when the Spirit of truth came to guide them into all truth.

The disciples were fearful to imagine life without their beloved Lord. Yet, the disciples were able to receive the Spirit because Jesus' life on earth came to an end.

Endings are often hard for us. Death, divorce, moving, job changes, the end of a relationship—these times cause us great pain. But these transitions may bring with them great possibility of change and renewal. In Christ, all life transitions can be moments when we are free to reevaluate our lives and decide how we are to live in and with the Spirit of truth.

Prayer: *O God of all transitions, give me courage to live my life allowing your Spirit of truth to lead me toward the future. Amen.*

Thursday, May 16   Read Acts 2:1-3.

The Spirit unites us

Although all the believers were gathered together in one place, they were still individuals, separate and unique. These people represented different nationalities, ethnic groups, languages, personalities. They each came with individual needs and wants, hopes and fears. In another setting, they might have left that place as strangers, unconnected and untouched by a mutual experience.

But they were gathered together on no ordinary day. What they experienced on Pentecost most certainly changed their lives forever. There came a rushing wind, swishing and swirling around, filling the house with its power. And then came the tongues of fire that somehow touched each person present.

And, as they experienced the wonder of what we now call "the birthday of the church," those disparate people became as one. Their differences were no longer so important. There was one spirit, one unifying presence that reminded them of their commonality and moved them toward a shared future.

That first Pentecost serves also as a reminder to all of us that in Christ, we are one. No matter what our particular theology and practice, we are ultimately one in Christ. What does it matter if we do not sing the same hymns, agree on fine theological points, or build our places of worship in the same styles? Jesus Christ came that we might let his Spirit radiate from within us as one unified people: followers of Christ.

Suggestion for reflection: *In what ways do I acknowledge and celebrate the oneness in spirit I share with other Christians? How do I focus on the differences among us?*

Friday, May 17   Read Acts 2:4-13.

The Spirit comes in unexpected ways

In our weekly women's Bible study, there are some faithful members who have carefully studied God's word as contained in the Old and New Testaments. These women speak of their lives and experiences from years of walking with God, and I am grateful for all that they share with me as their leader.

In the past year, a young mother has joined our group. Karen is new to the Christian faith, and she brings with her a rough past that includes alcoholism, emotional abuse, and drug addiction. Karen is genuinely searching for answers in her life, and it is exciting to see her make sense of her life as she studies the Bible.

Karen brings an invigorating earthiness to our study. Because all of what we study is so new to her, she is able to place the biblical stories in today's idiom—opening a window on the text for the rest of us. For instance, when discussing a passage in which the disciples misunderstood Jesus for the umpteenth time, Karen exclaimed, "I just don't understand how they could have been with Jesus and still been so thick-headed. You'd think if you were walking with Jesus, you'd stay on your toes!"

Karen's insights often make sense because they do not come in traditional theological language. In her "own tongue," she "tells the mighty works of God" just as those people did on Pentecost.

Pentecost reminds us that we can each speak about how God is working in our lives. It doesn't matter what language we speak or what theological terms we know. We can each share our faith in our own way.

Prayer: *Gracious God, help me share my life and faith in my own way. And let me be open to others as they share the ways they experience your power. May we know the unity to which you call us. Amen.*

Saturday, May 18   Read Acts 2:14-21.

The Spirit must be made manifest in us

We often think of Pentecost as a one-time event—a great day in the history of the Christian faith when the believers felt God's Spirit poured out upon them. But the Spirit was not for that time and place only. The Spirit is for each follower of Christ at each moment in our lives.

Peter eloquently connected what happened to the believers to the prophecy of Joel many years before. In so doing, Peter also connected Pentecost to the future. This friend of Jesus, this "rock," realized that the coming of the Spirit was the beginning of a new era in history. There would be prophecies, visions, and dreams—all leading the people of faith toward the future.

A friend of mine was raised in a devout Jewish family. She tells of reading the entire Bible at the suggestion of a Christian friend. At that point, the New Testament made no sense to her. Several years later, when she herself had converted to Christianity and was an active believer, she tried again to read the Bible from start to finish. This time she understood the Old Testament in a new way and was able to enter into the story of Jesus and the early church as well.

Gayle says, "Before I had the Spirit, it was just words on paper. But after I knew Jesus, the Bible simply came alive for me. It all made sense and has spurred me on to continue to read and study."

Once we feel God's Spirit within us, we are not at the end of our journey. Rather, we are entering a new phase of understanding and relationship with God.

Suggestion for prayer: *Sit quietly in a relaxed position. Imagine yourself being touched by the Spirit. Pray for understanding of where God's Spirit is leading you at the present time.*

Sunday, May 19 (Pentecost)
Read Psalm 104:24-34.

The Spirit gives new life

We cannot imagine the nothingness out of which God created the earth. We experience the world in an evolving form that includes rushing waters, mountain peaks, a vast array of animals and people, and even such miracles as rainbows, hummingbirds, and an unfolding flower.

Psalm 104 gives praise to God for all aspects of creation. We sense that the psalmist felt overwhelmingly compelled to give thanks for the grandeur of nature. This is a highly visual psalm. With the psalmist, we watch the earth as it is created. We see the mountains rise, the valleys sink down, the waters cover the earth. We see the abundance of animal and plant life that is so precious. And we cannot help but join the song.

The breath of God—that which gives life and renews the world—is the Spirit that is available to us in Jesus Christ. Whatever our past, present, or future, we are given the Spirit to renew and sustain us through whatever we experience. It is not always easy to define the Spirit, or to categorize or predict the Spirit's movement. But as we gaze on the intricacy of creation, we get a glimpse of the Spirit's power and majesty.

On this Pentecost Sunday, we can once again claim our partnership with the God whose Spirit reached out and formed the earth, skies, and waters. We can accept the gift that is so freely given—the gift of new life in Christ Jesus. And we can commit to sing praise to God in all the moments of our lives.

Suggestion for prayer: *Read Psalm 104 aloud. Read slowly and use your most dramatic voice, for this creation is high drama. Let verses 33-34 be your own prayer of thanks to the wondrous God whose Spirit renews the world.*

SHAPED BY GOD'S LOVE

May 20-26, 1991   **Willie S. Teague†**
Monday, May 20   Read Psalm 29.

While on vacation in Yellowstone Park, my sons and I saw a double rainbow. Now we never see a rainbow that we do not remember the fun, excitement, and togetherness of our trip to Yellowstone.

When reading Psalm 29, one cannot help but recognize that the psalmist is calling for the heavenly beings to ascribe glory to God. This call to give God glory comes amidst the noise and fire of a thunderstorm. The final call to give glory to God comes with the faith statement, "The Lord sits enthroned over the flood" and is enthroned forever. But the ends comes with a blessing: May the Lord give strength and peace to God's people.

Isn't it strange that in the midst of a thunderstorm so great that it shook the cedars of Lebanon the psalmist remembered God's victory over chaos? While in the midst of a thunderstorm many of us would not think of God. If we did, we might wonder how God could be so angry. No doubt the psalmist had similar thoughts; but they led the psalmist to remember that God is in control over the chaos and may even have remembered that many a storm is followed by a rainbow—the sign of promise first given to Noah.

Devotional exercise: *Sit quietly. Relax and breathe deeply. Breathe in, remembering that it is God's breath that you breathe. Hold the breath as you would hold God in your being. Slowly let the breath out as you would hesitantly leave God's presence. With each breath, remember a storm in your life. As you hold the breath, claim God's peace, remembering that storms are often followed by rainbows.*

---

†United Methodist minister; editor, *South Carolina Advocate*, Columbia, South Carolina.

Tuesday, May 21   Read John 3:16-17.

Few, if any, passages of scripture are more familiar than John 3:16. The reading or reciting of "For God so loved . . . " brings sentiments of warmth, security, and hope. But the radical nature of God's love is sometimes missed.

I remember as a little boy being told the story of Abraham's willingness to sacrifice his son, Isaac. I could not understand how a father could willingly kill his own son. As a son, I wondered how Isaac must have felt. When I asked questions about it, I was reminded that God intervened and stopped Abraham before he killed his son. There was some comfort in that, but not enough. It raised the question of the extent of my father's love for me.

Now as a father, I find the story of Abraham and Isaac perplexing. How could a father do that? Could I? Could any father really give his child to death like that? John 3:16 answers that question. Yes! God did just that. Unlike Abraham and Isaac, God's and Jesus' struggle did not end so happily. God actually stood by and let his son die! How could he? What could make him do that?

The answer to those questions is found in the same verse of scripture: "For God so loved the world . . . " Here is the radical nature of God's love for the whole of creation. This radical love is made even more so by the son's participation.

Devotional exercise: *Sit quietly. Relax and breathe deeply. Breathe in, remembering that God loves the world so much that he did what Abraham did not have to do. Hold the breath as you would hold God in your being. Slowly let the breath out as you would hesitantly leave God's presence. With each breath, remember that God loves you, and examine the nature and extent of your love for God and the world.*

Wednesday, May 22   Read John 1:14-18; 3:16.

The prologue to John's Gospel tells us that the Word became flesh. Words of love and caring are important to hear, but their real power is experienced when they are actualized.

Peter learned that words of love are not enough when the risen Christ asked Peter if he loved him. Three times Peter answered that he did, and three times Jesus told him to act on that love (see John 21:15-17).

What we know of Jesus and his love is not primarily a result of what he said about the nature of love. No! We know of Jesus and his love because he ate with sinners, healed the sick, fed the hungry, cared for the outcast, confronted the powerful, and paid the price for righteous living. The Sermon on the Mount has power not only because of the truth it contains but because of the way in which Jesus lived out the words he spoke in that sermon.

In his call to active faith, James wrote: "If a brother or sister is ill-clad and in lack of daily food, and one of you says to them, 'Go in peace, be warmed and filled,' without giving them the things needed for the body, what does it profit?" (2:15-16)

We know how much God loves us not because of words but because the Word became flesh. We know that we are loved enough not because of the words of Jesus but because of the actions of Jesus which give his words their real power to save and shape our lives.

Devotional exercise: *Sit quietly. Relax and breathe deeply. Breathe in, remembering that Jesus not only spoke words of love but also actualized that love in his living and dying. Hold the breath as you would hold God in your being. Slowly let the breath out as you would hesitantly leave God's presence. With each breath remember that the question is not only "Do you love me?" but also "How?" Examine your acts of love in comparison to your words of love.*

Thursday, May 23   Read John 3:1-15.

Nicodemus is easy to identify with. He believed in Jesus because of the miraculous signs attributed to Jesus.

How easy it is to believe in Jesus because of miracles, be they of healing or of meeting needs. The account of the exchange between Nicodemus and Jesus is important because it shows us that faith based only on miracles and signs is partial faith.

Apparently Nicodemus thought that Jesus was in God's presence in the sense that Jesus was approved or chosen by God. Jesus responded that only by being begotten by God can one be in the presence of God. Then Nicodemus asked, "How is that possible?" Jesus' answer is rather straightforward: A person becomes flesh and enters this world because of his or her earthly parents. Likewise, a person enters the kingdom of God because of her or his heavenly Father. Nicodemus still does not understand. He said, "How can this be?"

We live in a day when there are many who talk about being "born again." Often when asked how that is done, they respond, "Believe on the Lord Jesus Christ." Emphasis upon rebirth is at the heart of the Christian faith; however, that rebirth is only partial faith if it is based upon Christ's miracles, both biblical and contemporary. It is not the faith which is the breath of all citizens of the kingdom of God. Such faith comes only as a gift, not as evidence.

Devotional exercise: *Sit quietly. Relax and breathe deeply. Breathe in, remembering that true faith is a gift of God and is not a response to miracles. Hold the breath as you would hold God in your being. Slowly let the breath out as you would hesitantly leave God's presence. With each breath, remember that God has come to you in Jesus not to prove anything but to claim you. In the name of Jesus, pray that your faith might not be partial but whole and powerful as to give you new birth.*

Friday, May 24   Read Romans 8:14-16.

"Aha" moments come to all of us occasionally. They are those moments of profound learning or recognition. Have you ever struggled to solve a problem, only to have its solution come in an ordinary manner—only to say, "Aha, I knew that"? In today's scripture, Paul describes such a moment in our faith life: "When we cry, 'Abba! Father!'" When we know that we are a child of God, there is a deep awareness that we have finally come to the truth of our identity. We know ourself for the first time, but it does not feel new or strange; it feels natural and real. Our innermost being has an "aha" moment of awareness. Paul not only describes such a moment but also tells us how such a moment comes to be. "All who are led by the Spirit of God are sons of God." That seems simple enough. But why does the Spirit lead one person and not another? Paul does not say that the Spirit of God pulls or drives us to the knowledge that we are God's children. To be led requires a willingness to be led.

Paul goes on to say that the awareness comes from "the Spirit . . . bearing witness with our spirit that we are children of God." The Spirit does not force a new identity upon us. The process is one of cooperation. It is a result of the Spirit of God joining our spirit in a mutual journey of faith. Such a mutual effort requires an acquaintance that is more than casual. If we are to come to such deep faith, we must daily invite the Spirit of God into our life and respond to the Spirit's guidance.

Devotional exercise: *Sit quietly. Relax and breathe deeply. Breathe in, remembering that the Spirit of God is always more willing to lead than we are to follow. Hold the breath as you would hold God in your being. Slowly let the breath out as you would hesitantly leave God's presence. With each breath, ask God to grant you the presence of the Spirit and the presence of mind to receive and respond to the Spirit's guidance.*

Saturday, May 25   Read Isaiah 6:1-8.

In the Protestant tradition one speaks of being "called to ministry." In the Catholic tradition, one speaks of "making vocation." In either case the result is the same. A person "hears" God say, "Whom shall I send?" How can anyone have the confidence to respond, "Here am I! Send me"?

Isaiah's response did not come out of an immediate sense of worthiness or competence. It came as a result of experiencing the presence of God and God's holiness. In the year of King Uzziah's death, Isaiah was in the temple worshiping and heard the angels singing, "Holy, holy, holy is the LORD of hosts; the whole earth is full of his glory." Isaiah had an "aha" moment. In the presence of such holiness Isaiah had a keen awareness of his own lack of holiness. "Woe is me! For I am lost; for I am a man of unclean lips, and I dwell in the midst of a people of unclean lips; for my eyes have seen the King, the LORD of hosts." Then the angel touched Isaiah with the righteousness of God, and Isaiah recognized himself as a new person. Then and only then was Isaiah able to hear God's call and respond to it.

There is a shortage of ministers in the church today, both ordained and lay. Is God not calling enough people to ministry? Hardly! Most likely it is a result of too few of us having "aha" moments when we are faced with God's holiness and our own unholiness; moments of worship when we receive a new identity; moments of being led to say, "Here am I! Send me."

Devotional exercise: *Sit quietly. Relax and breathe deeply. Breathe in, remembering that God is holy and willing to touch you with God's own holiness. Hold the breath as you would hold God in your being. Slowly let the breath out as you would hesitantly leave God's presence. With each breath, ask God to grant you a sense of call or vocation that you might be able to say, "Here am I! Send me."*

157

May 26 (Trinity Sunday)

Read John 3:1-18.

Unlike most holy days in our church calendar, Trinity Sunday commemorates a doctrine, not an event. I am not sure of the formula $3 = 1$ and $1 = 3$, and I find the explanation that we are dealing with three expressions of the same essence to be less than helpful. Some claim that the Trinity is a mystery and not to be understood.

There are, indeed, mysteries which make large claims upon my life which I do not understand, and yet I know them to be true. There is the mystery of life itself. We understand the reproductive process to be sure; but do we understand the source of life? I remember the birth of my first son. David's presence could be explained, but the mystery of his being could only be received as a gift—a gift to be affirmed, loved, shaped, and freed.

In like fashion the Trinity is to be received as a gift. It is the gift of life from the Creator known as Parent. It is life freed from the dominance of evil by a Brother who not only inspires us to seek the fullness of life but also empowers us to do so. It is life led and shaped by the Spirit of love. Further, the doctrine of the Trinity is the result of the most unique event in human history: "The Word became flesh and dwelt among us" (John 1:14*a*). We may not understand the doctrines of Trinity or Incarnation, but we receive the fullness of life they can bring.

Devotional exercise: *Sit quietly. Relax and breathe deeply. Breathe in, not seeking understanding but seeking faith to live in divine mystery. Hold the breath as you would hold God in your being. Slowly let the breath out as you would hesitantly leave God's presence. With each breath, receive the life given by the Creator Parent, the fullness of life given by the Brother, and the guidance given by the Spirit.*

THE LORD PROVIDES

May 27–June 2, 1991   **Julie Rybolt Wilkerson†**
Monday, May 27   Read 1 Samuel 16:1-3.

This week's readings reflect an image of God as an ever-present parent who comforts, guides, and directs us. God supplies our needs despite our desire to have control.

God is not fooled by our games. God understands our need to try our hand at independence—just like a toddler who refuses to relinquish control over any skill he has learned. His mother hears "Mommy, I can do it" often at this age. But we adults are no different from the toddler. We often say to God, "I can do this myself," when, in reality, God's help would give us the direction we need. God overlooks our struggling desire to do it our way out of love for us.

In this first reading, we see a distraught Samuel who cannot get over the loss of Saul, Israel's first king. We do not know why Samuel is overcome with grief for this man. But we do know they once served the same Lord. And Samuel played a part in bringing Saul to power.

Samuel does not want to go to Bethlehem. He would rather stay where he is. Perhaps it would be easier to dwell on things in the past—to give up the fight. After all, Samuel was involved in one disaster—why would he want to anoint another king? How could he follow God's plans again? And anyway, Samuel could be in real danger if Saul heard of his plans in Bethlehem. How would you handle a similar situation?

Prayer: *Dear Lord, thank you for guiding us through our maze of choices. Be with us as we seek your will. Amen.*

---

†Graduate student of journalism; Bartlett, Tennessee.

Tuesday, May 28   Read 1 Samuel 16:4-13.

You can imagine Samuel's thoughts as he travels in search of the future king: *Lord, please help me find the right one, and forgive me for hesitating to do your will. . . .*

When Samuel arrives in Bethlehem, he is greeted with some fear by the townspeople. They wondered, *What is an important man like Samuel doing in such an insignificant town?*

Samuel keeps his mission a secret. He replies to the people's questions about his being there only by saying he has come to sacrifice. He invites Jesse and his sons to participate in the ritual. Of course, this gives Samuel the perfect opportunity to choose the next king of Israel, with God's guidance.

As each young man approaches, the Lord cautions Samuel: "Do not look on his appearance or on the height of his stature . . . for the LORD sees not as man sees; man looks on the outward appearance, but the LORD looks on the heart."

I wonder how many of us would listen to God's guidance as Samuel did in this situation. Many of Jesse's sons were handsome and strong—qualities that would help any man if he were king. And Jesse had seven—a holy number to the people of Israel—of his sons pass before Samuel. To another person, this could have appeared a sign from God that one of these men would be king. But Samuel listened to God.

None of these men was called to be king. Samuel asked if there were other sons. David was called in from the fields. As he passed in front of Samuel, God guided Samuel to choose David. Despite David's youth, God saw in him a king.

God always sees our potential and gives us opportunities to serve in the kingdom.

Prayer: *Father, help us to listen, as Samuel did, to your will. Open our eyes to the possibilities you have for us. Amen.*

Wednesday, May 29   Read Psalm 20.

A leader and his people are dependent upon each other. One must rule fairly; the other must be loyal to the government in order for there to be stability.

In David's time, the people offered more than their allegiance. They offered their prayers and relied upon God's guidance.

As the psalmist looks to God for help, he asks the Lord to remember the sacrifices and offerings of David. In a real sense, this is symbolic of his own obedience to God. As David was faithful, surely God will be faithful, too.

We are reminded in verse 6 that David was the anointed king. Because he was chosen by the Lord to rule, the people are confident God will grant him favor. Their faith is in the Lord.

Verse 7 is reminiscent of David's battle with Goliath, the giant Philistine. By all accounts, David had no chance of surviving a battle with Goliath. His inexperience and youth were against him, so the Philistine thought. But David had faith in God. His trust was so strong that he took only his sling for a weapon (see 1 Sam. 17:37-51).

How does this psalm speak to us today? Consider the concern over nuclear armaments. Is there greater strength in warheads or in our faith in God? Who are the Davids of the world today? And where do we, as God's people, fit in to our government's role in world peace? Do we, like David's subjects, offer prayers for our leaders and their decisions? And what about our stockpile of missiles—do we "boast of chariots" or do we "boast of the name of the LORD"?

Prayer: *God of peace, please grant us the courage to follow your will in all things, including the issue of nuclear weapons. Help us to listen to your voice, as David did, and believe. Amen.*

Thursday, May 30   Read 2 Corinthians 4:5-6.

Light is the absence of darkness. In this reading, we see that light shines through our hearts when we are one with God. This shining light testifies to the glory of God.

Once we were full of darkness. We did not know the Light (Christ Jesus), whose presence illumines us with his love. This light reveals the transformation which takes place within any believer who knows and loves God.

There are many references to light in the Bible. Because of the way it was used, "light" could signify one of the most important processes a Christian could go through—the transformation of the worldly, unsaved person into a member of Christ's king-dom—a person who is *becoming* more Christlike, or set apart (holy), through faith.

The light was also a reference to Jesus. He said, "I am the light of the world" (John 8:12).

In Ephesians 5:8-14, we see "light" as a symbolic identifica-tion of God's children: "Once you were darkness, but now you are light in the Lord; walk as children of light (for the fruit of light is found in all that is good and right and true), and try to learn what is pleasing to the Lord."

The light can be a sign of God's working within us. In Exodus 34:29, Moses returned to the Israelites after being with God on Sinai. This passage reads, "Moses did not know that the skin of his face shone because he had been talking with God."

This physical change in Moses' appearance was the result of his close relationship with God. When we truly attempt to live in the light of Christ, we too move closer to God, and our inner light shines more brightly.

Prayer: *Father, help us to live close to you so that our light may be a witness to your love. Amen.*

Friday, May 31   Read 2 Corinthians 4:7-12.

Children of God have access to an abundance of power. Through prayer and obedience to God's will, we are able to take part in God's plan. But we must consider the words in verse 7: "Power belongs to God and not to us."

We are not immune to mishaps and sadness. But we have prayer as our link to God, and God's strength will sustain us.

In today's reading, we are reminded that our living in this world will ultimately bring about physical death; but through grace, we have been given eternal life.

In life we experience fear, pain, sorrow, persecution. But, through Jesus, our lives take on new meaning. We are not left defenseless when problems come our way. Besides, Paul has told us that the suffering that we endure serves only to refine us, offering us opportunities to grow even closer to the Lord and to learn greater trust. He said in Romans 5:3-5: "We rejoice in our sufferings, knowing that suffering produces endurance, and endurance produces character, and character produces hope, and hope does not disappoint us, because God's love has been poured into our hearts through the Holy Spirit which has been given to us."

Psalm 27:1 offers this hope for us: "The LORD is my light and my salvation; whom shall I fear?" After all, who gave us life? What kind of power could create us "in his own image" (Gen. 1:27) or conquer death through the resurrection? The good news is this word in Romans 5:2: "Through [Jesus Christ] we have obtained access to this grace in which we stand, and we rejoice in our hope of sharing the glory of God."

Prayer: *O Lord, we desire to be able always to recognize your love and guidance. Help us to let go of our problems and to offer them up to you. In Jesus' name. Amen.*

Saturday, June 1   Read Mark 2:23-28.

The sabbath observance began as a Jewish ritual which reminded the Israelites of God's redemption from their Egyptian captors (see Exod. 16:22-30). This observance parallels the Creation story found in Genesis 2:3: "So God blessed the seventh day and hallowed it, because on it God rested from all his work which he had done in creation." In Exodus 20:8-11, the sabbath observance becomes a part of the Ten Commandments.

The sabbath is significant to Christians because of Jesus' exercise of compassion. Despite the protests of the Jewish leaders, Jesus performed miracles on this day. His emphasis was on the person, not the ritual. His actions seemed to say, "Ritual observance is useless without considering the person's intent."

Matthew 12:7-8 reads: "If you had known what this means, 'I desire mercy, and not sacrifice,' you would not have condemned the guiltless. For the Son of man is lord of the sabbath."

Even though Jesus healed the sick on the sabbath, he confounded the Pharisees with his observance of it. Jesus followed the command in Exodus 20:8 of keeping this day holy. His interpretation of what that meant lessened the importance of the many laws the Pharisees invented. There were so many laws that the people became slaves to them or "outcasts" for not observing them. God's day of remembrance and rest became a meaningless day of impossible demands and insignificant laws.

In Mark 2:27, Jesus reminds the people, "The sabbath was made for man, not man for the sabbath; so the Son of man is lord even of the sabbath." Mercy is more important than ritual.

Prayer: *Lord, help us to keep from thinking "rituals"—going to church, reading the Bible, and following our own code of ethics—signify our faithfulness. Help us to remember that having compassion for others is central to our worship. Amen.*

Sunday, June 2   Read Mark 3:1-6.

It is hard to tell someone how to act if no role model is offered.

During Jesus' time, life for the Jews was difficult. Were there any prophets, other than John the Baptist, who could lead the people? And what about the political problems the people faced—being Jewish in a Roman society? Who were the role models Jesus and his peers could look to for guidance? The prophets and kings were dead. They could only be remembered by the oral tradition of reciting stories of the ancient heroes.

Though the Hebrew people continued to observe their feasts and holy days, God's leadership seemed almost forgotten without someone leading the way.

Jesus came at a time when Jewish factions provided dogma that seemed to serve the purpose of no one but those who believed it. The worship of God was watered down with unimportant beliefs, even superstitions. Consider Jesus' anger with the money-changers and merchants in the temple (see John 2:13-16). The temple was a revered place of worship to any Jew. See how the reverence faded in this example!

Jesus taught us to look beyond the world's—even the church's—definition of being holy. His compassion for the man with the withered hand is a reminder that real love glorifies God.

It seems so simple in today's reading: Follow your heart and offer the gifts you can. In Jesus' case, his ability to heal urged him to say, "Stretch out your hand."

What skills has God given you to share with another? Whom will you ask to stretch out their hand?

Prayer: *Help us, Lord Jesus, to share our gifts with others. Help us to love those who need compassion and care. Remind us of your words and actions, and guide us as we try to follow in your way. Amen.*

THE TRUE SCALE OF THINGS

June 3-9, 1991   **John Carmody†**
Monday, June 3   Read 1 Samuel 16:14-23.

The books of Samuel form a single unit in the Hebrew Bible. Together, they describe the rise of kingship in Israel and the personality of David, the model king. The traditions on which our passage is based date to before 1000 B.C., yet the passage remains relevant today because it suggests some constant elements of the spiritual life.

Without the Spirit of the Lord, Saul is bereft. However, music soothes him when he is tormented by evil spirits. The irony is that David, the source of such soothing, will eventually supplant Saul as king. The Spirit of the Lord will pass from Saul to David. We can see that for Saul and David, their lives depend on the divine providence.

The Lord gives the Spirit that uplifts us, and the Lord ultimately controls the evil spirits that cast us down. Everything about our lives rests in the hands of the Lord, even our consolations and desolations. Certainly what happens to us externally, in the realms that concern medicine and history, is significant. But even more significant is what happens to us internally. The peace or distress that visits our spirits greatly influences what we can accomplish, what we can be. The mystery of such peace or distress reminds us that God alone can settle our hearts. When we realize this, the good news of the old and new covenants appears astounding. In faith, we can believe that all peace and distress serves God's ends.

Prayer: *The Lord gives and the Lord takes away. Blessed be the Lord. Amen.*

---

†Senior Research Fellow, University of Tulsa, Tulsa, Oklahoma.

Tuesday, June 4   Read Psalm 57:1-6.

Psalm 57 is what scholars call an "individual lament." As Israel's prayerbook, the Psalter includes materials for most states of the soul. Here the petitioner asks for protection from "the storms of destruction." Behind this request is a strong faith that God has purposes for each of us, and that God can rescue us from our troubles. Though our enemies seem like lions, God, the exalted Lord of heaven and earth, is stronger. The glory of God is magnificent and is always greater than any threat.

Though the drama of Saul and David may seem more significant, the search of the anonymous petitioner of Psalm 57 may be just as important. Who knows? Those we call kings can be peasants to God. Those God calls saints can change history. What is important is reaching out to God with all our might, so that our enemies do not blot out the sun. God is the only sun, the only One who finally matters. The martyrs, ancient and recent, witness to that truth.

The mercy of God, available any time we are sorely tried, means that nothing can separate us from God's lordship. We may think we are failures, but we don't have the final say. We may think we cannot endure, or are bound to make a mess, or are boring God with our constant whining, but all such judgments are up to God. Be merciful to us, O God, be merciful to us—that is the essence of many saints' prayers. Keep us, O God, by your grace. On our own, we are weak and inadequate, but we are not on our own.

Devotional exercise: *Think about those times in your life when you felt you had failed. How did you handle those feelings? What did you learn from them?*

Prayer: *Come upon us, O God, to wash what is dirty, to smooth what is wrinkled, to make us more closely reflect your image. Amen.*

Wednesday, June 5   Read Psalm 57:7-11.

This typical psalm of lament moves from an expression of heartfelt pain to self-forgetting praise of God. Like the rhythm of death and resurrection that punctuates the Gospels, the movement of those casting their fate into God's hands goes to the depths of their misery and then rises up. Strangely, facing our pains, our worries, our sense of wretchedness seems to cauterize us. Having looked at the worst, we can remember the best—the bedrock truth that God alone rules the world.

When we hit that bedrock, our hearts can be steadfast. We can sing and make melody with awakened souls, because we ourselves are no longer the center of attention. The outbreak of the soul in joy is like the release of a prisoner. Once we were bound by self-concern, fettered to our own tiny vision and impotence. But when we reach bedrock, where the Spirit teaches a realism that makes us blush, all things become possible again.

Those who praise God to the nations because they have experienced the steadfastness of the divine love know that lauding God is the highest truth. The heavens, the clouds, and the hosts above the heavens witness to what poor human beings only glimpse now and then: God alone is fully real. We are creatures of a day, and our troubles with us. At the bedrock of the human spirit, where the divine Spirit turns things around, psychology gives way to theology. Like John the Baptist, the psalmist must decrease so that God can increase.

Devotional exercise: *Remember a particularly difficult time in your life, a time when you were in a kind of emotional misery. Were you able to place that despair into God's hands? What was God's response?*

Prayer: *Dear God, teach us to come to you in all our distress and to let go of our self-concern. Amen.*

Thursday, June 6   Read 2 Corinthians 4:13-15.

The center of Paul's theology, all commentators agree, is the death and resurrection of Christ. In the section preceding ours, Paul has used the theme of death and life to encourage the Corinthians to think of their suffering as part of the process relating them to the dying and living of Jesus.

This reflection triggers a memory of the attitude of the psalmist who took faith as a warrant for crying out every trouble to the Lord (Ps. 116:10). In this spirit, Christians can express whatever is occurring in their hearts to God. The ground of such Christian confidence is what God did for Jesus, the model for Christians. If God raised Jesus, the followers of Jesus can be confident that God will raise them. The Spirit, made available through the resurrection of Jesus, guides Christians' growth in such confidence. Nothing can separate believers from God's love, because if they suffer they do so after the pattern of Christ, and if they prosper they betoken Christ's triumph.

Because the notion of death and resurrection is familiar, smoothed by words long handed down, we often forget the audacity of Christian faith. Where others may find only a void, Christian faith hopes, believes, and trusts that there is a plenum, a divine fullness cushioning all blows. The only reasonable warrant for such a view is the biblical record of God's support, which culminates in the raising of Jesus.

Devotional exercise: *Think about the suffering of Jesus and his rising from the dead. Relate the suffering you may be experiencing now to Jesus' suffering. What does God's raising Jesus from the dead say to you about how God sees and understands your suffering?*

Prayer: *May your grace extend to more and more people, O Lord, to increase thanksgiving and magnify your glory. Amen.*

Friday, June 7   Read 2 Corinthians 4:16–5:1.

Continuing with his reflections on the implications of faith in Christ, Paul shows why believers should not lose heart. If they suffer affliction in the outer world, the world of physical things such as money and politics, God may be renewing their inner selves. Besides, what is earthly life compared to eternity? Some commentators worry, rightly enough, that such a thought can take believers away from their worldly responsibilities or make them fail to appreciate the beauty of creation. In itself, though, the thought is the barest realism. All human lives are short, and God's everlasting life is longer than we can imagine. If we cling to God, the treasure we set our hearts upon outstrips anything we can achieve or enjoy in this time. The things that are unseen are eternal, Paul says; and Paul should be trusted, because he saw the Lord.

To live *in* the world but not be *of* the world—that has been the goal of many saints. As an incarnational faith, Christianity follows its Lord in blessing the good things of the earth and not turning its face away from people's sufferings. But as a faith directed to a God who lives beyond the physical world and is sovereignly free of all the limits that restrain creatures, Christianity cannot be contained in secular categories. Anyone who takes these verses of Paul to heart is bound to be an enigma to secular friends. In Paul's perspective, death becomes useful if not friendly. Can it be that our lives, our selves, escape the grave and meet a deathless God? In every fiber of his being, Paul believed so.

Devotional exercise: *What does it mean to you to live "in" the world but not be "of" the world?*

Prayer: *O God, secure our lives in your living Christ. Amen.*

Saturday, June 8   Read Mark 3:20-27.

The Jesus we meet in Mark's Gospel is mysterious. Full of power, he confronts the forces that warp people's lives like a divine warrior sent to battle Satan. In our text, Jesus has already established a reputation as an exorcist. The reaction of the crowd as he returns home is both painful and amusing: they think he has lost his mind. The scribes, who soon will be Jesus' enemies, go further: he has become possessed by the devil. Jesus' reply is the epitome of common sense: if what he does works against the kingdom of Satan, how can he be possessed by Satan or in league with him?

The kingdom of God that Jesus announces is dawning because he is strong enough to bind Satan and plunder Satan's house. So the combat that onlookers witness is more profound than they can suspect. At issue is the liberation of humankind, the radical conquest of what keeps people from being human.

We are tempted to apply this military scenario to lands such as Central America, where the divine and the demonic seem to clash every day. Can the Christian faith prove stronger than the hatred moving those, rightists and leftists alike, who think that violence is the answer? Those who meditate on the Markan Christ should have no doubt. To Mark's mind, Jesus accomplished a definitive, once-and-for-all conquest of the evil that has always been humanity's greatest sorrow. The cures and exorcisms of Jesus were pledges, or down-payments, on the liberated life that Christians can enjoy in heaven.

Devotional exercise: *Think about your response to the violence that occurs so rampantly in Central America. What does your faith have to say about such violence? In what ways can you help others to understand the futility of physical and verbal violence as a way of life?*

Prayer: *We believe, O Lord; help our unbelief. Amen.*

171

Sunday, June 9   Read Mark 3:28-35.

Finally at issue in the charge that Jesus was in the thrall of Satan was the integrity of those making the charge. To accuse Jesus of demonism, they had to blind their eyes to the good effects of Jesus' power. Or, they had to fear the overturning of the status quo so much that they sold their souls. The kingdom of God that Jesus was demonstrating was the antithesis of sin and disorder. All of Jesus' power pointed to his heavenly Father, so to associate him with Satan was to sin against the Holy Spirit, the divine custodian of right human conscience. That is the unforgivable sin, because it is the sinner's ultimate self-warping. By refusing to honor the deepest structures of conscience, the sinner twists all of morality out of shape and loses the knowledge of God that the prophets considered necessary for humanity to survive. "Humanity" is people who still love the light, even though their weakness may cause them to fail on occasion.

The editor of Mark has followed this discussion of Jesus' power with a saying about true membership in Jesus' family. If we recall that Jesus' own family was quick to write him off, we can also wonder whether their subsequent asking for him was sincere. At any rate, Jesus clearly subordinates earthly ties to doing the will of God. In his view, God always has the first claim on human conscience. Only by honoring God's claim can people gain healthy family relations.

Devotional exercise: *What are the treasures of your life? Think about each member of your family, regardless of the nature of the family to which you belong. How do you honor those persons?*

Prayer: *O God, yours is the kingdom, and the power, and the glory. May we love your power and honor your light. Help us make these our great treasures. Amen.*

Seeing with the Eyes of Faith

June 10-16, 1991   **Jean M. Blomquist†**
Monday, June 10   Read 2 Corinthians 5:6-10.

"Seeing is believing," the old adage goes, but seeing with the eyes of faith often challenges us to see in new ways—not only with our eyes but with our hearts, our whole beings.

An art professor once challenged me to draw what I *saw*, not what I *thought* I saw. In reality there are many subtle lines, folds, and shadows that are pared down to what we think we see. When those subtleties are ignored, a drawing looks crude and incomplete. Only when we put the tricks of our mind aside and see clearly does the object to be drawn emerge in all its complexity.

In today's reading I thought I saw an other-worldly focus with a Manichaean tinge, a crude and incomplete picture based on Paul's expectation of the imminent parousia. How could this image speak to us today? A closer look, however, reveals Paul's understanding of the complexities of life, of how the burdens of our everyday existence—the pressures, anxieties, responsibilities—draw us away from our true home in God. Paul challenges us to see that when our lives are guided by our faith in God's reality rather than by what we *think* is reality, we can live fully, confident that even now we belong to God. The complexities and subtleties of our everyday lives are part of the divine picture.

Devotional exercise: *Slowly repeat verse 7 several times, pausing and reflecting as the word and Spirit speak to you amidst the challenges and pressures you face today.*

---

†Lutheran free-lance writer and editor, Berkeley, California.

Tuesday, June 11   Read Mark 4:30-32.

I grew up on a ranch in the San Joaquin Valley of central California. In late January and early February, bright yellow mustard bloomed and flourished between the rows of rain-darkened almond trees and wizened grape vines. To farmers, the mustard was a weed, something to be plowed under. To animals, it was a source of food and shelter. To me, it was a bright promise of spring during the long, gray winter days.

The mustard was always a wonder and a delight. Bright and beautiful in the winter dreariness, it was plowed under and forgotten during the rest of the year. Yet beneath the surface of the soil the tiny seeds lay waiting to live again.

Mark uses the process of growth shown in this parable as a metaphor for the proclamation of and response to the kingdom. He reminds us that insignificant beginnings can blossom unexpectedly and luxuriantly, yet the growth itself is a mystery. Perhaps Jesus told this parable not only for others but also for himself—to renew his own hope and that of his disciples in the coming of God's reign.

Although I know both the mustard plant and the mustard seed parable well, I often fail to connect them. Yet if I can hold this parable close in times of discouragement—those times when it seems that the work I do is so small, so insignificant that nothing will ever come of it—I can also remember the bright yellow hope that came in the midst of winter darkness.

Prayer: *Gracious Creator, the seeds of faith we plant often seem so tiny. We struggle to believe they can grow into something strong and flourishing. Help us trust in your mysterious ways, knowing that you can bring to life our feeble attempts at being faithful. Amen.*

Wednesday, June 12   Read 2 Corinthians 5:14-17.

When writer Madeleine L'Engle was eight years old, she attended a school that emphasized athletic prowess and popularity. Since she did not excel in either, her peers labeled her "dumb." Unfortunately her teachers did also, and nothing she did was acceptable. Consequently she quit doing her homework and spent her time reading, writing stories and poems, and playing the piano.

One day she entered a school poetry contest and won. Her teacher objected, saying that Madeleine must have copied the poem, because she wasn't very "bright." Fortunately her mother came to her defense, sharing other poems and stories Madeleine had written. Her teacher then determined that Madeleine had written the poem after all. The next year she transferred to another school.

This story is particularly disturbing to me because I know how L'Engle has touched me and many others with her writing. How easily this human judgment could have stifled her gifts!

At one time or another, most of us, including Paul, have been misjudged. In today's reading Paul is responding to his critics' charge that he doesn't have the appearance, skills, or social status to be a true apostle. Neither does he have the correct achievements or religious experiences. Jesus, too, failed to meet the expectations of society. Today effectiveness, expediency, and appearances tempt us as society's ultimate criteria. But Paul says that we are not to judge as the world judges. Instead we are to live for Christ, to be a "new creation," allowing love to govern all our perceptions and actions.

Prayer: *Gentle God, we often judge ourselves and others easily and harshly. Help us to see people, especially those who vex and trouble us, with the eyes of faith, that we may live fully as a new creation. Amen.*

Thursday, June 13   Read 2 Samuel 1:17-27.

David grieves for his dear friend Jonathan and the love they shared. But does David really grieve for Saul? Given their problematic relationship and David's imminent anointing as king, we can't help but wonder about the nature of his lament. In David's time, the funeral dirge, in this case a personal lament, was obligatory. Refusal to participate was tantamount to slander. Does David really grieve for Saul, or is he simply being politically astute? Or are his feelings and motives mixed? For David, mourning was probably mingled with a range of emotions—grief, relief, sadness, regret. It is often the same with us.

When people die, especially if their deaths are untimely, why do we always speak well of them even though our feelings may have been mixed when they were alive? Does grief cloud our eyes? Do we deceive ourselves? Or, perhaps, do we see and experience the person in a new way after he or she is gone? Certainly death can evoke guilt and regrets, but can it also help us see with the eyes of faith, seeing the person in a new light? Can we experience a measure of reconciliation in that moment of death that we somehow were not able to experience in life?

Death reminds us of our faulty vision. What do the eyes of faith see? Can we catch a glimpse through faith's vision even when our motives or feelings are mixed? What can our laments—political and unpolitical, unfelt and keenly felt—teach us about others and about ourselves?

Prayer: *God of love, remove all that blinds us and binds us in our grief. Help us acknowledge our feelings and motivations, and use those to bring us ever closer to you and to those around us. Amen.*

Friday, June 14   Read Mark 4:26-29.

I like to be in control, but I don't always like to admit it. From planning my work day to organizing household chores, I want things done in a certain way, at a certain time. I keep my life orderly, I tell myself, so I will have time for more important things. And that is true—but only to a point.

But in my garden I can't be in control—at least not in the same way. I can plant and water, mulch and weed, but I cannot force the plants to grow. Perhaps that is one of the reasons I love to garden: the mystery and miracle of life surround me. They invite me into the freedom of letting go, of living responsively rather than compulsively. Because I can't control the mystery and miracle of the garden, I can relax and till the soil with confidence that someday the fruit and flowers will beckon me to share in their harvest, to enter responsively, communally into their abundance.

I often want to know the how, when, where, and why of everything I'm involved in; I want to control, but that is not my business. I am simply called to be ready. I see with the eyes of faith when I am patient, waiting, and trusting that God is working even when I am unaware of it.

Prayer: *Loving God, I try so hard to keep everything under control— my family, my friends, my work, my faith. Help me step aside for a moment, marvel in the mystery of your reign among us, and refresh myself that I may be ready when you call me to the harvest. Help me to trust that your reign goes on even when I am not in the middle of it. Amen.*

Saturday, June 15　　　　　　　　Read Psalm 46:1-7.

As I write this in November of 1989, the San Francisco Bay Area, where I live, is recovering from a major earthquake. On October 17, the mountains trembled and shook in the heart of the sea. The quake was so powerful that people living west of the San Andreas Fault now live twenty inches higher and twenty inches further north than they did before.

Yet in the midst of the death and devastation, there was "a river whose streams [made] glad the city of God." God became present in people caring for one another, in rescuers risking their own lives to save strangers trapped in homes or in the collapse of the I-880 freeway structure, in a massive outpouring of relief goods—clothing, food, and shelter. In this fast-paced urban area where it often seems people can't find time for themselves or their loved ones, much less for anyone else, we were amazed, heartened, and even delighted by the fullness of our own human-ity, by the presence of the living God within us and around us. The quake reminded us that God comes to us in unexpected ways, at unexpected times, when we open our hearts and see, when we open our hearts and reach out to those around us.

This psalm, the inspiration for Luther's "Ein Feste Burg" ("A Mighty Fortress"), honors the Creator who struggles against chaos and brings peace. In the midst of the chaos of our lives, whether the cause be natural or economic disasters, relationship struggles, or professional difficulties, God struggles with us and offers us a safe and peaceful refuge. How ironic that we some-times best experience that peaceful place when we are in the midst of chaos.

Prayer: *Refresh us and gladden us with your streams of life-giving water, Creator God. When we are in chaos, when the world trembles and our lives overwhelm us, help us place our hearts in the refuge of your love. Amen.*

Sunday, June 16   Read Psalm 46:8-11.

I once led a workshop on peace and the inner life called "Does Peace Really Begin with Me?" I asked participants whether they had ever experienced the peace that passes understanding in a chaotic or violent situation. Nearly everyone had. One man shared this story:

While a missionary in Africa, he was awakened during the night by shouts and screaming: "Fire! Fire!" The dormitory of the mission boarding school where he taught was engulfed in flames. Feverishly he worked with others to lead all the children to safety. Then, because of an inadequate water supply, they stood silently, watching the dormitory and school burn to the ground. Though the financial and physical losses were devastating, he was flooded with peace and assurance that all would be well. He then gave thanks.

Today's reading reminded me of his story: the chilling encounter with chaos, the feverish activity, the silence, the experience of peace—and then the exaltation or thanksgiving. The silence particularly stands out because that is where we know God. Yet we often fear silence and surround ourselves with noise to protect ourselves from it. When the San Francisco Bay Bridge was closed for repairs for several weeks after the earthquake in October 1989, people living nearby on Treasure Island couldn't sleep because it was too quiet. They had become so accustomed to the noise that the silence was disturbing. Being silent and listening to God *can* be disturbing—it can change our world, our way of perceiving things; it can change our hearts. Silence can also be reassuring, for there we can know the peace that passes understanding, the very presence of God.

Suggestion for meditation: *Be still and know. Be still and listen. Be still—and be. Be—still—and know that I am God.*

To Be Close to God

June 17-23, 1991   **Paul Escamilla†**
Monday, June 17   Read 2 Samuel 5:1-5.

This week's readings from 2 Samuel, Psalm 48, and Second Corinthians communicate a message of our closeness to God in terms of likeness, affection, and mission. Then the reading from Mark counter-balances this message in a profound way.

David has been established as king over Judah, the southern kingdom. And now a popular movement from Israel, the northern kingdom, would make David king over Israel as well. "Behold, we are your bone and flesh" cried the tribespeople of Israel to David. Notice the phrasing: the people gathered around David do not say, "You are our bone and flesh—you are one of us." Rather, they say, "We are your bone and flesh—we are like you."

When we consider a leader to be "one of us," we take pride in knowing that a great person's background includes our hometown, home church, or high school. However, it is quite another thing when a leader leads in such a way that others begin to see qualities and gifts in themselves which are like that person's own. The first kind of leader generates admiration from a distance; the second cultivates strengths within the admirer.

The gospel of the incarnation is that Jesus is like us, to be sure. But it is also that we are like Jesus. We are indeed his bone and flesh, sons and daughters loved by God, fashioned in God's image, and empowered to serve by God's grace.

Prayer: *God of wonder, show us how like Jesus we are, that our own lives might embody and express his compassion and faith. Amen.*

---

†A pastor in the North Texas Annual Conference, The United Methodist Church, Forney, Texas.

Tuesday, June 18   Read Psalm 48:1-3, 9-14.

The closing verses of Psalm 48 present us with a delightful metaphor for getting to know God. The image comes as an invitation to explore Zion, that is, Jerusalem, considered in the Old Testament to be the city of God: "Walk about Zion, go round about her, number her towers . . . that you may tell the next generation that this is God, our God . . . " In this way, the subject begins as "Zion" but ends as "God." In this way, the reader has the sense of being invited to traverse not only a city but God's very nature. The reader is asked to explore not only the walls and walkways of the city of God but the very towers and trellises of God the city. "Live in that city," the psalmist is saying. "Let it be your home, your place of security and enjoyment."

Such allusions to approaching God in wonderment and affectionate curiosity are not foreign to scripture, although they may appear "too playful" for our tastes. The psalmist is surrounded and absorbed with these thoughts of God, but not in a frivolous or pointless way. As an outcome of finding God in this way, the psalmist's trust is deepened and assurance firmly established: "this is God . . . [God] will be our guide for ever." This psalm brings expression in a beautiful way to the classical phrase from the Shorter Catechism of the Westminster Confession regarding the chief end of humanity: to worship God, and to enjoy God forever.

Prayer: *God of mystery and wonder, free us to answer the call of the psalmist. Help us grow each day in exploring and enjoying who you are, and in partaking of your very nature. Amen.*

Wednesday, June 19   Read 2 Corinthians 5:18-19.

In these two beautifully worded verses, a powerful and poignant message comes through: God trusts us. Twice in the text is this message expressed: God gave us the "ministry of reconciliation" (v. 18); God entrusted to us "the message of reconciliation" (v. 19). To entrust something to another person, in the thought of Joseph L. Allen, is actually to place ourselves or something that we value in the other person's hand. In light of this definition, what Paul is saying is quite radical: God has placed in our hands something of God's very own—the message and ministry of reconciliation in Christ. God's own gospel has been entrusted to us, placed in our hands to be shared with others. The words from an old Anglican hymn speak the same language.

> We are thy stewards; thine our talents, wisdom, skill;
> Our only glory that we may thy trust fulfill . . . *

Awesome and beautiful indeed is the realization that God trusts us with such a precious treasure as the gospel. The first few words of these two verses from Second Corinthians frame the whole text, and they speak volumes about God's nature of beneficence and trust toward us: "All this is from God."

All this is from God, the apostle declares. Not only is the act of reconciliation from God; the trust in us to be messengers of reconciliation to others is also from God. The fact that God trusts us suggests that bearing and sharing the message of reconciliation have to do not only with responsibility but also with how God esteems us. After all, to entrust a precious gift to another is to deem that person worthy of such trust.

Prayer: *O God, thank you for esteeming us so highly as to entrust to us the treasure of your gospel. Through Christ our Lord. Amen.*

---

*George B. Caird, "The Claims of Love."

Thursday, June 20   Read 2 Corinthians 5:20-21.

God having reconciled us (vv. 18-19), we now are called to respond by appealing to others, becoming "ambassadors for Christ." Paul writes so naturally here of the connection between God's gift and our response that the distinction between the two becomes blurred. Indeed, a part of God's gift is that we respond. "In Christ God was . . . entrusting to us the message of reconciliation" (v. 19). Likewise, our response is still very much God's gift: "God making his appeal through us" (v. 20). For the apostle, gift and response are two dimensions of the same reality. Paul has no problem seeing the first infusing the second.

Listen to that gift-response rhythm as Paul uses it in the opening words of this letter: "Blessed be the God and Father of our Lord Jesus Christ . . . who comforts us in all our affliction, so that we may be able to comfort those who are in any affliction, with the comfort with which we ourselves are comforted by God" (1:3-4).

Why would Paul emphasize this theme of gift and response to the young Corinthian church, struggling as it was with its share of problems and doubts? Perhaps because the twofold message undergirding this theme speaks to the heart of what it means to be human in any age, any place. As human beings we are always seeking to understand both our own worth and our relationships with others and with all creation. Paul's twofold message, simply put, is this: "We are gifted, and we are responsible." We are blessed and we are to bless; we are comforted and we are to comfort; we are loved and we are to love. God's gift always precedes, infuses, and follows after our response. Always, we love because God first loved us (see 1 John 4:19).

Suggestion for meditation: *Meditate on God's gifts to you, then consider with whom God would have you—and help you—share them.*

Friday, June 21   Read 2 Corinthians 6:1.

"Synergism" is perhaps not a word we normally associate with traditional Christian faith. A term to describe the blending together of more than one force, it sounds as though it might have emerged in the modern era. Curiously enough, the apostle Paul uses the Greek form of that very word in this verse to describe his working relationship with God: "Working together (*sunergeo*) with [God], then, we entreat you not to accept the grace of God in vain."

Paul has been writing about the dynamic of God's gift and our response (5:18-21). In this verse, by using this term, he goes so far as to suggest that even our response is a gift from God. That is, our living, working, and sharing the gospel in response to God's gift in Christ is enabled only by God's working with us.

So synergism is not so foreign a concept after all. To rely, as Paul does, upon the principle of synergism—God and humans working together—is to balance Christian life and doctrine between two extremes. The first extreme assumes that God does everything and we do nothing in the work of reconciling persons to God. The second extreme assumes that we alone manage and control how and to what degree persons (including ourselves) are reconciled or made whole, and that divine forces really have nothing to do with the matter. Paul understood the task of reconciliation as initiated and completed by God, who employs as instruments in the task any who will receive and extend God's reconciliation. (See 1 Cor. 3:6; Phil. 2:12*b*-13 as examples of this duality.)

Suggestion for prayer: *In prayer today, pray as though everything depended on God. In life, work for reconciliation as though all things depended on you.*

184

Saturday, June 22   Read Mark 4:35-39.

Mark leads us into the raging tumult of a windstorm with characteristic immediacy: in one verse we are moved from a calm, quiet scene on the water, away from the crowd, to a tempestuous storm and a capsizing boat. Whatever other reasons there may be for Mark's sense of suddenness here, it certainly reflects the reality of everyday life, in which crises can erupt in mid-sentence, sweeping over us and threatening to submerge us like a giant wave in a windstorm.

Jesus poses a study in contrasts here. While wind and water beat and batter against the boat, he sleeps on a cushion. While the disciples are at the front of the boat frightened for their lives, fighting a tumult beyond their own resources to subdue, Jesus is napping.

The question with which they awaken Jesus seems to be a mixture of desperation and sarcasm: "Teacher, do you not care if we perish?" That particular combination—desperation and sarcasm—is where many of us end our conversations with God, before moving on to cynicism and disbelief. Sarcasm *toward* faith often masks desperation *for* faith, so that "God doesn't care!" is sometimes more a yearning for God's help than a dismissal of divine benevolence.

Jesus responds to the disciples' desperate plea by rebuking the wind and quieting the storm, until there was a "great calm." The calm of which Mark speaks describes the elements, and not, as we shall see, the disciples.

Prayer: *In sudden crisis, O God, help us trust that you do care for us, and will come to our aid when we call upon you. Amen.*

Sunday, June 23   Read Mark 4:40-41.

Jesus' commanding words and actions toward the wind and sea have just quieted a raging storm. To say the disciples are filled with awe is to understate the Greek text, which speaks rather of a "great fear" which has overcome them. If the seas are now calmed, the disciples are in greater tumult than before. They are forced to raise a profoundly important question regarding the identity of their teacher: "Who then is this, that even wind and sea obey him?"

We can picture the scene: Jesus has just raised a hand and stilled the wind and sea, so that the waters are suddenly very calm, very still. He now turns to his disciples, whose looks of trepidation have not gone away, but only changed their focus, and asks: "Why are you afraid? Have you no faith?" (In this context, we must wonder to which fear he is referring—the fear of the storm, or the fear of Jesus.) The disciples, who still do not understand what Jesus has done, respond by raising their own question. Notice the question is not asked of Jesus directly but is raised among the disciples. For them, this Jesus is, for the moment at least, unapproachable.

We began the week with an identification of the people of Israel with King David. "We are your bone and flesh" (2 Sam. 5:1). The image suggests closeness—bonding and kinship—demonstrated with King David and anticipated with the Messiah. By contrast we end the week with a sense of the radical mystery of God, as expressed through the words of the mystified and terrified disciples: "Who is this?" In scripture, as in the experience of faith, the incarnation of God always remains firmly poised against the otherness of God.

Prayer: *God of mystery and wonder, nearness and delight, give us faith to love what we see of you and trust what we do not. Amen.*

LIFE'S INTERRUPTIONS/GOD'S BLESSINGS

June 24-30, 1991   **Cheryl Hammock†**
Monday, June 24   Read 2 Samuel 6:1-15.

A victory march! One great big parade! A celebration of a
new day for Israel and for King David! Everything was set to
bring to Jerusalem the Ark of the Covenant, the very physical
representation of Holiness-in-the-midst-of-humanness.

But just like all the best-laid designs of human beings, these
plans were interrupted. The oxen stumbled. And the presence
and power of the Holy fell into the hands of Uzzah, one who had
taken no precautions to handle it with ritual preparation and
cleanliness. And Uzzah died in the midst of all those spectators.

What could David do? He did just what we, even with all of
our enlightenment, are prone to do in the face of tragedy and the
interruption of the course we've laid out for our lives. He got
angry. And then he got scared. He decided that God-tabernacled-
in-our-midst was too unpredictable, too risky. He sent God away.
He put a safe distance between himself and the Holy—until he
saw the benevolence of God poured out on a Philistine, an
outsider in a border region.

Maybe God was not so unpredictable after all. Maybe that was
and is the God of both Israel's history and our lives: a sovereign
God who cannot be appropriated by any government or kingdom
or individual for gain, a God who blesses at will and with
inclusion and for God's own sake. What a surprising God!

Prayer: *Surprise us again, O God, by drawing near to us even when
we have sent you away, by quieting us even when we are afraid, by
blessing those we are not even sure are part of your household—even
us, O Surprising God, even us. Amen.*

---

†Ordained minister, The Christian Church (Disciples of Christ) serving as a
chaplain for Hospice of Central Florida, Inc., De Land, Florida.

Tuesday, June 25   Read Mark 5:21-34.

Jairus, a dignitary of the synagogue, had come to Jesus in the kind of desperation each of us has experienced in hospital corridors or at bedsides. He threw himself shamelessly at the feet of Jesus. The two of them set out for Jairus' home, and the crowd formed a spontaneous parade, thronging around Jesus.

A woman in the shadows of an alleyway saw them coming. What she was about to do was risky. A woman had no place in the company of these men on a mission. A sick woman, ceremonially unclean, was sure to be shunned—again. She would contaminate anyone she touched.

When she burrowed through the mass of muscular bodies, she grabbed hold of God, or as close as she thought she could get to God. *Healed,* she breathed to herself. *Healed*! Then just as silently she started slipping away unseen to the edge of the excitement. But Jesus stopped in his tracks and stopped her, too.

You can't do it that way, Jesus seemed to be saying. You can't hit-and-run with God. You are healed not by your own reach to God's power but by God's open hand extended to you. I'm more than a mysterious miracle worker, and you are more than an unclean outcast. I'm God's son and you're God's daughter. This whole exchange is built on that relationship. What has happened here has happened because of both of us, not just one.

It was then she knew she was fully restored to life. So when all was said and done, Jesus bade her his warm Hebrew *Shalom*— "saved by God!" And he gave her, for all to hear, the good Greek blessing "Be healed!" And the daughter of God, reclaimed from the edge of life, slipped past the anxious, hopeful Jairus.

Prayer: *O God of interruptions, stop us in our tracks when we think we have laid hold of you for our healing. Help us to know instead that you have laid hold of us, for now and for always. Amen.*

Wednesday, June 26   Read Mark 5:21-43.

Can there be a more desperate human being than a parent whose child is near death? Wouldn't a mother or father do anything, no matter how difficult or painful, to restore the child to health? Wouldn't you or I be willing to change places with the helpless little one, if we could? But the fact is, we can't.

Just like us, Jairus was sick from watching the agony of his little girl, and he was helpless as she moved from life ever nearer to death. Jesus was his last hope. But after he pleaded with all his might and persuaded Jesus to go home with him, his mission was interrupted by a woman who had been sick as long as Jairus' child had been alive.

What he saw gave him hope. Surely Jesus had the power to restore his daughter to health. But just as they turned to go, the awful word came: It's too late; she's already dead.

If only! If only I! If only you! If only God! The words went spinning around in his shocked and disoriented head.

And then, the greeting of every encounter with God throughout faith's history: Fear not! Fear not, Jesus said. For you are looking with your own frightened parent's eyes. But I am looking with the eyes of my Eternal Parent.

Jesus took his three most trusted team members, sent away the noisy hired mourners, and closed the door on all but the agonized mother and father. Then Jesus took the young girl's hand. And he talked to her. And he claimed her for life again.

Later, when the world was very, very sick, he did what every paralyzed parent wishes to do—he changed places, on a cross, with his helpless children. And he claimed us for life again.

Prayer: *O God, who refuses to believe in the death of your children, help all who wait at bedside or at graveside. Touch each hand, speak to each child, and feed us on your love in life everlasting. Amen.*

Thursday, June 27   Read 2 Corinthians 8:7-15.

Interruptions can interfere with the best intentions of communities and churches. And those who would manipulate God for their own purposes or franchise God's blessing through corporate channels can disrupt benevolence efforts for the needy.

Corinth was a center for extremism in almost every human appetite: commerce, luxury, sexual liberties and abuses, sports. It was a Roman colony with Roman citizens running it, but there was also a strong Hebrew presence and a synagogue.

It was difficult enough for Paul to proclaim the gospel and to plant a church in this diverse culture. He and Corinthian Christians also faced interruptions from self-styled "super-apostles." These opponents of Paul challenged his leadership as the servant of Christ and his integrity as one who shared in the suffering of Christ. Their presence threatened the very relationship between Paul and the new, growing believers in Corinth.

The disruption was severe. Reconciliation between Paul and his friends was delayed for nearly a year. And the crucial goal of famine relief for Jerusalem was put on hold.

Finally, when peace had been restored, Paul encouraged his friends to finish what they had started: to feed the hungry and care for the homeless. Their love in Christ, he said, should become tangible care for those in need.

Now as then, love calls us back to our original mission: to love, to feed, to shelter, to heal and comfort, and to follow Christ—whose richness in the form of God was interrupted and depleted for our sake.

Prayer: *Help us, O God, to be reconciled not only to you but also to one another, both near and far. Help us to know that both Spirit-filling and stomach-filling are in your design for all your children. Amen.*

Friday, June 28   Read 2 Corinthians 8:9.

Corinth. It was a city at the crossroads of almost every kind of trade. It was a city where you could buy anything and almost anybody. It was a city of great diversity: Romans, Greeks, Jews; slaves and liberated ones; men, women, and children. And there was a price of one kind or another on each of them.

For everyone there was a god of one kind or another, too. There were the worship centers for a host of deities, including a temple for Aphrodite which provided slave-prostitutes in a cult of what today would be considered unrivaled sexual abuse.

Here Paul found people who were eager to hear the word of liberation in Jesus. They were so eager that they were easy prey for self-promoters. These "superlative apostles," as Paul calls them in ridicule, peddled a brand of feel-good religion that diluted the authority of Christ and the autonomy of the church.

Our world is not so different. There is a price attached to each of us. Our days no longer belong to us but to the corporation, or at least to the credit cards. Sometimes we are owned by our unaddressed fears, our unmastered passions, our unfulfilled dreams. We are owned by the urgency of today, the getting and the keeping of what really cannot be kept anyway. We are not so far away from Corinth.

But we are, like Corinth, not so far away from salvation, either. Jesus poured out all that was rich in God-ness and bought us back from all that is not. Now the wealth of God—of creation, of redemption, of reconciliation—is ours. God interrupted the buying and the selling and bought us back—for keeps.

Prayer: *O God who buys us back, help us to buy back your world of people and creatures and even creation itself. Help us, like Jesus, to embrace poverty and sacrifice that all of your earth may be rich together in your love and our care. Amen.*

Saturday, June 29   Read Psalm 24.

The whole earth belongs to God. And all that live on it, in it, under it, over it belong to God, too.

Those who live marginally belong to God. Those who live in migrant worker camps and drug-infested trafficways belong to God.

Our swimming mammal-kin, drowning in tuna nets, belong to God. Voiceless fur-covered victims of cosmetic testing belong to God. Vanishing forests and suffocating springs belong to God. Dirtied skies through which missiles soar belong to God.

We are giving back to God a very dirty gift.

Who may ascend the hill of God? Who shall stand in God's holy place? Those whose hands are unpolluted and whose hearts are given to purifying the earth again.

What can we do? Once again our human designs prove inadequate, and the sheer vastness of our wasting interrupts our wholeness and the wholeness of God's creation.

What can we do? The answer is as ancient as this psalm. We must understand, as those early worshipers of Yahweh understood, that we cannot fashion this life to our users' schemes and insatiable appetites. We must let God's redemption claim us.

And now, just as surely as we were utterly without hope except for the sacrifice of Jesus, there is no hope except for our learning to sacrifice for this fragile earth and all who are a part of it. Then will the blessing of God come. Then another generation of those who seek God's face will have a chance to find it.

Prayer: *Help us, O God, to give ourselves to the redemption of this incredibly wonderful home. Help us to give ourselves to all who live on it, in it, under it, over it—that it and we may once again be fit for the God of glory to come in. Amen.*

Sunday, June 30   Read Psalm 126.

Life's interruptions and God's blessings go hand in hand. In this week's readings we have seen every kind of dilemma and God's consistently loving response. The plans of a leader and a nation are delayed. A woman's disease isolates her from the fullness of life and love. A child dies awaiting a cure. A church, its relationships and its ministry to the poor and hungry are disrupted by power-gatherers. A planet faces poisoning from the very tenants it feeds and shelters.

We are in those stories. Crisis diverts us from the paths we chart for ourselves, our families, our fortunes. Our circumstances seem irrevocable. Our own wisdom fails us. Our strength withers. Our hopes for human intervention fade. And life seems like a bad dream from which we cannot awake.

The psalmist reminds us that Israel faced these nightmares of failed plans and broken spirits. But God's steadfast love empowered them to bear the present and to hope for the future. God still gives blessings beyond what we can imagine, like rivers greening the barren desert: not just restoration, not just healing, not just comfort—but resurrection.

And resurrection is not out there somewhere. It is the giving of new life here and now to all who are broken by life's interruptions, to all who are lost in despair, to all who know pain of flesh and of spirit. The past and the present and the future become one in hope. Life may give us weeping, but in resurrection, the last laugh, the laughter of joy, comes from God.

Prayer: *O God, when we are delayed, dejected, denied by all of life's interruptions, help us to remember and to rest in you. When we go forth in weeping, bring us home to your heart in joy. Amen.*

GOD THROUGH A PERSON AND A PEOPLE

July 1-7, 1991   **John Oliver Nelson†**
Monday, July 1   Read Mark 6:1-3.

In this week's lectionary we will deal first with Mark. This story of Jesus' visit to his "home church" is obviously a particularly honest and frank account.

We sympathize with the Master as he encounters his neighbors and family. After all, we are in on the secret of who he really was. Yet by nature surely we are much like the members of that Nazareth congregation: like them, we can tell everyday people from divine ones. Especially are we slow to accept as extraordinary any 30-year-old preacher we have known as a boy. Besides, he shows abilities that exceed ours and announces truths which we cannot comprehend.

But did a few among all the neighbors and kinfolk discern authenticity in Jesus? Surely there were thoughtful ones, unaffected by the group's judgment, who said to themselves, "This is real!" Can we be among them, recognizing the wonder? Can we judge for ourselves, no matter what the townsfolk say?

Such discerning attention leads us to go deeper, to put study and inquiry into our ideas, to look beneath the surface for essential truth. Eagerness and attentiveness, no matter who comes to town, are the keys to discovering extraordinary truths and persons. Such discovery can involve shock and surprise—and growth. Let us not allow the Master to leave our village without reaching for the life and meaning he brings us.

Prayer: *Save us, O God, from hearsay, rejecting the truth. Free us to embrace with eagerness and dedication the way of Christ. Amen.*

---

†Presbyterian minister; founder of Kirkridge Retreat Center, Bangor, Pennsylvania.

Tuesday, July 2   Read Mark 6:4-5.

During Jesus' teaching and healing ministry, people near his boyhood home flocked to hear him. He did what older translations have called "miracles" and many more recent ones call "mighty works." Ah, but this success was not to come in his hometown. Here, to reassure themselves that he was nobody special, people numbered out his brothers—James, Joses, Judas, Simon—his sisters, and his mother, Mary, to remind themselves that Jesus himself was just a carpenter.

Honesty as a biographer—telling it as it was—led Mark to relate that our Lord "could do no mighty work there." All he could manage was to lay "his hands upon a few sick people and [heal] them." No, nothing very dramatic or divine. As his neighbors brought serious cases, such as he dealt with in nearby villages, did Jesus try, and fail, to make them whole? The account reads as though he did. His boyhood friends and his family "took offense at him" (v. 3). This made the Master himself marvel. He was astonished. His failure he traced simply to "their unbelief." (Later in his ministry these same people followed him eagerly and sought his presence. Indeed, his mother, who apparently didn't believe him at home, stood by him at the cross.)

How often we ourselves take Jesus for granted! We speak the dull, familiar phrase, addressing this wondrous announcer of God as part of our surroundings. His name can become as timeworn and unexciting as that of the boy next door. Jesus himself bids us see him, not with "unbelief" but in the prisoner, the hungry or homeless one, the genuine one, the rejected one.

Prayer: *Give us power and saintliness, O God, even when we are unrecognized. May we remember that Jesus calls us to do mighty works in his name, especially with those who are numbered among the poor. Amen.*

Wednesday, July 3   Read Psalm 89:20-37.

Psalm 89 has four sections: preface (vv. 1-4); hymn of praise to God (vv. 5-18); oracle on the Lord's promises to David (vv. 9-37); and lament on behalf of the king (vv. 38-51). Today's reading tells of God's covenant with David, a covenant that is eternal in spite of what David or his descendants might do. Since the king both incorporates and represents the people, the covenant extends to the people under the king's rule. Here, the psalmist shows us a God who doesn't exist in a vacuum, a God who has chosen to use us as agents to help bring about the divine will, a God whose nature is such that companionship is valued, a God who shares the creative process with us.

But a warning comes with this promise (vv. 30-32). The next section, the national lament (vv. 38-51), bears out the warning. The enemy (probably Babylon) has torn down Jerusalem's walls, left the king's (probably Jehoiachin's or Zedekiah's) forts in ruins, and taken away the royal scepter and throne.

Ultimately, however, in spite of the people's disobedience, God's purpose will prevail. What a message of hope for our time! A time when our planet's very life is endangered. A time when many times more money is still spent on weapons of destruction rather than on those things that sustain life for God's people. A time when the distribution of goods and capital is way out of balance. We are realizing that we have not lived according to God's commands, and we—or our children and grand-children—will suffer because of that failure.

So where is the comfort? "But," God says, " I will not stop loving David or fail to keep my promise to him" (TEV). Unconditional love is good news, and it extends to all of us.

Prayer: *Keep us aware, O God, of being a worldwide family to whom the good news has come. Amen.*

Thursday, July 4   Read 2 Samuel 7:1-17.

King David was sure a building would better honor God. His own mansion made of cedar—ah, the aroma of it!—made shamefully inadequate the shaky, temporary tent where the Lord dwelt. David asked his trusted prophet Nathan. Nathan took the situation seriously and had a vivid dream about it that very night.

He came up with a famous "not yet" answer. King David, originally a herdsman and always a man of war, was no builder. Rather, the building should be done by the next generation. Upon it, and the builder, God would heap all the blessings of Israel.

But why, in this story of Israel, did the divine promise to prosper and protect his people come in relation to a *building*? Why did God agree that the Presence could be localized and honored by a great wooden temple, even overlaid with gold? This was the way neighboring pagans enshrined their idols.

One answer is that even though Israel's deity was unseen, a human response to God was and is to erect the most lovely, magnificent structure possible. Through the centuries, people have bespoken their worship in the finest houses of worship they could build—from Saint Sophia in Istanbul to Cartres Cathedral in France or First Church in Appleville.

"Where there is no vision, the people [and their church designs] perish." Yet we must build, even among skyscrapers and in desolate deserts. For this is an indelible medium for glorifying God. To acknowledge that Presence, and also to witness to our neighbors, we are again and again called to build.

Prayer: *To you, God, we lift the highest praise. We glorify you as we build our houses of worship. May we glorify you more as we build loving relationships that can become the building blocks of your kingdom. Amen.*

Friday, July 5   Read 2 Corinthians 12:1-6.

The apostle Paul's writings abound in person-to-person relationships with the unseen Jesus or God. This is one of Paul's vast contributions to the story and experience of the church. It is all the more remarkable, then, that in these six verses, he describes an impersonal, philosophic entering into a realm of consciousness otherwise strange to him. Here we find terms and diffidences exactly like those of many mystics of all the world's profound religions. He precisely dates this one-time access to such mysteries. Almost reluctantly, and in third-person witness, he presents unutterable claims.

What is this "third heaven" or the "paradise," in which Paul had realizations which "cannot be uttered"? Since he says it cannot be described, we must place it in the mystical treasury—by no means exclusively Christian—to which classical mysticism testifies in countless writings. Their claim, and Paul's, is that this voyage into the inexpressible is always made alone. Its vividness makes ordinary life seem unreal. As "a call," it revolutionizes persons. It is a wonder that Paul, reluctant to write about the experience at all, told the whole church at Corinth about it and said he could boast about it but would probably be misunderstood. It was evidently a one-time revolutionary event of a lifelong quest for faith in God.

What can his halting description mean for people today? It shows us that Paul, in a vision which is neither Jewish in imagery nor Christ-oriented like most of his other writing, identifies with the worldwide witness to unutterable truth. It also may inspire us to seek for ourselves some inkling or echo of mysteries of which we may dream in our workaday seeking after the reality of God.

Prayer: *Expand, O Holy One, our small horizons of expectancy, that we may be caught up to visions we have never had before. Amen.*

Saturday, July 6   Read 2 Corinthians 12:7-10.

In the last paragraphs of his letter, Paul sent along to the family of faith in Corinth the news—almost a warning—that he would soon visit them (v. 14). His word here is what in musical notation can be called *sforzando,* sudden roughness and gentleness. He says he might well brag of his own spiritual achievements, but prefers to be humble and even helpless about them.

What checks him is of course the "thorn in the flesh" which reminds him of his human weakness. The phrase has long been a part of our everyday secular language. Nobody has satisfactorily discovered what Paul meant, though thousands of scholars and other readers have tried. Was it a speech impediment? Could it have been a nagging other person? What could be "a messenger of Satan, to harass me"? He says he three times asked God to deliver him from it. But the reply has been, instead, that he will always be given strength to deal with it.

Yet, it is only a thorn, not some tragedy, that stalks him. We may well question why Paul wrote about it to the Corinthians when it was only a personal discomfort. Possibly they had found him suddenly deficient at some point and wondered why. Whatever the situation, his telling about it was surely a strange comfort to them—as it has been for countless hearers who have been pricked by some such nettle ever since.

Not all of us have such a persistent difficulty. But the main purpose of the apostle's telling everybody about it, apparently, is to show that God does pledge sufficient power for us to overcome again and again. For this lesson and assurance, we thank both God and God's uncomfortable apostle!

Prayer: *O Eternal One, inspire us to elation in your gospel, reminding us always that in our weakness your strength is our salvation. Amen.*

Sunday, July 7   Read Mark 6:5-6.

Return to the poignant incident with which these meditations began six days ago: Jesus' visit to his hometown and family and his sorrowful realization of their unbelief.

The great learning from this situation is that we can refuse the power of God, even if this means continuing to be fevered or paralyzed. Oddly, it was immediately after this that he called the twelve disciples together—all of them witnesses to their Master's failure at home—and sent *them* out two by two to heal.

How did Jesus equip them? And how does he instruct us? Jesus' primary question was nearly always, "Do you believe I can do this?" "Are you sure I can heal you?" His disciples were undoubtedly bidden to ask that same question.

In our time, for victims or patients, the query is the same—for healers, counselors, and even medical doctors. For religious groups dedicated to healing, or secular therapy groups, this is where the path to wholeness begins.

When seeking forgiveness in prayer or repeating a request in a general confession, most of us surely don't expect anything to happen unless we are confident that the Hearer of our prayer is able to heal and forgive. A learned teacher said, "The worst sin is false piety"—sounding holy but knowing it isn't so.

What do we expect? That is the whole question as we meet Jesus in our home or in church. It is within our power today to say—despite our familiarity and *casual* belief—"Lord and Master, I believe with all my heart that you can bring me complete wellness in God." Then, though kinsfolk marvel at my belief, the healing and grace are available to me as Jesus goes on his way to the cross, to resurrection, and to ascension.

Prayer: *O God, grant me this day to be and do what you ask of me. In Jesus' name. Amen.*

IN CHRIST

July 8-14, 1991   **Jaime Potter-Miller†**
Monday, July 8   Read Ephesians 1:1.

As my mail crosses my desk each working day, I notice the letterheads on incoming correspondence. Without reading a line of the content, I can perceive a wealth of information about the one who writes to me. The color of the paper and ink, the logo, if any, the arrangement of the lettering—these visual symbols speak a message and put into a context the words that follow. I look at the stationery that sends my communications to others. Before the text is read, the receiver knows my name, my title, and my denominational affiliation. The name of my church evokes memories of others who have served there before me. Using that letterhead places my ministry in the midst of a great cloud of witnesses.

The writer of the letter to the Ephesians paints a picture with words that serves as a letterhead for this message to the believers in Ephesus and wherever else the epistle would be circulated. The writer, if not in fact the apostle Paul, at least shares the inspiration Paul knew and can boldly proclaim the connection. It is no accident of fate that calls this servant of God to put pen to paper. It is the intentional decision of God that these words should be spoken to the saints, the community of those who act as sanctuary, the dwelling place of holiness, those who are faithful in Christ Jesus.

Suggestion for meditation: *Allow the words* apostle, called, saints, faithful, *and* in Christ *to meander through your mind. Reflect on the images that this pondering produces. Are these comfortable metaphors for the letterhead of your life?*

---

†Pastor, Dormont United Methodist Church, Pittsburgh, Pennsylvania.

Tuesday, July 9   Read Ephesians 1:1-2.

Our daughter was born when my husband and I were both students in seminary. She began attending classes, chapel services, and choir practice, where she was surrounded by Christians before she achieved her first month of life. Surrounded by music, she sang as often as she spoke, concluding her nursery rhymes in the same fashion that she heard the hymns at church end. Her broad repertoire included "Jesus Loves Me" and "Day by Day" as well as "Take Me Out to the Ball Game."

The first song Janna learned to sing came, however, as a shock to us. Although she was ordinarily limited to visiting Sesame Street and The Neighborhood of Make-Believe, she discovered how to turn on the television while we were studying and learned to keep the volume low. One day, hearing her padding down the hall, I looked up at her angelic face in time to see her fling her arms wide, throw back her head, and solemnly intone: "When you say 'Budweiser' you've said it all! Amen."

The writer of the letter to the Ephesians, however, sings a hymn of richer depth and texture. In this letter to Christians hungry for exhortation, thirsty souls are refreshed with recurring offerings of "grace and peace to you from God." Indeed, grace is offered twelve times and peace imparted seven times in this letter. Over and over again the flavor of this communication is enhanced with the use of these words. Grace and peace, when used in a secular context, connote hospitality and safety. But when spoken "in Christ" these words encompass a dimension that no intruder can violate: *God's* grace, *God's* peace—wrapped in God's arms, held close to God's heartbeat. When you say "grace and peace . . ." in Christ, you've said it all.

Suggestion for prayer: *"Inhale" God's grace; "exhale" God's peace. Spend a few minutes absorbing the quietude that comes from resting in Christ.*

Wednesday, July 10   Read Ephesians 1:3.

E. Stanley Jones's twenty-third book is a compilation of daily devotions. Brother Stanley, as Ashram devotees lovingly refer to him, writes in the introduction to *In Christ:*

> The phrase "in Christ" is the ultimate phrase in the Christian faith, for it locates us in a Person—the Divine Person—and it locates us in Him here and now. It brings us to the ultimate relationship—"in." Obviously this "in" brings us nearer than "near Christ," "following Christ," "believing Christ," or even "committed to Christ." You cannot go further or deeper than "in." *

The New Testament epistles overflow with the concept of being "in Christ." The phrase or its equivalent is spoken repeatedly in the letters traditionally attributed to the apostle Paul. In the first ten verses of Ephesians the words appear like a refrain, tying up the threads of the mystical concepts and theology. "In Christ" provides a context for the doxology that follows the letterhead and greeting in this letter. By being and becoming "in Christ," believers already benefit from the spiritual blessings that belong to and emanate from the heavenly realm. This is not merely a lofty wish for "pie in the sky by and by." Living "in Christ" consolidates a union that grafts us into Christ's suffering and exaltation. Spiritual union represents no esoteric musing; to be "in Christ" joins believers into the Body of Christ that Paul celebrates. "In Christ" the faithful are joined inexorably to one another. To be "in Christ" is to be in community.

Suggestion for meditation: *Stand beside the Christ and picture yourself walking into his arms. As you experience his strong embrace, feel your life joining with others around whom you can also picture his arms. Join arms with them "in Christ."*

---

*New York—Nashville: Abingdon Press, 1961, p. 8.

Thursday, July 11   Read Ephesians 1:4-6.

Sometimes disciplines other than religion assist us in interpreting the faith. I have been impressed with the work of Carl Jung, a psychologist who probed the caverns of personality theory, allowing the shadows to exist alongside the illuminations. Jung hypothesizes a "collective unconscious" where memories and dreams bump into each other, allowing persons to feel linked with the past and the anticipated.

Quite separate from what Jung calls the "self" or the "soul," the unconscious psyche ties us to one another and offers us, through our dreams and visions, a glimpse of how God intends that we become whole. In this collective unconscious, time unscrolls like waves upon the seashore. Those in the Judeo-Christian tradition have always known that spiritual time is not gauged by a Timex; any given moment in time leans backward and strains forward while stretching out its arms in many directions. Time, for the believer, unfolds in a multi-directional field, not on a linear, logical graph. Jung has simply given a name to what we have long known intuitively.

In this unconscious place, the work of prevenient grace begins. In Christ, we are chosen for holiness before the creation of the world. Drawn from the collective story of humankind, our lives begin before birth to spin a tale, a story that weaves threads from the past with hope for the future on a loom named "chosen." Those loved by God are called from preconsciousness into life and light. Holiness is the result of, not the prerequisite for, God's choice of the believer. Being "in Christ" focuses the call of God with a purpose: we live for relationship with God.

Suggestion for meditation: *Consider the relationship and call expressed by the essence of the Westminster Catechism: The chief end of humanity is to glorify and enjoy God forever.*

Friday, July 12   Read Ephesians 1:7-8.

Citizens of the world of the first century were familiar with the ideas and customs of the Romans. Words from Roman thought and practice have made their way into our faith vocabulary as well. "Redemption" allowed for the freeing of a slave through the practice of paying a ransom fee. So it was not unusual for the leaders of the church to draw the analogy between those in bondage to sin and those in bondage to a human owner. However, the ransom price is no cash settlement. We are redeemed by the death of Jesus.

Once I heard a sermon in which the preacher made a case for doing away with the use of the cross for jewelry. Wearing a cross, he stated, was the ancient equivalent of sporting a miniature electric chair or gallows. Insisting that no one would morbidly display execution devices on necklaces and earrings, this preacher made a plea for abolishing the cross and allowing the believer's life to become a vigorous metaphor for resurrection.

I affirm resurrection. But I need the cross. I know that if I were to stand before God's holiness without the shadow of the cross falling across my life, I would be unable to bear the gaze of holy eyes. To constantly remind me of my redemption, I wear a cross fashioned from crystal. It is inconspicuous; it blends in with whatever I am wearing without clashing or calling attention to itself. But whenever anyone looks at me, they are seeing me through this crystal cross. Frequently throughout the day, I find myself fingering the glass, holding the cross in the palm of my hand. Sometimes intentionally, often unconsciously, I am reminding myself that in Christ I am redeemed! I am forgiven! God lavishes on my life wisdom and understanding sufficient to grace me with fruitful life.

Suggestion for meditation: *What does the cross mean to me?*

Saturday, July 13   Read Ephesians 1:9.

The young adult Sunday school class I teach was reviewing the life of King David. Interest heightened when the intrigue and shame of Bathsheba's pregnancy was rehearsed. Quoting Psalm 51, I spoke of David's confession and repentance. The question was posed: Did David really think the death of the child ended the controversy between him and God? Was his sin forgiven? One class member shot back, "No, that doesn't get him off the hook!" Almost as a reflex, the response leaped from my tongue, "Yes! God's forgiveness is complete! David was completely, utterly forgiven!" Ken's face reflected the look of one who has been shocked by cold water. He later came to me with tears and shared his joy that something in him had been released by the starkness of my reply. He had experienced the mystery of forgiveness.

The mystery of God is often revealed through the tension of paradox. Jesus is human; Jesus is divine. The Holy Spirit is like a gentle dove; the Holy Spirit is dynamite. The same voice that compassionately sang out, "Come to me, all who labor and are heavy laden, and I will give you rest" stated matter-of-factly, "Let the dead bury the dead." For Ken, the pronouncement of God's justice ran head-on into God's mercy. In confronting the paradox, Ken understood the mystery.

God does reveal the mystery of faith to those who are in Christ. Those willing to allow the conflicting tensions of apparently opposing truths to exist side by side will understand. Some might think that the heaping of paradox upon paradox would result in a harvest of confusion. I believe instead that the plural of "paradox" is actually "paradise."

Suggestion for meditation: *Are my images of God sufficiently diverse to embrace paradox and mystery?*

Sunday, July 14   Read Ephesians 1:10.

In July of 1989, my family vacationed in Western Europe. Unexpectedly, we had a four-hour layover between flights in West Berlin. As we toured parts of the city, we walked along a stretch of the Berlin Wall. Deep within my soul was an urgency. I told my fourteen-year-old son, "Jordan, this wall is coming down—I can *feel* the hope of it coming down."

In the spring of 1987 and 1988, I had chaperoned groups of teenage youth leaders from the northeast United States on trips they called "Mission of Peace." After briefings in Helsinki, Finland, we spent ten days in the Soviet Union. The difference between the first and second trips was profound. I could *feel* the hope that accompanied the relaxation of tension. Even the air was easier to breathe. The cross-topped onion domes glimmered in the sun as a quiet testimony to the truth that had never been silenced: God is still God. Even in the face of odds that appear insurmountable, God is still God, and God is bringing all things in heaven and on earth together under one head. All things are being gathered "in Christ."

Within five months after our trip to Europe, the Berlin Wall changed from a symbol of division into a symbol of hope. As I write in these latter days of 1989, signs of the fulfillment of this passage in Ephesians are blossoming all around me: Lech Walesa addresses American workers; Gorbachev plays the role of a modern Cyrus and visits with the Pope; Wenceslaus Square overflows with hopeful Czechs; certain Southern African beaches are integrated; the Malta summit sails stormy but promising. I can *feel* the hopeful contractions of new birth. All things are being brought together in heaven and on earth.

Suggestion for prayer: *Use the headlines of the front page of the newspaper as seeds for intercession. Imagine the nations of the world together in Christ.*

JESUS CHRIST IS OUR PEACE

July 15-21, 1991   **Bruce C. Birch**†
Monday, July 15   Read Ephesians 2:13-14.

In this last decade of the twentieth century we desperately hope that real peace is drawing closer, and there are many hopeful signs. Yet, we are also aware that conflict, injustice, oppression, and poverty are all too real in our world and stand in the way of lasting peace.

In Jesus Christ we see a peace which goes beyond the uneasy quiet between conflicts. In him we see the dividing wall of hostility broken down and we are made one. If we are to follow Christ, we cannot settle for tolerance or mutual self-interest with those we have considered our enemies. We must seek those paths that end hostility and move us to unity.

Behind this text is the Hebrew concept of *shalom*. This word can be translated as "peace," but its basic meaning is "wholeness." It encompasses all of those things which make for wholeness: justice, compassion, health, righteousness, and love. To seek *shalom* is to actively work for wholeness rather than settling for the absence of conflict. As long as any of our neighbors in the global community of humankind live in brokenness of body, mind, or spirit, then we ourselves cannot experience true peace.

Jesus Christ, in his openness to all persons and his concern for all who were broken in body or spirit, showed us the path of seeking *shalom*. In this week of readings we shall try to discover more of what it means to follow his path to peace.

Prayer: *O Lord of all the earth, who desires our wholeness in all things, make us instruments of thy peace. Amen.*

---

†Professor of Old Testament, Wesley Theological Seminary, Washington, D.C.

Tuesday, July 16   Read Psalm 53.

There is no shortage in our time of "those who work evil" (v. 4). I work in a city where drug-related violence is a constant source of concern. We all live in a world where poverty and injustice create brokenness and deny us the peace for which we hope.

The temptation in the face of evil is to think that if we can just find the right program or the right security system or the right political initiative, we can neutralize evil in the world by our own efforts. This psalm teaches us that this is a false hope.

God is the true source of opposition to evil in the world. Those whose actions and words fail to acknowledge this are no better than fools (v. 1). Yet, we continue to mount program after program as if our crises had no spiritual dimension.

In our own lives we often compartmentalize God into "church" activities and live the rest of our lives by the values of our workplace or our politics or our cultural setting as if God were not the source of true peace in all our doings.

Of course we are to use our own resources to oppose evil in the world. But if we do not understand God as the source of power for wholeness standing behind and beneath our efforts, then we too are lacking in understanding and fail to call upon God (v. 4). Despite our best efforts and intentions we may then be numbered among "those who work evil."

Prayer: *O God, the source of genuine understanding, cleanse our hearts and minds of the foolish belief that our power alone can save us. Amen.*

Wednesday, July 17   Read 2 Samuel 11:1-15.

No other story in the Old Testament better illustrates the abuses of power which make for brokenness than this tragic tale of David, Bathsheba, and Uriah. David is at the height of his power and is idly pacing on the roof of the palace when he sees a beautiful woman bathing on her roof. There is no hesitation. He sent. He took. He lay with her—even though he was told that Bathsheba was the wife of Uriah, one of his own commanders.

Unfortunately this story demonstrates the way in which our intentional breaking of *shalom* compounds itself. A child is conceived, and what follows is an attempt to bring Uriah home and deceive him into believing the child is his. When this does not work, due to Uriah's ironic faithfulness to David, the king resorts to murder. David, the greatest of Israel's kings, the royal line from which the Messiah will come, is now reduced to acts of violence in order to cover his own acts of greed and power. What has gone wrong?

A small clue may lie in this observation. All through David's story it has been clear that God was at work. Even in his victory over Goliath when David was a young man, it was to God that David gave the credit. But there is no mention of God in this story. It is as if David had grown so powerful and successful that he left God behind. He believes that he is the source of his own power; therefore he acts in his own interest. He casually tells the messenger who brings news of Uriah's death, "Do not let this thing be evil in your eyes" (v. 25, AP). But the last line of this story says, "This thing was evil in the eyes of the Lord" (v. 27, AP).

Prayer: *O Lord, forgive us when our own sense of power blinds us to the source of wholeness which lies in you alone. Amen.*

Thursday, July 18   Read Mark 6:30-36.

From yesterday's story of broken *shalom* we now come to a story of need for *shalom* and those who minister to that need. The disciples have returned from a mission of preaching and healing, and Jesus hears their report. Still people throng to them so that they "had no leisure even to eat" (v. 31). They decide to seek some quiet time away so "they went away in the boat to a lonely place by themselves" (v. 32). But the crowd ran around the shore of the lake and got there ahead of them. Seeing them, Jesus had compassion and taught them. As the hour grew late the disciples worried about how the crowd would be fed. Jesus and the disciples, seeking their own peace (*shalom*), find themselves in the presence of human need, both spiritual and physical.

How common it is to think of true peace as a pulling apart from the world. Yet God constantly reminds us that wholeness is most needed where there is brokenness. Elijah flees in discouragement into the desert to Mt. Horeb seeking God's still, small voice, only to have that voice send him back into the turbulent world of Ahab and Jezebel (see 1 Kings 19). At the Mount of Transfiguration the disciples want to build booths and remain there, but Jesus calls them back to their ministry of teaching and healing among the people (see Luke 9:28-36).

The peace (*shalom*) of Jesus Christ is found in the presence of need and in willingness to serve that need.

Prayer: *O gracious God, in our desire to be alone, empower us anew for the task of service to a broken world. Amen.*

Friday, July 19   Read Mark 6:37-44.

"Feed all of these people?" The disciples are amazed. They did not object to Jesus' teaching of the crowd, even though they had hoped for some time alone. But they assumed they had no responsibility for the people's physical needs, only their spiritual needs.

What follows, of course, is that well-known story of the feeding of the five thousand from only five loaves of bread and two fish. When the disciples take responsibility for the people's need, there is enough. Even twelve baskets over!

The church has often tended to limit its ministry to the spiritual realm, but God's concern for our salvation has to do with God's desire for our wholeness in every respect. In a broken world we, as God's people, are to be present to the needs of all who are denied wholeness in any way. We are to feed those hungry in body as well as hungry in spirit.

When Jesus took the five small loaves "he looked up to heaven, and blessed, and broke the loaves, and gave them to the disciples . . . " (v. 41). This language is a reflection of the breaking of the bread at the Last Supper and reminds us of our breaking of bread at the Lord's Table. For us as the church there is a connection between life's bread and the bread of life. Out of brokenness we are made whole.

In the feeding of the multitude Jesus calls the disciples and us to a new awareness of our ministry to bring wholeness (*shalom*) wherever we find human need and in whatever form that need takes.

Prayer: *O God, the giver of bread and of the bread of life, feed us by thy word, that we may feed the needs of a troubled world. Amen.*

Saturday, July 20   Read Ephesians 2:11-15.

"He is our peace" (v. 14). In Jesus Christ the brokenness of the world is restored to wholeness. It is not accidental that the early church chose to refer to Jesus by the title found in Isaiah 9:6, the "Prince of Peace [*shalom*]."

If we are to seek peace in our world as followers of Jesus Christ, then we must attend carefully to the model of peacemaking here.

The peace of Jesus Christ breaks down the dividing walls of hostility. What remarkable times we have been through in recent years. Political and social barriers we thought impregnable have begun to come down in Eastern Europe and South Africa and the Soviet Union. But it is remarkable how often the walls of our hostility stay in place. We don't easily give up our enemies. And it is remarkable how tenacious the walls of hostility created by racism, nationalism, economic injustice, and ignorance can be erected in new places even as they come down in others.

The peace of Jesus Christ is incarnational. God in Jesus Christ took flesh in our midst to show us a new humanity of oneness in the midst of our divisions. So too, we must take flesh in the midst of the world's division. To bring peace, wholeness, to a divided world we must dare to be physically present as the church wherever hostility still divides us. As the church we must constantly and prayerfully seek to face the issues that divide us in our congregations, in our communities, and in our world. To avoid them is to remove ourselves from the peace of Jesus Christ.

Prayer: *O God, give us the courage to seek wholeness of life in all of those places where hostility yet divides us. Amen.*

Sunday, July 21   Read Ephesians 2:16-22.

The peace of Jesus Christ is not without cost. It comes through the cross (v. 16). Jesus faced the hostility of a broken world and brought wholeness (*shalom*) by his willingness to suffer and die for the sake of that broken world.

This is not the way in which the world seeks peace. We speak in our political forums of peace through strength or peace as the prize of victory over enemies. The peace of Jesus Christ is the peace which comes from an ability to love our enemies, to seek out the outcast, to give ourselves for the needs of the world rather than our own needs.

The church too often imagines that it can serve Jesus Christ in the world without paying any price. We want the new life of resurrection without the pain of the cross. But it cannot be.

When we gather at the Lord's Table we break the bread and remember Christ's broken body, but then we take that brokenness into ourselves as a reminder of the broken world for which Christ died and to which we are sent.

We are called in the preaching of the peace of Jesus Christ to bring the far-off near, to make their pain ours, to seek wholeness not as the result of our own success but at the cost of our sacrifice and commitment to the way of the cross. Who are the far-off in our lives and in our communities who must be brought near? Can we sacrifice our own comfort and success for the sake of true peace in Jesus Christ?

Prayer: *O God, strengthen us to take up the cross in our world as followers of Jesus Christ, who alone is our peace. Amen.*

July 22-28, 1991   **Penny Bargo†**
Monday, July 22   Read 2 Samuel 12:1-6.

Self-sentencing

David's sin, which began with lust, had mushroomed into a jealous act of malicious maneuvering that resulted in a perfectly planned murder. Without putting his hand to a weapon, David connived to accomplish his purpose. And he got what he wanted—Bathsheba was his. However, David had neglected to include in his calculations the all-seeing eye of God.

God prefers to deal with us personally when we fail. He does so through his word when we allow him to. But the wedge of sin often separates us from communion with God, and God must then employ human instruments. For example, "The Lord sent Nathan to David" (v. 1).

The prophets often used the reigning king as a court of appeal in behalf of the oppressed. Therefore, Nathan's visit did not seem out of the ordinary at first. But the prophet's mission is clear: Nathan's parable reveals not just the impurity of David's deed but also the injustice of what he has done.

Nathan confronted David in a way that forced the king to condemn his own act. Surely a shepherd would pity the plight of a poor man being exploited of his one little ewe lamb! The king, in his outrage, demanded justice. "The man who has done this deserves to die" (v. 5). Little did David know that, but for God's mercy, he had pronounced his own sentence.

Sin separates us from God. Turning back to sin results in self-sentencing. How much better to accept God's grace!

Prayer: *Search me, O God, and know my heart. Amen.*

---

†Free-lance writer and speaker; ordained minister presently serving as Bible College instructor and dean of students, Harrisburg, Pennsylvania.

Tuesday, July 23   Read 2 Samuel 12:7-10.

David's sword

David's sin is symptomatic of a deeper problem. Evidently, he had not learned to trust God in every situation. David's distrust led to dishonesty and became a sword in his hand that damaged his relationship with God.

Nathan's message to David demonstrates the New Testament teaching that prophecy convicts and discloses the secrets of the heart (see 1 Cor. 14:24-25). The prophet's verdict, a poisoned arrow, struck the heart of David with intolerable grief. "You are the man" (v. 7). God's beloved David had embraced evil.

The testimony of scripture concerning David was forever tainted. He was not like Job, "blameless and upright." David was not a man "who feared God, and turned away from evil" (Job 1:1). Something had gone wrong. Perhaps the difference between David and Job is best revealed in Job 2:3. God informed Satan: Job "*still maintains his integrity,* though you incited me against him to ruin him without any reason" (NIV, italics added). Unlike David, Job had suffered loss and experienced sorrow which few have had to bear; yet he continued to trust God.

Like David, we are not sinless. But we are perfect in God's eyes because of the finished work of Christ at Calvary. God sees us through the blood of his Son. David's sword returned to his own house; he would never live down the seduction of Bathsheba and the death of Uriah. Christians possess the sword of the Spirit, which is the word of God. For the redeemed, "you are the man" is no longer an accusation but an invitation.

Suggestion for meditation: *Recall the special gifts and callings with which God has graced your life. Have there been times when you sought something that was unworthy of God's blessings? Take time to receive God's forgiveness.*

Wednesday, July 24   Read 2 Samuel 12:11-14.

Facing up

"David said to Nathan, 'I have sinned against the Lord.'"

As a shepherd boy, tending his father's flock, David learned the helplessness of the little lambs in his care. He watched over the flock, leading the sheep into green pastures. He spotted wild animals lurking in the shadows and was swift to drive them away. The shepherd treated injured sheep when they stumbled on the rocky terrain. He assisted in the birthing process and posted himself nearby at lambing time.

Did David play his harp beneath a star-speckled sky as he protected the sheepfold? Did the shepherd, now become king, sing in the pastures while tending his father's flock? Were some of David's insights, expressed in the truths of the psalms we cherish, first experienced in the pastures? David had slain the giant Goliath in the Lord's strength; yet he had failed the most crucial test of all: that of ruling his own spirit.

The consequences of David's failure would be grave. The king would lose the son in whom he delighted—this fruit of his passionate love affair with Bathsheba. His daughter Tamar would suffer defilement; his son Amnon would be killed in revenge; the kingdom of David would be divided after his death; and Absalom would be killed.

Yet when David the shepherd-king became a helpless lamb and repented of his sin in sorrow, God's restoring power reached to the depths of his helplessness. So it is with us.

Suggestion for meditation: *How is the Lord Jesus our Great Shepherd? Ask Jesus to help you trust him in every area of your life.*

Thursday, July 25   Read Psalm 32.

Penitence

"Many are the pangs of the wicked; but steadfast love surrounds him who trusts in the Lord" (v. 10).

There was a man, active in the Lord's work, who joined a group of other disciples to learn about the ways of Jesus. He witnessed miracles, healings, and the salvation of many souls. Although money was scarce, meals were miraculously provided as the group traveled about spreading the gospel. Then one day this disciple moved into a place of responsibility. His accounting ability and apparent trustworthiness combined to make him the logical choice for the position of treasurer.

However, somewhere along the way covetousness entered into this disciple's heart, and he became greedy. Before long, he treated the treasury as his own, rather than the Lord's.

One night, while the disciples broke bread together, Jesus revealed there was a cancer within the body. The guilty disciple felt the conviction of the Holy Spirit. However, rather than repenting, he entered into even shadier transactions, and plunged deeper into sin. He had betrayed his friends and his Lord.

Later, after his sin was discovered, the enormity of his acts engulfed him. Who would trust him again? The people to whom he had bragged would shame him. He wept with anguish because he had been caught, yet he did not repent. He could think of only one way out. So Judas went out and hung himself.

Penitence for the Christian stretches beyond traditional rites; it is a matter of the heart. Those with repentant hearts turn from relying upon themselves toward a deepening trust in God.

Suggestion for meditation: *This psalm is the second of the seven Penitential Psalms (6; 32; 38; 51; 102; 130; 143). Read one each day and follow your reading with prayer.*

Friday, July 26   Read Ephesians 3:14-19.

Fullness

". . . that you may be filled with all the fulness of God" (v. 19).

Rushing through the shopping mall, I almost collided with a friend I hadn't seen for several years. "Where are you attending church?" I asked, after catching up on the news. "Truthfully, I'm just visiting here and there. With all the corruption, even in churches, I don't want to get involved." She fumbled with her purse nervously, then said brightly, "I feel so free now." I might have accepted her explanation if it were not for the message of today's scripture passage.

In the Epistle to the Ephesians Paul has much to say about the true nature of the church. The first part of the letter is doctrinal and forms the foundation upon which the living of the Christian life rests. In today's prayer Paul addresses the issue of the fullness of the church (v. 19). According to Paul, this fullness is attained in Christ through his Body, the church.

The Christian who grows and matures into the full measure of Christ is filled with the presence, power, and wealth of Christ. He or she is no longer a child who can be easily influenced. The conduct of others, whether within the church's walls or outside, does not uproot the grounded Christian, nor does it undo the fullness of the church.

True freedom in Christ is found within the church. So it is no wonder that Paul prays for the empowering of the Spirit (v. 16) and the indwelling Christ (v. 17). They are the means to function within the Body. We are incomplete apart from our involvement in the church.

Prayer: *Gracious God, may I take my place within the Body of Christ, and discover the fullness of your love. Amen.*

Saturday, July 27   Read Ephesians 3:20-21.

Love's powerline

I hope I never forget the lessons I learned while working with the mentally retarded some years ago. Perhaps the most valuable (and least obvious) lesson was the power of love.

Nothing is quite so discouraging as laboring day after day and witnessing little or no response. In my work with the mentally retarded, I never really knew how much I was communicating to them.

I was especially frustrated by my inability to communicate to the more seriously impaired persons. When after months of trying a child failed to direct a spoon to his mouth without losing half the food on the way, my energies dwindled. Then, when I realized this was the child's best attempt, love took over. I thought, *That's why I am needed*. The child would never again miss his mouth with my hand to guide his.

When Paul bowed to dedicate the Ephesian Christians, he prayed that the full measure of God's gifts would fill their hearts. The mystery of God is not grasped through human experience alone. It is only fully realized through the guidance of the Spirit.

Each of us can attest to struggles and failures in our walk with the Lord. But the mystery of redemption that weaves through the spiritual Body of Christ is that God's great love and power can guide us to the spiritual goal for which we strive in spite of our weakness. God is more than able to give us victory and cause us to live triumphantly.

Our reason for living, the object of our worship, the fruit of our labors, is God. God's love is the power that enables us to receive the full measure of God's gifts.

Prayer: *Help us to trust the power of your great redemptive love, O God. In Jesus' name. Amen.*

Sunday, July 28   Read John 6:1-15.

Plentitude

"When they had all had enough to eat, he said to his disciples, 'Gather the pieces that are left over. Let nothing be wasted'" (v. 12, NIV).

One commentator has called the Gospel According to John the unveiling of the divine mystery. John portrays Jesus as God's self-interpretation. It was John who wrote, "No one has ever seen God; the only Son, who is in the bosom of the Father, he has made him known" (John 1:18). In his Gospel, John presented miracles as vehicles of larger truths, bridges upon which Jesus sought to bring the multitudes to deeper understanding.

The Jews were well-versed when it came to miracles. Their ancestors in each generation had told the stories to their children of God's power and outstretched arm. God had delivered them from Egyptian bondage, parted the seas, and sweetened the waters of Marah. God had fed them manna in the wilderness.

Now, the Jews were face-to-face with this man who had chosen to dwell among them. He would break bread with them because he was God, and God is love. Love is always aware of human need. By distributing a few loaves, Jesus used the miracle to communicate the meaning of his presence; he was the manna that came down from heaven. He would later remind them of the loaves and tell them, "I am the bread of life" (John 6:35). Our God is a God of plentitude. But our sights must be raised so we can comprehend that God is the sustenance for all our needs. The church will fulfill its mission when we recognize that God is the bread of life and that the tabernacle in which the glory of God resides exists for our enlightenment.

Prayer: *Gracious God, may the miracle of your love be reproduced in us to reach the world for you. In Jesus' name. Amen.*

DIVINE YEAST

July 29–August 4, 1991   **Sr. Marcella Clancy, S.S.J.**†
Monday, July 29   Read John 6:32-33.

Jesus used many images to vividly portray the kingdom of heaven. It is like a sower going out to sow . . . like a mustard seed . . . like a treasure hidden in a field . . . a merchant in search of fine pearls . . . like a dragnet . . . like a vineyard . . . or like "the yeast a woman took and mixed in with three measures of flour till it was leavened all through" (Matt. 13:33, NJB). How warm, how welcoming this parable of the yeast to portray God womanlike, motherlike with flour-coated hands and arms absorbed in the kneading of her dough. Unlike the other kingdom images, this image is an image of the home.

How long does it take for our hearts to understand the mystery of this parable? Who among us has not been tempted to discouragement, if not despair, when we see ourselves repeatedly doing the evil we wish to avoid and avoiding the good we wish to do? We cry out with the apostle Paul, "Who will deliver me?" (Rom. 7:24) And God's eternal response remains constant: God, who "comes down from heaven, and gives life to the world." It is precisely those places in us where we are poorest and most wounded that we most need Christ's life to penetrate.

It is not only the Father who gives us the true bread which comes down from heaven and gives life to the world. The parable of the yeast suggests that, motherlike, our gracious God takes her divine yeast and kneads it with the totality of our humanity until we are made into bread divine.

Prayer: *God, who art in heaven, make of us your daily bread. Amen.*

---

†Sister of St. Joseph who is Director of Nazareth House, a home for senior citizens, Detroit, Michigan.

Tuesday, July 30   Read 2 Samuel 12:15*b*-24.

How greatly favored and loved by God was David! Yet David was also a sinner. David coveted his neighbor's wife and committed adultery with her. When Uriah, her husband, unwittingly did not cooperate in the cover-up of the child conceived by this illicit union, David had him killed by an enemy's sword.

It is easy to wonder why David is not more devastated by his sin and its implications for his innocent child. On closer scrutiny, however, we see a stark simplicity and a beautiful honesty, even humility, expressed in David's stance. He is not obsessed with his sin; he is not morose or self-recriminating. David is neither surprised by his sin nor confused and embarrassed by the experience of himself as a sinner. When confronted with his sinful deed, David acknowledges and owns his sin with a simplicity possessed only by a truly humble soul steeped in his own truth: "I have sinned against the LORD" (v. 13).

David does not treat lightly the gravity of his sin. Rather, he believes that the forgiveness of God is so much greater. Even when his penance and his pleas do not prevent the death of his child, despair does not claim David. Never does he doubt he is a friend of God. He comes into the sanctuary, falls prostrate before God, and surrenders to God's boundless mercy and love. And then, with astounding confidence in God's forgiveness, David again takes Bathsheba to himself. She conceives and gives birth to Solomon. God makes known his love for this child by naming him Jedidiah, meaning "beloved of God." The sin is forgiven; the wound is healed. God's grace, deposited in the very brokenness of David, becomes the source through which God's purpose is accomplished and God's promise is fulfilled.

Prayer: *Gracious and merciful God, help me remember that even my sin when surrendered to you can become a source of grace. Amen.*

Wednesday, July 31   Read Psalm 34:11-22.

In the film *Crimes and Misdemeanors,* a prominent and wealthy physician, an essentially upright and moral man, has an affair. When he attempts to end the relationship, the woman threatens to expose him. In panic and in fear, he consents, though with grave misgivings, to have her murdered. After the deed is done, however, we are left with the sense the doctor has gotten away with murder not only before others but before God. We recognize that the character and the plot represent a familiar reality: evil frequently is rewarded while the good suffer.

How can we reconcile that reality with Psalm 34? Do we really believe that God is close to the brokenhearted? Does God really help those who are crushed in spirit? Perhaps we would be more comfortable if God kept an account of good and evil and meted out rewards and punishments accordingly. At least then we would know where we stood and what we could expect. We might be able to make sense out of life.

Jesus gently reminds us that God lets the sun rise on the evil as well as the good and allows the rain to fall on the honest and dishonest alike (Matt. 5:45), and that God did not send the Son into the world to condemn it but to save it (John 3:17). Jesus is the fulfillment of what is promised in Psalm 34.

We want to be forgiven. We want to go to heaven, but there is something in us that would like to deserve it, to earn it. The best we can do is open wide our hearts, our entire beings, and let the untold mercy and goodness of God flow into us. The question Do the evil pay for their sins and are the good rewarded? becomes irrelevant. Our prayer is only that all people everywhere and at all times be held in the tender embrace of God's mercy.

Prayer: *Lord, feed us with the bread of your mercy. Let us remember that mercy means you always regard us as your children. Amen.*

Thursday, August 1   Read Ephesians 4:1-2.

When we are young, we are tempted to wonder why Christians who are years ahead of us are still so imperfect. When we are older, we wonder if we will ever feel anything other than mere beginners, novices, on the spiritual journey. In the beginning, we think a "life worthy of the calling" means doing great things: ardent prayer, enormous sacrifices, magnanimous charitable activity. But later on, holiness seems to be more a matter of being kind and patient and gentle with oneself and others.

It is not that we give up on our dreams of great holiness; rather, we realize we have used the wrong words to define it. To lead a life worthy of our calling means not that we outdistance others in goodness. Rather, it means that our goodness becomes a soothing ointment, a healing balm. Goodness may confront evil, but it treats weakness with gentle kindness. An unmistakable sign of truly holy people is that in their presence we experience more of our goodness than theirs. We come to feel more at home not only with them but also with ourselves.

Bearing with one another charitably, unless it is characterized by selflessness, tends not to be charity at all. Rather it is more self-righteousness and is experienced as oppression by those who are the "object" of our charity. Sincere charity is not something we can put on from the outside to cover up interior condemnation. True charity rises from within, born in a heart who knows itself to be a loved sinner always forgiven, found, redeemed. Such a heart has learned from the gentleness and patience of God how to be gentle and patient with itself.

Prayer: *Lord Jesus, you have given your peace to us as your "farewell" gift. Your peace is a power that does not eliminate the burdens we must bear but rather gives us your ability to absorb and transform them with love. We are grateful. Amen.*

Friday, August 2   Read Ephesians 4:4-6.

How long does it take for infants to realize that the hand or the foot they study with their eyes is a part of their own body? How long does it take for us to recognize that the stranger, the foreigner, is no more separate from our "body" than our hand, our foot, or our heart? We hear that our planet is becoming smaller and smaller. Yet we know that it is not our earth that is becoming smaller; it is our consciousness of others—even continents apart—that is becoming greater and greater.

What is true on a natural level is likewise true on a spiritual plane. We are made in the image and likeness of God. We can never be our truest self, we can never be whole or holy, unless we are involved with others—giving and receiving, pouring out and being filled up. Jesus himself has provided us with an example. No one is too poor, too little, too repulsive, too weak to be united and identified with Jesus. "As you did it to one of the least of these my brethren, you did it to me" (Matt. 25:40).

From the beginning Jesus declared that his followers would be recognized by their love for each other and their love for their enemies. Sometimes we think it is difficult to love others because they are our enemies, but actually the reverse is true: others are our enemies because we are unable to love them. They reflect back to us our incapacities, our limitations, and our inability to be like God, and we are tempted to hate them for that. Jesus knew that to be fully human we had to love with the fullness of our being. And he increases in us each day our capacity to love more by giving us himself and his Spirit. Jesus' command to love one another cannot be fulfilled unless we also faithfully obey his teachings.

Prayer: *God most gracious, open wide our hearts, our souls, our entire beings and fill us with your love. Amen.*

Saturday, August 3   Read John 6:24-26.

Jesus told the crowd, "You seek me, not because you saw signs." Yet earlier, John tells us it was precisely because the people had seen the sign that "they were about to come and take him by force to make him king" (John 6:15). There was nothing wrong with the eyesight of the crowd; it was their hearts that could not "see."

Before we allow ourselves to condemn the crowd too easily, can we not appreciate its impulsiveness? If daily provisions were a constant worry and someone stood in our midst and, moved to compassion, multiplied our meager fare, would not we be inclined to invest him or her with power and authority?

Then "Jesus withdrew again to the mountain by himself" (John 6:15). And isn't that often our experience of Jesus? We feel his care, concern, love, comfort. And just as we are about to settle back and settle in, Jesus moves beyond us. He goes to the hills, to the desert, to the mountaintop, to the garden, to the cross. But Jesus does not escape from us; rather, he beckons us to follow him. He is always leading us where we would rather not go. "If anyone wants to come with me, he must forget himself, carry his cross, and follow me." (Matt. 16:24, TEV).

What must Jesus have been thinking that evening when he bent down and washed the feet of his disciples, knowing that each pair of feet would ultimately follow him to suffering and to death? Yet Jesus never apologized for involving his followers in his mission. In fact, he told them they would be persecuted and warned them that if they looked back, they were unfit for his kingdom. He predicted that their lives would be full of suffering, but asked that their hearts be full of joy.

Prayer: *Lord Jesus, let me this day, in your name, lay down a piece of myself for one of the least of my brothers or sisters. Amen.*

Sunday, August 4   Read John 6:27-35.

Jesus never threatens or intimidates us; he tells us over and over not to be afraid. And to insure that we will never be afraid to draw close to him, he leaves himself for us in the forms of bread and wine. Who can be afraid of bread, of wine? Jesus knew full well the risk he was taking. We could become so accustomed to this simple gift that we could begin to take Jesus for granted. We could fail to recognize his transforming power.

We could not hunger and thirst for God unless God first hungered and thirsted for us. Yet so often, we do not even recognize our hunger. We do not take the time to be silent, to be still, to listen long enough and at sufficient depths to hear the yearning of our own hearts.

We were not made for anything less than God, and we will never be satisfied until we feast on him. Why do we, who are made for God, continue to evade God? What is this deeply-rooted fear that possesses us? For though we ardently long for God, we constantly try to compromise the gift of ourself to God.

Our God is an all-or-nothing God. God can never give just a part or a piece; God's self-emptying is total, complete, absolute. Nothing is left. Yet God is also patient and kind and gentle. So each time we receive the magnificent gift of Christ's body and blood, his death and resurrection, hidden quietly and simply under the forms of bread and wine, Jesus deposits in us his hunger and thirst not only for us but for God. He does this so that with us, in us, and through us his prayer may be fulfilled: "I pray that they may all be one. Father! May they be in us, just as you are in me and I am in you" (John 17:21, TEV).

Prayer: *O Holy Spirit, create in us the hunger and thirst the Father has for the Son and the Son has for the Father, that Jesus' prayer for unity may find its completion in us. Amen.*

WE WHO WOULD LEAD

August 5-11, 1991   **Barbara W. Short†**
Monday, August 5   Read 2 Samuel 18:1, 5, 9-15.

Leadership. Always a word of authority and aspiration, it became a buzzword in the power-driven 1980s and a hope for the 1990s, touted as the decade of decision.

What mother or father has not looked into the small, wrinkled face of a newborn and wondered whether this would be a future president of the United States or a world leader!

Surely David, reflecting on his own humble beginnings and how far he had come in leading Israel from the rule of judges into a monarchy, must have held the tiny Absalom and crooned lovingly and hopefully those now-fateful words: "O Absalom, my son, my son!" And Absalom himself would aspire to leadership, but by a path not of God's design.

The reign of David is the major topic of Second Samuel, and the narrative speaks a clear message of the price of leadership. Even though David was a God-chosen leader, he was also a father. In the midst of battle, when he realized his errant son now-turned-enemy might be killed, he allowed his parental concern to override his kingly responsibility.

But the price of leadership still was exacted from David. His followers recognized that it would be David or Absalom, but not both, who survived. The fate of Israel hung on their decision, and not even David's plea to spare his son in battle could deter David's followers from the necessary deed. David, the leader, gave his son to a greater cause.

Prayer: *Too often we who lead see the beautiful without the bad, the gain without the grief, O God. Give us the vision of a true leader. Amen.*

---

†President/CEO, InfoMarketing Inc.; administrative board chair, McMannen United Methodist Church, Durham, North Carolina.

Tuesday, August 6   Read Psalm 143:1-8.

True leaders understand the source of their power, and that it is unfailing. They can acknowledge that, while they may lead others, they fall short when measured against God. They are men and women who acknowledge temporary defeat, even as they lift their head to face the future with confidence.

The psalmist looks to God from a confined position, perhaps a prison built by human beings, perhaps a prison that was self-imposed. But he looks to God sure in the knowledge that the answer he seeks will be born of God's faithfulness, that his spirit—lifted to God—can be revived to lead again.

We who would lead today seek ways to escape our own prisons. At times, we are fearful and pray with the psalmist that we will be spared what we know we deserve. At other times, we are strengthened in the remembrance of what God has done for us in "days of old," and in God's promises that hold for the present age. Just the memory of past blessings is enough to create a new thirst for the cup God offers.

The Psalms, the poetry of the Hebrew people, sing of God's loyalty and God's love. The meter may change with the mood, but the underlying theme is that all we are depends on God. God alone is to be trusted. God alone gives power.

The true leader, in any age, is not spared sorrow or imprisonment or despair. Indeed, the leader may carry an extra measure of the hurts in this world, but does not carry this burden alone.

Prayer: *If we would be leaders, dear God, we know that much is expected. Never let us forget that if we are true leaders, much is given through your grace. Amen.*

Wednesday, August 7   Read John 6:35-39.

The leader in the group was no more than 17 years old. A band of six teenagers, they were part of a teen theatre, visiting churches and acting out situations that young people face today.

As I watched their improvisation where one was excluded from the "in" crowd, another alienated from parents, and a third left alone with an unwanted pregnancy, I felt the old anxiety of adolescence clutching at my insides.

What was it? Why should I, in my mid-fifties, feel those teenage hurts so acutely? Their pain was my own.

These scenes were universal, threatening at any age because the situations were so basic to us all. No one was really opening up to another; they could not get beyond their own insecurity to truly share with family or friends. It did not matter that the actors were under 17 and that the audience ranged to 70 and above. All hungered and thirsted.

In the discussions that followed, the age differences fell away. The communication that had been missing in the vignettes the teens portrayed from life came alive as we struggled together for answers to the problems of humankind.

"But how can we do better?" one parent pleaded. "You can listen," one of the troupe replied. "Just listen."

The message was clear. If we would lead, then we first must listen—to our children, to our neighbors, to our world, to God.

Prayer: *Dear God, don't let us be so taken with our roles as leaders that the sounds of our own voices drown out the cries for help that are all around us. Help us remember that today's children are your leaders for tomorrow. Amen.*

Thursday, August 8   Read Ephesians 4:25-32.

"What does our leader want us to do?" That is the question that had awakened me as an employee called in the early morning hours, wondering how to deal with the weather.

A look outside determined my advice: "Stay home."

The sudden winter storm also stopped the maddening rush of my life for that day. Isolated by a 10-inch cushion of snow, I acknowledged the gift of unexpected time at home—time to look outside at the cold whiteness of the world and inside at the icy darkness that enveloped my soul.

Some leader I was! For months I had harbored a hurt—a perceived injury from one I had regarded as Christian and cherished in a bonded relationship. Much as the banked snow insulated me from visits by friends or family, I had insulated my spiritual wound from the forgiveness and acceptance that might bring healing.

A flash of red against pristine whiteness startled me. It was a cardinal seeking food in a barren land. That bird seemed to me the blood of Christ—a red offering in a pure white life seeking peace for humankind. My small injustice rankled still; but it eased as I recalled the ultimate injustice—Christ's death for the sins of others, including my own.

Jesus was the real example of leadership. When others offended him, he forgave them. If we would learn his leadership style, we also must show kindness, mercy, and forgiveness.

The ice inside me melted a little, as I prayed anew that I would be led to a right relationship with Jesus Christ and would follow his example with a warm heart and a forgiving spirit.

Prayer: *Forgive me, Lord, for my unforgiving ways, and melt the coldness of my heart. In the name of Jesus, who forgave even those who killed him. Amen.*

Friday, August 9   Read Ephesians 5:1-2.

Mama was very proud of the four bright red blooms on an amaryllis big enough to dwarf the windowsill of her room in the retirement home. The hardy plant was a holiday gift from a thoughtful nephew, on the last Christmas of her life.

She gave me careful instructions on how to care for the big bulb to insure its flowering in future seasons. I tried to follow that advice, especially after her death the following September; but the blooms never materialized again. It was as if the bulb had run out of strength, much as Mother had in her waning years.

As a last measure, I decided to plant the bulb in a well-tilled flower bed, heavily mulched against the cold. Even though our climate was ill-suited for amaryllis to survive outside, I hoped a mild winter might spare it; instead, there came record snow, ice, and low temperatures.

As winter dragged on, I thought often of the bulb, its robust beauty lost to me, just as Mother's was toward the end of her life. She had been such a strong and dynamic person: a role model, a leader among women; but ill health and pain left her weak and sad.

I wanted so much for that flower to blossom again, but I realized there was little hope. When spring's first warm days caused other bulbs to break through, I fearfully postponed looking for Mother's amaryllis. When at last I dug, prayerfully, under the dead leaves and pine needles, there it was—one thick green leaf pushing aside winter's buildup and death's threat. It lived. And in living, it brought hope and the assurance that Mother also lived, with strength and beauty regained after her long winter of dying.

Suggestion for prayer: *Pray for the leaders who set examples for your life.*

Saturday, August 10   Read John 6:41-51.

The apostle John along with his brother James was given the nickname "Son of Thunder." What a name for a leader of the church! Certainly John earned it with his outspokenness. Whether or not the Gospel that bears John's name was actually written by one of the "Sons of Thunder" or by John the Elder or by yet another John, the Gospel rings with the authority of one who had firsthand knowledge of Jesus, the ultimate leader. This Gospel is required reading for those who would follow him.

John is different from the other Gospel writers. He tells different miracle stories and then goes on to explain what they mean. He never stops reminding us that Jesus was both human and divine, and that the Jesus of spirit and of flesh and blood was totally good.

Unlike many of the Jews of his time, John recognized Jesus for who he was. Others argued among themselves about the audacity of the man from Galilee who would define himself as "bread which came down from heaven." After all, they knew his family and his ordinary upbringing. By all appearances, how could this man possibly be a messenger from God, let alone God's son?

Well, John knew all that, too. Indeed, some believe he actually was related to Mary, the mother of Jesus. But John saw more in Jesus than others did. He recognized the qualities of leadership that Jesus possessed, and he followed him.

John accepted Jesus not on appearances but at his word that he was the "bread of life," "the bread which came down from heaven," the staple that made life possible and that makes eternal life a reality.

Prayer: *Dear Jesus, when we meet you in the ordinary byways of life, help us recognize you as the one worthy leader for our lives. Amen.*

Sunday, August 11   Read John 6:51.

The little boy painstakingly stretched his small stride so that he followed exactly in his father's footsteps. The father was busy with his yard work and did not notice that his son was imitating his every move, intent on being just like his daddy. There was a sweetness to the scene, as the one who looked so much like a junior version of the older man struggled to be at one with this all-important figure in his life.

Of such is the heart of Christianity. Today, when we read the words of Jesus that speak of eating flesh and drinking blood, they sound uncomfortable and strange. However, to the people of his time the concept of being at one with God was less strange. Indeed, the passion plays associated with the mystery religions of that age had one common element—an identity with God so strong that one became part of God, and God united with humanity.

Love at its deepest levels adopts this characteristic of oneness. When two people marry they bond in a union of singularity. A mother carries as part of herself her child in the earliest stage of life. And the love of Jesus Christ at its deepest level embodies an identity so strong, so keenly felt, that he lives within us. His blood keeps our heart at work, and his Spirit invades the being that is our soul.

We who would lead others to Christ can do so only when we accept him as our own, when he is truly at home in our lives. We will lead only after we have followed, after we have been joined to the leader.

Prayer: *Our Lord and our leader, please make us one with you so that our following will be as natural to us as our every breath. Amen.*

BAD NEWS AND GOOD NEWS

August 12-18, 1991   **Paul N. Franklyn†**
Monday, August 12   Read 2 Samuel 18:24-30.

Good news can be a facade for bad tidings. The circumstances of war are always bad news, no matter how glorious or effective the military performance in battle. So it is absurd for the first messenger, Ahimaaz, to greet King David at the battle front with "All is well!"

The body language of the messenger suggests contradiction. The gatekeeper in the tower can tell from a distance, "by the way he runs" (NEB), that this first lonely runner is Ahimaaz, the Zadokite. David assumes with confidence that good news and truthfulness will proceed from a good man with a pedigree from the priestly class. But this Zadokite is so eager to glorify the power of the Lord in battle that he "sincerely" throws his body to the ground in obeisance before the king. He states that David's enemies are vanquished. He evades and ducks when asked if David's son is well. Does he, perhaps, think that there will be a tip or a promotion if he sticks with the good news story about God's victory? David tells him to stand aside for the truth.

We are often required to deliver a report to those in power over us. How truthful can we be? Will my boss approve of my words? Am I being used? We should hesitate and consider how the truthful report can be aimed self-servingly to wound a friend or colleague. Sometimes we do cleverly twist a version of the truth to suit our competitive advantage. But too frequently we duck the truth because we would protect our place in the order of things, secure our livelihood, or enhance our reputation.

Prayer: *Help me, O Lord, to speak truthfully and carefully. Grant me wisdom to choose my words in love. Amen.*

---

†Editor, Professional Books, Abingdon Press, Nashville, Tennessee.

Tuesday, August 13   Read 2 Samuel 18:31-33.

The unnamed Cushite messenger who appears with the truth about the battle is an African slave or mercenary, if not a member of the enslaved Edomite tribe. General Joab originally sends the Cushite because it would be no great loss, he presumes, if David kills this alien messenger of bad news. Bearers of bad news are often eliminated, especially by David, who killed the messengers that announced the deaths of Saul and his son (see 2 Sam. 4). David must know if his rebellious son was harmed. With audacity the Cushite does not bow in obeisance but invokes a startling curse on the king's enemies, without naming Absalom. Now David knows. This clever messenger will survive, for David is consumed with unbearable grief.

No parent is consolable after the loss of a child, even in a patriotic war, and especially in a civil war which pits father against son. Once again, as with Uriah the Hittite, David would rather be the dead man sacrificed in battle.

Children should outlive their parents. The loss of a child is so threatening to our survival because it signifies the loss of our past and our future at the same time. We give part of our self, which we obtain from someone else, in order to form a new self who will one day honor us and preserve us. Thus in the ancient world of King David (and still in much Jewish belief today) a literal existence is not possible after death for the self, apart from what our offspring and heirs continue or preserve in memory and honor.

Suggestion for prayer: *Think of a parent who has lost a child in war or at an early age, and pray for God's presence to console that parent.*

Wednesday, August 14   Read Psalm 102:1-12.

We do not like to read publicly psalms which mention our enemies. Certain psalms offend our modern and civilized sensibilities with vengeance, anger, or violent predictions about God's wrath. We remove offensive passages from hymnals and lectionaries because this dark side of life, death, and God is inconsistent with scrubbed and whitewashed forums for worship. We have no enemies. And surely God is never our enemy!

The psalmist insists on a quick answer to a prayer for deliverance from enemies. As in other psalms, God's "face," or presence, is unavailable, hidden. "How long wilt thou hide thy face from me? . . . How long shall my enemy be exalted over me?" (Ps. 13:1-2) "Wake up, Lord! Why are you sleeping? . . . Why are you hiding your face?" (Ps. 44:23-24, AP)

Some of us, in our comfort, dismiss these psalms as religiously immature. But oppression is horrible. There is no food to eat, and when nourishment appears, bitterness is so great that one forgets to eat. Sleep does not come, and my enemies taunt with curses about a weak God. God is angry with me. God has "taken me up and thrown me away." God is my enemy, too.

Some persons are never aware of others, let alone God, as enemy. But most persons do experience others as enemy and may be comforted falsely with cliches or pious formulas that derive from inexperience or sentimental theology. The psalms help us face honestly these dark moments, so that we can admit, announce, or confront our oppressors. We cry out to God, we wrestle with God, until there is an answer. Sometimes we take matters into our own hands, in the name of God.

Suggestion for meditation: *Think back to a time when God was hidden from you. How do you explain this circumstance? What did you do about it?*

Thursday, August 15   Read Ephesians 5:15-17.

Prudent sages of ancient Israel instructed their disciples about poverty which surely will come to the sluggard who will "be broken beyond healing" (Prov. 6:6-15). Folk wisdom teaches us that idle hands are the devil's tools. The writer to the Ephesian church invokes a general moral principle about evil tendencies which overwhelm persons who fail to discipline their time. This ethical injunction sums up previous warnings (in vv. 3-14) against three common evils which are familiar from the Ten Commandments: sexual evil (fornication), verbal evil (demeaning or silly language), and material evil (coveting a neighbor's property).

The prudent follower of Christ will pause along the way to examine carefully his or her life for evidences of this common behavior. The thoughtful and reflective person will recognize the evil circumstances which arise inevitably when no meaningful purpose or action can be discerned in the ordinary events of life—often when one has too much or too little time on hand.

Often we attach our understanding of God's will to the spectacular episodes or experiences that we seek—the dramatic events which make juicy news for gawkers. But a wise person will see the folly of temporary or sporadic satisfactions. For example, famous persons often regret the loneliness of their stardom.

The will of the Lord will be discerned instead in the balanced and careful walk, regardless of occupation, which will return the wise person again and again for worship together with other persons who seek the intoxication that comes during our praise of God's love and self-sacrifice.

Devotional exercise: *Look for an example of God's love this day as you go about your normal business. Give thanks as you see this love in action.*

Friday, August 16   Read Ephesians 5:19-20.

A man came to dinner. He appeared with an untrimmed, foot-long beard and disheveled clothing. In our conversation he scattered religious phrases about the Lord and God's will at odd and disconcerting times. I was reminded of family ancestors who seemed to speak to one another with "psalms, hymns, and spiritual songs" as part of daily Elizabethan language.

Is this what was meant by the writer to the church at Ephesus in urging a state of being so "filled with the spirit" that a person's language is incessantly thankful to God? Some persons read this encouragement so literally that they spiritualize their circumstances to the point of mental or social imbalance. Still others subtly develop an insider rhetoric or Christian spirituality, a code language with often hidden or mysterious meanings, which only their enlightened community can discern or share.

Of course we cannot be thankful or jovial about everything that happens or is reported to us. King David could not thank God for the rebellion and subsequent murder of his son, Absalom—no more than we can say that God the Father is spiritually exhilarated when allowing the son Jesus to be spread upon a cross.

The author of Ephesians asserts that Christians should experience a wise and balanced ethic for wholesome living. This ethic requires that instead of gathering for evil purposes, we come together in regular assembly, where we express thanks and love for one another and for God's forgiving grace.

Prayer: *Help me, O Lord, to speak clearly about my Christian values, to join regularly with others who help me examine my faith and with whom I can sing in praise of you. Amen.*

Saturday, August 17 Read John 6:51-52.

The Old Testament does not give a clear promise of whether the individual self or soul shall survive personally after death. A similar insight into life after death is apparent when Jesus is making a startling claim about himself. "Our ancestors ate [manna] and died, but the person who feeds on this bread will live forever" (v. 49, AP). First Jesus disturbs us with bad news that the God-given manna in the Exodus was not enough to sustain a lasting life. This mysterious food—which nourished the people of God in their liberation from oppression—is temporal and soon replaced by other tastes or appetites.

In the Good News of John, which is possibly the last book written for our scriptures, the Word of God, made flesh, grants life its meaning now. The risen Christ grants life in the present and in the future. We know or taste this life each time we consume the flesh and blood, chew the bread and sip the wine, of the risen Christ.

As the evangelist John tells it, Jesus did not convince most people who heard his claim about real food and literal drink. The Jews argued sharply among themselves. They wondered if Jesus was proposing a cannibalistic ritual of eating human flesh. The disciples protested and walked out, too.

Despite our diversity when applying Jesus' self-revelation about the Lord's Supper in our prayer and worship before God, this teaching, set in the synagogue at Capernaum, does establish one crucial norm for the people who would call themselves followers of Christ: Specifically, we experience extraordinary life now, and we prepare for new life eternal, each time we eat together at the Lord's table.

Prayer: *Merciful God, help me prepare for eternal life with you each time when I find you present in the Meal. In the name of Jesus, in whose name we gather to remember. Amen.*

Sunday, August 18   Read John 6:53-58.

How often should we eat at the Lord's table? Most of us know that we Christians have differences about the meaning and frequency of Holy Communion. Catholic priests observe the sacrifice of Jesus in the Mass on a daily basis—they take these words of John's Gospel very literally. Catholic, Anglican, and Lutheran laity eat at the Lord's table each time they gather for Sunday worship. Methodists, Presbyterians, Baptists, and many others gather for the Lord's Supper less frequently.

We might obtain guidance on this matter from Jesus' analogy to the gathering of manna. The people of Israel in the wilderness collected their bread six days of the week, with instructions to secure twice as much manna on the sixth day, so that they may have some left over for the sabbath (see Exod. 16). Now Jesus reveals himself as the bread of life which lasts for the six days of ordinary time, and as the bread which brings eternal life to those who rest in Christ and eat on the sabbath.

Just as we give thanks to God as the provider for our daily manna, so we would be well advised to remember and thank God each week on the sabbath when we experience new life and prepare for eternal life.

During times in my life when God seems absent, or the circumstances of life are unjust, the Lord's Supper sustains my life by a crumb, even if the preaching is dull or the music sounds like clanging cymbals. The Lord's Supper disciplines me spiritually to experience God's work of salvation in Christ. When I recall those persons who are dead in Christ, such as our baby son who came and went on an ordinary August day, the Lord's Supper restores to me the hope of resurrection "at the last day."

Prayer: *We seek you and you find us each time, O Lord, in the eating of the bread and the drinking of the fruit of the vine. We are grateful. Amen.*

FREE TO CHOOSE LIFE

August 19-25, 1991   **Elizabeth Dreyer†**
Monday, August 19   Read 2 Samuel 23:1.

In the tenth century, under David's leadership, Israel changed its focus from looking inward toward its own federations to facing and becoming a part of the larger world of ancient Near Eastern culture. The resulting adjustment to a pluralistic culture forced Israel to a new self-understanding.

Israel discovered a new maturity under King David. He faced the challenges of his time with a new sense of freedom and responsibility. He was no longer a child, running to God to solve all his problems. Rather, he seemed to exult in the capabilities and gifts he had as part of the human community.

During David's time, human beings were seen as trusted by God. We read that David was anointed by God. The community not only recognized David's new-found maturity but saw this new behavior as blessed by God. David's freedom to act with creativity and responsibility was not seen as arrogant or self-serving but rather as a result of his commitment to God.

The freedom David felt also says something about God. God was not watching over David's shoulder, worried about possible failure. No, God has enormous confidence in humans and trusts them to handle well life's ever-changing situations. David's kingship challenges us to see that side of God that truly trusts in and celebrates the marvel of the human person, made in the very image and likeness of God.

Prayer: *O God of trust, help us accept your unreserved confidence in our abilities. Help us love well and act with insight and responsibility to make this world a "home" for all its inhabitants. Amen.*

†Associate Professor, Ecclesiastical History Department, Washington Theological Union, Silver Spring, Maryland.

Tuesday, August 20   Read 2 Samuel 23:2-7.

David's last words reflect the assurance he felt that the Spirit of God was indeed working within him. God had touched him, and he willingly communicated this message to his people. Throughout his life, through doubts and struggles, David had acted consistently to bring life to the community. He had the community's well-being at heart and was willing to own the grave responsibility of leadership. He also trusted in his and the community's ability to discern what was good for the community and to act to make that good a reality.

This description of a good leader is powerfully moving. Such a leader dawns on the community like the morning light, like the sun and the rain that make grass sprout from the earth. We can allow these beautiful images to emerge in our imagination. And we can begin to connect them with the kind of good and just leadership that is indispensable to any community.

David's freedom to use his gifts responsibly on behalf of the community did not come only from within. The writer of this passage sees just rule as deeply connected with God. David leads the nation in light of God's awesome presence, and he is empowered by a covenant with God that will last forever.

How might David be an inspiration today? Above all, David models for us his willingness to translate God's trust into confidence in his own ability. He sees himself and the community as able to decide what is good. Leader and people can behave in mature, responsible ways, bringing life and love to the community. He sees himself as a mature partner with God.

Prayer: *Help us grow in our appreciation of sincere, committed leaders, O God. Grant us the courage to own our own gifts and to use them creatively and responsibly for the welfare of all the world. Amen.*

Wednesday, August 21   Read Psalm 67:1-2.

Psalm 67 begins with the familiar blessing, "May God be gracious to us and bless us." Scholars suggest that this psalm is either a request for blessing or a national thanksgiving for a fruitful harvest. But the amazing element in these first verses is the implied connection between God's blessings on Israel and salvation for all the nations.

Often, Israel saw and defined herself as distinct from other nations. But in this psalm the net of inclusivity embraces the wider world. God's blessings are invoked with others in mind. God's graciousness to Israel can function as a herald, announcing both God's ways and God's saving power to all.

In the New Testament, Jesus and Paul continued this movement toward inclusiveness. Jesus was drawn to and embraced all kinds of outcasts—persons who were on the margins of society, regarded as unworthy or unclean. And Paul traveled from community to community in the Hellenistic world preaching the good news to anyone who wanted to hear.

These examples suggest that the life of God is not intended for some narrowly exclusive community. God intends that *everyone* have abundant life. However, God's desire to share the fullness of life with all people depends on human beings. By our thoughts, words, and actions, we can nurture and celebrate life or we can be instruments of death. This biblical thread of inclusiveness challenges our tendency to exclude others because we want to feel different from or better than them. The idea of inclusiveness confronts the way in which, by judging others, we bring death to ourselves and to the community.

Prayer: *Enlarge our hearts, O God. Make us a truly magnanimous people. Free us from narrow, petty concerns so that in choosing life, we might recognize and celebrate your life in all the world. Amen.*

Thursday, August 22   Read Psalm 67:3-7.

The psalmist exhorts all people to praise and fear God. The phrasing and repetition of these verses communicate a sense of energy and enthusiasm. These words create a feeling of exuberant life and call us to such an existence. Praise, gladness, song, and joy are hallmarks of one who is truly alive.

The reasons for such revelry are two: God's just rule and an abundant harvest. The former reminds us of the previous meditations on David. We reflected on the ways in which David brought life to the chosen people through his attitudes and actions on their behalf. Psalm 167 refers to the source and model for David's leadership—God's just rule of the world.

The second reason for joyous celebration and praise is the fertility of the earth. Attention to the harvest brings an awareness of nature's cycle of life and death. The seed is planted and dies so that the crops may come forth bearing fruit—fruit that both lives and brings life by being consumed.

An understanding of life outside the context of death will be a naive and superficial one. We are constantly discerning between authentic life, which will inevitably involve authentic death, and what we might call pseudo-life. The latter fears and avoids death, preventing the emergence of new life. Grasping control, cynicism, envy, and resentment are signs of this deadness. Joyous praise is a sign that we are free and truly alive. And praise in time of trouble is an even more telling sign of life. The poorest among us are often those who, having nothing to lose, are the only ones truly free to praise God with abandon. They are witnesses to our own poverty and to the choice to praise God in spite of hardship.

Suggestion for meditation: *Reflect honestly on the presence or absence of praise in your life. If it is absent, why? If you are one who praises, celebrate and be grateful.*

Friday, August 23   Read Ephesians 5:21-33.

The Letter to the Ephesians focuses on Christ alive and risen. The church is portrayed not as persons sitting around waiting for the *Parousia* but rather as a productive, involved, developing community. In Ephesians, the church is seen in an inclusive and universal context rather than in its local dimension.

This passage is problematic for many in the Christian community today. In a general sense, these verses are part of a larger context in which the early Christians struggled to articulate how all aspects of their lives might be suffused with the spirit and witness of Jesus. Similarly today, Christians desire to model their lives on the example of Jesus. But we are keenly aware that each life is embedded in a particular socio-cultural context, and that our Christian life is deeply affected by our time and choice.

These rules for wives, husbands, and children are an adaptation of the ancient "household code" in which order was maintained solely through male authority. We now know that subjection of one human being by another for any reason— slavery, indenture, or marriage—is dehumanizing and antagonistic to the divine life within us. Our mature responsibility to nurture life in the Christian community demands that we become aware of the effects of sexism and racism in our history and that we become actively engaged in their eradication. What we can take from this passage is the invitation to imitate Jesus in a universal and mutual way—to care for, respect, revere, and cherish not only all other human beings but indeed every living thing.

Prayer: *Lord of life, give us the courage to identify and struggle against the death-dealing effects of racism, sexism, and ageism in our own lives and in the world around us. Renew our sense of awe and wonder before every person and before all creation. Amen.*

Saturday, August 24   Read John 6:55-59.

In this passage the theme of life comes dramatically to the fore. Our daily experience of the connection between nourishment and life assists us in our understanding of the meaning of this passage about Eucharist.

The idea of eating and drinking the flesh and blood of Jesus was almost impossible for the Jewish community to understand. In Hebrew, the phrase "to eat someone's flesh" meant to slander that person, and the law forbade the consumption of blood as food. But since the biblical expression "flesh and blood" stood for human life, the author of John may have wanted to stress that it was the total Christ that was received in the Eucharist.

The symbol of eucharistic eating suggests an intimate connection between Christ and the Christian community. Food consumed and digested becomes part of the very fiber of one's existence. Reception of the Eucharist symbolizes the communion of life that is the believer's goal, both in this life and the next.

The call of the Christian life symbolized and effected in the Eucharist is to become "other Christs." God took on flesh in Jesus so that we might take on the divine life in its fullness. The Eucharist is an invitation to us to enter into and share in the infinite love and generosity of the Creator.

Our creation in the image and likeness of God takes on concrete form in a life of generosity, praise, and thanksgiving. The celebration of Eucharist sacramentalizes this life, celebrating and nurturing the gratitude that is present in our daily lives. The Eucharist also reminds us to renew our resolve to think and act in ways compatible with the divine life we share.

Suggestion for meditation: *Reflect on the connections between meals shared with colleagues, family, and friends and the Eucharist. In what ways do daily meals uncover and support the divine life you share?*

Sunday, August 25   Read John 6:60-69.

This passage and much of the rest of John's Gospel deals with what it means to be a disciple of Jesus. Jesus is aware that not everyone who is called will believe. He knows that even within his intimate circle of friends, some hesitate and stumble. But Jesus' words reveal a message that will bring spirit and life to those who can hear it. The author of John emphasizes that the ability to hear this message does not lie in our human strength but is above all a gift of the Spirit.

The message of the good news—communion of life with God—is freely offered and must be freely accepted. There is nothing magical or automatic about God's invitation to share in the divine life. Some choose freely to stay with Jesus; others find the message too scandalous and walk away from him.

While Jesus' followers had to grapple with the mystery of this person in their midst who said he was from God, later Christians must struggle in a different way with the invitation to enter into a very personal, intimate relationship with God.

Reflection on human relationships can shed light on the meaning of this invitation. Our relationships with others can help us see why we too are tempted to walk away from the challenges of Jesus' invitation. To become intimate with another person involves enormous joys and rewards but also great suffering and self-sacrifice. We are required to open ourselves and become vulnerable, to die to certain aspects of ourselves in order to accommodate the other. And wondrously, the more we become one with the other, the more we become who we are truly meant to be. How much more wonderful is communion with the Creator of the universe in unconditional love?

Prayer: *"Lord, to whom shall we go?" Draw us into the tender and dynamic communion of your life. Amen.*

CLAIM THE POWER

August 26–September 1, 1991 **Harvey Estes†**
Monday, August 26 Read Psalm 121.

I used to preach in the mountains of North Carolina. One summer while I worked as a pastoral intern, my assignment was to preach the 10:00 service on Sunday at a campground by the lake. As I drove up and down the mountain roads, I often thought of this psalm: "I lift up my eyes to the hills." As we sang hymns together on log benches by the lake, we often felt a special closeness to "the Lord, who made heaven and earth."

This week we will look at the lectionary passages from the perspective of claiming God's power to live the Christian life. The psalm for today reminds us that power begins in intimacy with God. One of the most comforting paradoxes of the faith is that the Lord who watches over all of Israel is also the One who keeps "your going out and your coming in." God's power is not limited to history or nations in general. God also cares intimately for each of us as individuals.

How different would our churches look if we lived with such assurance? If we felt the Creator of all things, the Lord of all history, to be present and intimately involved in our lives, what a powerful witness we could make! Before we can find the power to fulfill our calling to minister to others, we must first find that private chapel of the heart where we experience an intimate relationship with our Maker.

Devotional exercise: *Think of a time when you felt close to God. Think about the details that help you recapture that situation: a song, a smile, a word, a touch. You may want to return to this moment at times when you need sanctuary.*

---

†Ordained United Methodist minister on leave of absence, presently working as a psychiatric aid at John Umstead Hospital, Butner, North Carolina.

Tuesday, August 27   Read 1 Kings 2:1-4.

Skepticism haunts me when I read a passage like this one. Follow the Lord and you will prosper in all that you do. How can we understand prosperity from a responsible perspective? For me, the operative word is *all* (v. 3). We can put prosperity in the context of the wholeness of a life lived in fellowship with God. This helps us put material prosperity in its proper place as one of many facets of a godly life.

But this way of thinking confronts us with a possibility that we may not want to face: what if God wants my *material* wealth to decline so that my *spiritual* wealth may increase? Would we dare to pray, "Lord, give us the adversity that will make us strong"?

This is a difficult prayer, but we must pray it to claim the power. If we wish to become stronger, we will have to face stressful situations that involve making sacrifices so we can share our wealth with others.

Several years ago I spent a week with Jubilee Partners, a community in northeastern Georgia that helps resettle refugees from Central America. The members of that community lived on less than $3,000 per person per year, but they prospered greatly in the wealth of relationships that grew as they worked with people from another land. The joy I found among them reminded me that we can discover many ways to be rich without possessing (or being possessed by) a lot of money.

Devotional exercise: *Think about the times in your life when you didn't have much money but felt blessed by God in other ways. You may want to list those times in a journal or diary. After some quiet time, conclude by praying, "Lord, help me find the abundant life in the way that you want me to live."*

Wednesday, August 28   Read Mark 7:1-5.

"How dare your friends sit down to dinner with hands that are ceremonially unclean!" the Pharisees said, in effect, to Jesus. It wasn't that the disciples had come straight from making mud pies to eat chocolate pudding; personal hygiene had nothing to do with it. The problem was that the Pharisees observed a complicated labyrinth of rules that covered even how to ritually purify your hands before eating, and here some of the disciples ran astray of the regulations.

We shouldn't be too hard on the Pharisees, though. They believed they should honor God in every life situation, and so over the years they developed a tradition to cover every situation imaginable. (We should be so conscious of God's presence! But at times the Pharisees carried out their traditions with extreme attention to detail, as we can see in this scripture by the way they denounced others for omitting the finer points of the system.

Perhaps we dislike the Pharisees because we are so much like them. True, not many of us get upset about people who eat with "unwashen hands" (KJV). But whether the tradition is speaking in tongues, protesting oppression, or constructing bigger church buildings, almost every group in the church follows a standard that at times gets pushed to the extreme.

If we want to claim the power of God in our lives, we need to recognize this barrier that confronts people of all times and not just the Pharisees. Whenever the details of our tradition become an end in themselves rather than a means to communion with God and service to others, we change our churches from redemption centers into museums.

Devotional exercise: *Think about the times you have been judgmental and picky about details. After some quiet time, pray, "Lord, forgive me for putting the details first. Help me become both diligent and flexible in serving you."*

Thursday, August 29   Read Mark 7:5-8.

"Isaiah was talking about you actors," Jesus was, in effect, saying to the Pharisees. The word *hypocrite* comes from the Greek word that originally meant "actor" and came to mean someone who pretends to be what he or she is not. Jesus applied this word to the Pharisees because he knew that Isaiah's words fit them so well: "You honor me with your lips, but your hearts are far away" (AP).

All of us are actors; sometimes just trying to be polite at a finance committee meeting could merit an Academy Award. But if we hope to claim God's power in our lives, we need to ask ourselves, "When is the acting helping me? When is it hurting me?" At times all of us fall into the trap of acting as pretension. Like the Pharisees, we can become so entangled in pretending to have arrived that we never get where we want to go.

But not all acting is harmful. We can also participate in the acting of growth. Instead of pretending to be something we are not, we can strive for what we hope to become. Holy Communion is an example of a dramatic event that invites us to participate in the play as actors until it becomes a reality. When we go to the table, take the bread, drink from the cup, we are not yet the disciples we could be; yet Christ's presence in this drama pulls us in that direction. In the same way, if we sing with enthusiasm like the first Methodists, if we do acts of mercy like the first Christians, if we continue to *act* like God's children with the intention to grow, we begin to *become* the part we are playing.

We can act to pretend in order to hide our weaknesses. Or we can act to grow into powerful witnesses.

Devotional exercise: *Think of a Communion service or other worship during which you felt especially drawn into the dramatic presence of Christ. After some quiet time, pray, "Lord, help me act like a powerful witness until I become one."*

Friday, August 30   Read Mark 7:21-23.

"Sometimes I think I'd rather deal with physically messy situations than with emotionally messy ones." A preacher who had once worked in a rest home told me this. He had often cared for physically incapacitated residents. He had cleaned them up, diapered them, fed them, and bathed them every day for years before entering the ordained ministry. I would marvel at his capacity to do unpleasant chores, but he would shrug it off. "I got used to it," he would tell me. "But I never have gotten used to how church people often treat each other."

A graphic illustration, perhaps, but no less graphic than Jesus' own words. Referring to the Pharisees' long list of ritually unclean foods, Jesus tells them that people are not made unclean by what goes into them, enters the stomach, and passes on. People defile themselves by what comes out of the heart. The evil thoughts and intentions that erupt into sinful living serve as a far more accurate reflection of what we have become, and these defile us and reveal our need for redemption far more than any physical aspect of our lives.

Look at the power we lose when we get bogged down in the messy emotions and intentions clogging up our hearts. Like sprinters trying to run knee-deep in a swamp, we often seem to be just churning up the muck without getting anywhere.

If we want to think clearly and feel clearly so that we can carry out the Lord's ministry, we need to ask him to drain the swamp within us, to dry up the grudges, lusts, ill feelings, and hurts that have clogged up our souls. Then we can have firm ground on which we can build a new creation as we minister to others.

Devotional exercise: *Think of the unresolved ill feelings you harbor that hold you back from making a strong witness. After some quiet time, pray, "Lord, create in me a clean heart."*

Saturday, August 31   Read Ephesians 6:10-12.

I saw a basketball game at the gym recently that reminded me of church. Some fellows were playing "shirts and skins," which requires one team to take off their shirts in order to distinguish them from the other team. Probably without realizing what they had done, they chose sides this way: the four who didn't want to take off their shirts played against the four who would strip to the waist in a minute for some good basketball. As you might imagine, the skins almost devoured the other team because they had stumbled into a situation where the four most aggressive played against the four most timid.

I fear that this type of timidity characterizes too many of us in the church. Unlike Paul, we don't seem to grasp that we confront not flesh and blood but powers, principalities, and spiritual hosts of wickedness (see v. 12). Being nice and going to church occasionally will not cause the overwhelming powers of evil to back down. Such timidity will not help drug addicts kick the habit, reduce teen pregnancies, lower the crime rate, feed the hungry, house the homeless, or heal the many other casualties of a world where evil constantly wages war against creation. To face powerful opposition, we may have to lose our Sunday apparel and put on some work clothes.

Claiming God's power in our lives is not just exciting and fulfilling; Paul reminds us that it is also *necessary*. We simply cannot survive spiritually and emotionally without a powerful source from which we can draw strength. The love of God will finally triumph, but to claim the power of that victory we must confront the powerful forces of evil around us.

Devotional exercise: *Think of some examples of the power of evil that especially concern you, whether as obvious as drug addiction or as subtle as creeping affluence. After some quiet time, pray, "Lord, give us the strength to overcome."*

Sunday, September 1   Read Ephesians 6:13-20.

I felt invulnerable the day I got my first football pads and helmet. When we played on the vacant lot in the neighborhood, some of us had equipment and some of us didn't. After smashing my unprotected body over and over into the fiberglass armor of others, I began to realize that determination alone was not enough. When I finally got the right equipment, I was ready to jump into the battle headfirst.

Looking back, I realize that playing ball in such an unsupervised and unprotected way was dangerous. But isn't vacant-lot football much like the rest of the world? Doesn't the evening news each day confront us with a world that seems largely unsupervised, unprotected, and dangerous? Whether you're looking at a line of homeless people in a soup kitchen or the latest line of nuclear missiles, you can't help but feel that we're all as vulnerable as kids playing football without pads.

I wonder whether this feeling of vulnerability holds us back from claiming God's power in our lives. If you claim the power, you have to use it; there's no point in putting on the helmet if you're not willing to knock heads. But it will still hurt some. Whether you face criticism for unpopular stands on social issues or emotional fatigue from shouldering the grief of others, ministry can hurt, even when we're wearing the Lord's armor.

But in the long run we're better off even with the hurt. Paul tells us to put on the armor "that you may be able to withstand in the evil day." Hardship eventually comes to us all. I prefer wearing the armor with a few bumps and bruises to hoping the battle never finds me.

Devotional exercise: *Think about the things that are your armor (for example: prayer, fellowship with others, singing, or solitude). After some quiet time, pray, "Lord, thank you for all the ways you protect me and equip me for your work."*

September 2-8, 1991   **Elaine Blanchard Brewer†**
Monday, September 2   Read Mark 7:31-37.

Two women are busily choosing meats and fruits for their families in a dusty, noisy marketplace. One woman leans toward the other. "I just heard that merchant say he passed Jesus earlier on the road. He says the healer is coming here."

The other woman stops her shopping and stares blankly for a moment. Yes, she's heard of this man and his miracles. Her chest suddenly fills with a great hope that is almost painful in its intensity. Her mind goes home before her feet begin running. Her son would be home, alone and lonely in his deafness. This just might be it, the chance she's waited for all along. Now is the time to tell her son about her dreams. And as she tells him they will run together, hurrying to meet Jesus and to beg his healing for the boy's ears and his tied-up tongue.

Our ears are opened; our minds and hearts are made sensitive by the struggles that touch us where we live. The parents I have known who live and love with physically and mentally challenged children seem to be blessed with extra patience, the rough edges worn smooth by daily accomplishments that often seem like major victories. Their ears seem to be open for a kind word or for the opportunity to listen when a friend needs to talk.

The woman who passed along the news that Jesus was coming had found healing, knew wholeness, before Jesus arrived. Her ears had been opened by faith and she spoke words of hope to a friend, leading her to Christ. Perhaps we can be motivated by her example to spread the good news of Jesus to others.

Suggestion for prayer: *Listen for God in silence for five minutes.*

---

†Registered nurse; candidate for the ordained ministry in The United Methodist Church, Fulton, Kentucky.

Tuesday, September 3   Read Mark 7:31-37.

Healing is a community process; all are affected. His loosened tongue allowed the man to speak plainly, but scripture doesn't tell what he said following Jesus' healing touch. The gathered community is reported to have exclaimed of Jesus: "He has done all things well."

Asking about someone's grandchildren or someone's health often has the power to loosen a tongue. Speaking ill of someone often causes other tongues to join in. How easily our tongues can be loosened! The most loosened my tongue has ever been was when I was eighteen and caught in the act of shoplifting. I was motivated by extreme fear, and my mouth spewed slick and speedy words that convinced the store's manager I would never steal again if only he would allow me to leave freely.

Our prayer, as faith communities in moments more holy and silent, is that our tongues might be loosened by pure love of God. We pray that we might be enabled to speak what is true, noble, right, pure, lovely, admirable, excellent, and praiseworthy. Paul tells us: "Do not let any unwholesome talk come out of your mouths, but only what is helpful for building others up according to their needs, that it may benefit those who listen" (Eph. 4:29, NIV).

Jesus had a purpose in this healing event—all were made aware of the pattern of perfection in his works. Perhaps the man, no longer deaf or tongue-tied, spoke first to affirm the goodness of God. Whatever his words, we know that the members of the faith community affirmed the perfection of Christ among them.

Each of us will require a touch from Jesus so that our tongue might truly be loosened for the edification of his community and the glorification of his name. We are his witnesses.

Devotional exercise: *Reflect on all you have said in the last twenty-four hours.*

Wednesday, September 4   Read James 1:17-18.

In the study of ecology we learn that all systems are interrelated. The air, soil, and water interact with one another. Living organisms compete for a limited supply of nutrients to sustain life and to reproduce their species. No system is isolated. Life affects life. God has created the world in a complex and interrelated design.

Human beings are unique in that we are the firstfruits of God's creation. In the ancient world it was law that all firstfruits from the harvest belonged to God. God has created us so that we might interact with the world, with our faith communities, and also with our Creator, recognizing that we have great meaning to God. As far as we know, a fish holds no hope when the last worm and algae are eaten. The fish falls to the bottom of the lake with no expectation for resurrection. It is of no consequence to the fish that its dead body will provide nutrients for next spring's growth.

But when God sent the Son, God invited all of us to have hope above all other attitudes. We are free to see ourselves as firstfruits, as important members of God's family. We gather together at the table where provision has been made for each of us and for all of us. There we see how interdependent we are on one another and on the perfect gifts of God.

As we live together, listening with the ears of the reborn and speaking with loosened tongues of the redeemed, do we hear the word in all its truth and power calling us out of the dust and into the light? Do we respond with obedience so that the harmony God plans might become a reality?

Prayer: *Allow me to hear your word, Lord, that I might assist my faith community in moving toward holiness. Amen.*

Thursday, September 5   Read James 1:19-27.

I am an alcoholic, and the major act of my recovery was to associate myself with the fellowship of Alcoholics Anonymous. We admit to ourselves daily that we have been defeated by alcohol. We decide to turn our lives and our wills over to God, then seek through constant prayer and meditation to know God's will for our lives. The work involved is a lifetime process.

Part of the recovery process is a personal moral inventory. Here we search our souls for the truth of who we have allowed ourselves to become in allowing alcohol to destroy our moral fiber. We write down the names of all those we have harmed, detailing situations so we cannot deny the damage we have done. Much time, prayer, and encouragement from the community is involved. I call this process "carrying out the garbage."

Then we make amends to all those we have harmed, except where doing so would bring further damage to someone else. We spare ourselves no pain. Again and again we look into the faces of those from whom we have stolen, those to whom we have lied, those we have heartlessly used, and those we have bitterly resented. We say "I'm sorry." Honesty, willingness, and action are our first lines of defense against falling back into the powers of darkness.

Alcoholics are not the only ones who develop roots of negativity in their spirits. Spiritual housecleaning is necessary for all members of God's family if we are to work together in harmony, to be more than merely "hearers" of the word. It is up to us to take action as reconciliators against the pride, addiction, anger, jealousy, resentment, prejudice, and isolation that threaten to extinguish the light of the Spirit in our midst.

Prayer: *God, give me the courage to see myself as you see me and the power to carry out the garbage. Amen.*

Friday, September 6   Read Psalm 119:129-136.

True love for the law is born from experience with obedience. Obedience grows out of a healthy prayer life.

Carol had finally been relieved of working on the midnight shift as a nurse, following six years of going into the hospital late and going home in the mornings to sleep during the day. She felt her prayers had been answered as she moved to a new city.

For several months the family's finances were such that Carol didn't have to seek employment. During that time she enjoyed times of solitude and quiet meditation at home. One Sunday she noticed that Leigh, a committed member of the church, was missing for the fourth week in a row. "Is Leigh sick?" The answer was no, but both of Leigh's parents were ill and required constant care. Carol learned that Leigh, an only child, was struggling to care for her elderly parents as well as for her own household. Leigh had little time to sleep and no time for Christian fellowship or for attending worship. "She needs a nurse for her parents at night," somebody said. "But it's hard to find regular private-duty help."

Washing her Sunday dishes, Carol knew who could be helping Leigh. It wasn't that Carol wanted to work during the night, but she recognized an opportunity to help balance a burden. It might not be comfortable or convenient, but she knew obedience had its own rewards. Carol drove out to offer her services as a nurse.

Leigh gave Carol a hug. "I had to get out for a good cry this morning," she said. "I walked out to the barn and prayed. It's funny. Your name came to my mind while I was out there."

Devotional exercise: *Meditate on the importance of obedience to God and God's commands.*

Saturday, September 7   Read Proverbs 2:1-8.

Breakfast at Fellowship Hall

Strong smiles come from grandparents,
some circular and some bent,
all with beauty of aging and belonging
as plates are passed, filled.
Sitting politely but sending
some impish message dancing
through the mind,
clear to the heart.
Hot, humid day outside
simmers over ancient code—
parallel to the wrinkles of their faces.
I am not old; I am not young.
Public school no longer provides
wisdom for my dance.
My partners, now, are miles apart.
There is more to be eaten
than pancakes this morning.
Here a nutrition
for souls against loneliness
and weary of casual contacts.
Encircled by a sweet sea of wisdom, love—
we are fed in fellowship hall.

The church is in the business of bridge-building when it is at its best. First we create a solid foundation by celebrating ourselves, and then we find we have strength to share.

Those of us who are raising children, working at a marital relationship, or struggling to know ourselves more fully need the settled wisdom that can come from our friends who are older. When the bridge has been crossed, a treasure is discovered.

Suggestion for prayer: *Pray by name for the elderly members of your congregation who are away from all that once was home.*

Sunday, September 8   Read Proverbs 2:1-8.

Power emerges from true community. But this kind of community goes unborn if persons are unable or unwilling to come together. A community motivated by love brings forth an extra dimension in living that cannot be known in any other way.

We hunger for wisdom both personally and within our Christian fellowship. Too often, however, our search takes us nowhere near those persons who have physical or mental disabilities. Our faith communities often lack the enrichment that might be added by persons with different gifts and abilities.

We tend to avoid disabled persons. Institutions that house these persons keep them from our sight, and too often they are out of our thoughts as well. The bureaucracy that seeks to serve disabled persons knows only their names and numbers. Human service workers and nurses, even with their best intentions and top efficiency, cannot meet all the needs for so many children of God. Families themselves, no matter how attentive they are, cannot fill the roles of good friends.

Persons with disabilities will always be a minority, but they should never be left out of the majority. Remember the story of the ugly duckling? Imagine the type of loneliness experienced by the little duck when he had no place to belong, no circle of family or friends.

Wisdom appears whenever the commands of Christ are being obeyed. Wisdom appears wherever the Spirit of Christ is evident. The Word is among us to be shared, to be lived.

Suggestion for prayer: *In five minutes of silence, wait on the Lord to direct you toward new avenues for wisdom-seeking and sharing the word.*

IN GOD WE TRUST

September 9-15, 1991 **John K. Stoner†**
Monday, September 9 Read Psalm 125.

The words "In God We Trust" are printed on every coin minted in the United States. The Bible speaks often about trust in God. There must be something very important about trusting God. But do we really trust in God? It is ironic that the nation which above all others trusts in its wealth and military power should write on its coins "In God We Trust."

Could it be that the empty slogan is there by some mysterious divine appointment as a challenge to the church to do what the nation itself has no intention of doing?

In Psalm 125 we read, "Those who trust in the LORD are like Mount Zion, which cannot be shaken but endures forever" (NIV). What astonishing security and permanence are given to those who trust in God! Mount Zion was the southwest hill of Jerusalem, an elevation of land which became synonymous with Jerusalem itself, and also gave its name to the temple. Zion was viewed as the place where God dwelt (Ps. 48). The mountain itself proved impregnable, although not the city and temple.

Trust in God meant believing and acting on the belief that God will vindicate those who do good. It includes trusting God for defense against enemies (Jer. 39:17-18). Those who trust in God do not trust in human strength or in wealth (Jer. 17; Prov. 11:28).

When we look at the Appalachians, the Rocky Mountains, or the Cascades, we have a sense that here is something firmly in place. So are the people who trust in God.

Prayer: *God, I do not trust in money or armed force. I trust in you. Amen.*

---

†Ordained minister, Brethren in Christ Church; writer, peace activist, spiritual director, Akron, Pennsylvania.

Tuesday, September 10   Read Proverbs 22:1-2, 8-9.

Rich and poor alike

Prosperity has a tendency to reduce our trust in God, and poverty has a tendency to increase our trust in God. These are tendencies, not absolute laws. But they are consistent tendencies, and because of this they have to be taken seriously. We might name this observation "the principle of the diverging tendencies of prosperity and poverty."

Insofar as our relationship with God is concerned, the principle offers in the first instance a warning to the rich and encouragement to the poor. Our reaction to this is probably negative if we suspect that we are closer to being rich than poor. It sounds unfair. Why should middle-class American comfort give any disadvantage to the poor in trusting and knowing God?

On the other hand, if we are poor it may sound like good news. There is a lot that we don't have, but somehow we are standing in a place from which God is just a little more visible.

Human societies, and even churches, make distinctions between the rich and the poor. We are class-conscious. The Bible also recognizes that there is a difference between rich and poor, but it interprets that in its own way. It warns of the danger of riches, encourages generosity, and gives hope to the poor. Jesus' words in Luke 6, "woe to you that are rich" and "blessed are you poor," pick up very familiar biblical themes (see Jer. 22:13ff., 1 Sam. 2, and Ps. 69:33).

But the rich and the poor have the most important thing in common: "The LORD is the Maker of them all" (Prov. 22:2, NIV). Their need to learn trust in God is equal.

Suggestion for meditation: *Allow God to influence your thoughts as you meditate on the ways in which wealth may produce hindrances and poverty produce helps in the path of trust in God.*

Wednesday, September 11   Read James 2:1-5, 8-10.

Rich in faith

The history of discrimination and oppression based on greed and racism in America is a long and depressing story. Perhaps that is why not many white Americans know it.

When James said, "My brothers, as believers in our glorious Lord Jesus Christ, don't show favoritism" (NIV), he warned against a sin with which the church in the United States is well experienced, if not well acquainted. Many times we would understand the Bible better if we knew our own history better. James was describing the stuff out of which the colonial rape of the Native American was forged. He was depicting the mindset which conceived and nurtured the kidnapping and breeding of African slaves for economic advantage. He was explaining what horrendous oppression can be practiced by people who sit piously in straight rows on Sunday morning at 11:00. The words "In God We Trust" may be true, according to some strange idea of trust and an even more unusual concept of God, but it will also have to be said that we have been handy with the gun and we look with considerable deference to a good supply of cheap labor.

And yet, says James, the poor, the victims of oppression, have been chosen by God to be rich in faith. Feeling keenly the pain of oppression imposed by humans, they have put their trust in God. In this they have become examples to all of us. We can learn from them.

Prayer: *Crucified God, loving us from the cross, from the lynching tree, and the electric chair, help us to trust you to secure our place in the world. In Jesus' name. Amen.*

Thursday, September 12   Read James 2:14-17.

Living a faith

Trust in God is not only a way of thinking. It is also a way of acting. It is a way of living.

In James 2:17 we read, "Faith by itself, if it has no works, is dead." Martin Luther is said to have called the Book of James an "epistle of straw." Luther was strong on faith (as he understood it), and we are indebted to him. But it would be unwise for us to limit our definition of faith to Luther's experience and words.

James has something to tell us about living faith. The practice of good works as evidence of faith is praised throughout the Bible, and if the idea of righteous works has gotten a bad name in Protestantism, then we shall have to boldly say, "So much the worse for Protestantism." Righteous works are not the same thing as works-righteousness. In the Book of Revelation the bride of Christ is said to be clothed in fine linen, which "stands for the righteous acts of the saints" (19:8, NIV).

Not all good works are done to convince God that the doer of them is more good than bad. It is true, the Pharisees, the apostle Paul, and Luther knew what it was to try too hard to impress God. But there is a proper impulse to please God and to help people with good works, and we should be very cautious about denigrating that impulse.

Jesus put it well enough when he said, "Your light must shine before people, so that they will see the good things you do and praise your Father in heaven" (Matt. 5:16, TEV). More often than not, a good deed or right action is possible only on the basis of faith. If we do not have faith in God, we will do something easier, or safer—something which looks to human eyes more likely to succeed, or which in any case will cost us less.

Prayer: *Help us, Lord, to act our faith, not just talk it. Amen.*

Friday, September 13   Read Mark 8:27-30.

Peter's flawed confession

Peter seems fated to receive both more praise and less than he deserves. In the Mark 8 passage today we look at how the church traditionally may have praised him more than he deserves.

Who is Jesus of Nazareth? It is a question which has intrigued millions of people for centuries. Jesus himself first asked it of his disciples one day as they walked the road toward Caesarea Philippi. As Peter was to find out, it is a question which goes to the heart not only of what we know about Jesus but also of what we know about God.

Peter said, "You are the Christ." "The Christ" and "the Messiah" both mean "the Anointed One"—the One dedicated by God for a special task. Peter and his contemporaries hoped that God would send the Messiah in their time to deliver them from their enemies. One popular image of the Messiah was a political and military leader called the Son of David.

Josephus, the Jewish historian, records incidents of horrendous repression by the Roman troops who occupied Palestine during Peter's lifetime. In one incident two thousand Jewish insurgents were crucified. In such circumstances it is not surprising that Peter (and others) saw in Jesus potential for deliverance from their national enemies. So when Jesus asked Peter who he was, Peter readily replied, "You are the Messiah."

Jesus reacted to Peter's words by warning the disciples not to tell anyone about him. We wonder why. Certainly Peter wanted everyone to know that the Messiah had come. That would have been his prayer. Perhaps Jesus' response to the disciples, to Peter's words in particular, was an indication that Peter's confession was somehow lacking.

Suggestion for meditation: *What was wrong with Peter's confession?*

Saturday, September 14   Read Mark 8:31-33.

You don't trust in God

Would Jesus say to Christians in the United States essentially what he said to Peter: "You don't trust in God"? Would he say with the same vehemence, "Get behind me, Satan!"

Peter must have been shocked speechless when Jesus used such strong language. Do we understand what brought it on?

The scripture says that after Peter confessed that Jesus was the Messiah, Jesus began to teach them that the Son of Man must suffer many things and be rejected by the elders, chief priests and teachers of the law and that he must be killed and after three days rise again. Then it says, "Peter took him aside and began to rebuke him" (TEV).

Imagine the scene: Peter grasps Jesus by the arm and begins to give him a lecture. Peter is rebuking Jesus. For what? Obviously for saying that he is going to suffer and die. (Did Peter even hear the words about rising again?) Peter had just confessed that Jesus was the Messiah, powerful king and military hero, son of David. What was this talk about suffering and death?

Now it was Jesus' turn to be upset and angered. He rebukes Peter in the strongest language possible. In effect he calls Peter Satan, and he says, "You do not have in mind the things of God, but the things of men" (NIV). What "things" is he talking about? He is talking about Peter's idea of power, about the kind of power God's Messiah will use to deliver the people from oppression.

Peter is tempting Jesus with military power to fulfill his messiahship. Is it any wonder that Jesus was angry with Peter? I wonder if Jesus is angry with those of us in the twentieth-century church as well?

Prayer: *O God, keep me silent about Jesus if I don't know who he is, so that you will not be misrepresented. Amen.*

Sunday, September 15   Read Mark 8:34-38.

Was Peter ashamed of Jesus?

Today's reading has probably been removed from real life by spiritualization as much as any text in the Bible. Let us try to allow it to speak in its historical context.

There has just been a heated conflict between Jesus and Peter over the way Jesus is going to fulfill his role as Messiah. Jesus has spoken of rejection and suffering. Peter has vehemently objected. Now Jesus proceeds to say that *anyone* who would follow him must take up a cross. So the suffering, the cross, is not only for Jesus but for all of his followers as well.

The word *cross* on the lips of Jesus, and in the ears of his disciples, meant execution. It meant specifically execution for political offenses. The cross of Jesus was not the share of suffering which is the common lot of humanity. No, it was the consequence of speaking truth and living love in the midst of political and religious systems that suppressed truth and ridiculed love. There is no reason to think that Jesus called his disciples to take up a fundamentally different cross.

When Jesus was arrested in the garden, Peter was not ready to lose his life for Jesus. By all evidence, however, he was ready to take someone else's life for Jesus. He had a sword and tried to use it. When Jesus failed to join the struggle on Peter's terms and healed the wounded man, it was too much for Peter. He could not stand to be identified with the nonviolent Jesus. In a word, he was ashamed of Jesus and denied that he even knew him. But later Peter experienced his own resurrection to a new understanding of life. That is the gospel of Jesus Christ.

Prayer: *Let me not be ashamed, dear Jesus, of you and your words of nonviolent love for enemies. Teach me to trust your way, that as I confess you as Messiah I shall follow you as Lord. Amen.*

GOD'S WISDOM IN OUR LIFE

September 16-22, 1991 **Marian Yagel McBay†**
Monday, September 16 Read Job 28:20-28.

Wisdom as understanding

"Whence then comes wisdom? And where is the place of understanding?" So often as a pastor I wonder when I will achieve a level of knowledge and experience that makes maturity and forbearance come easy. Job is in despair when he speaks these words—but not so deeply in despair as to abandon philosophical rhetoric as a means of relief from his suffering.

How like Job we are! In the midst of tragedy our first cry is so often "Why?" When we find ourselves in crisis we want to know how we got there and why. It is as if by retracing our steps and mapping our arrival we can somehow orchestrate our departure and gain relief. Sometimes it even works. Through self-understanding and a grasp of our situation we are often able to alter our course for the better. Other times—many times—we cannot. Such is the instance in which we find Job. What at first seems to be a crisis of understanding is really a masquerading crisis of faith. The answer that comes to Job reflects this knowledge on an intellectual level: "Behold, the fear of the Lord, that is wisdom; and to depart from evil is understanding."

Wisdom is an *act*—an act of faith. But faith is not an intellectual endeavor. Plentiful discourse follows for Job, characterized by proclamation and complaint, before he fully experiences the meaning of those words: "I had heard of thee by the hearing of the ear, but now my eye sees thee" (42:5). So it is with us.

Prayer: *Dear Lord, if we are to be wise we must first be ourselves. And being ourselves is an act of courage. Courage is a gift of faith and belief. Grant us such faith that we may act wisely in the world. Amen.*

---

†Co-pastor, Hobson United Methodist Church, Nashville, Tennessee.

Tuesday, September 17   Read Psalm 27:1-6.

Wisdom as fearlessness

"The LORD is my light and my salvation; whom shall I fear?" Verses 1 through 6 of the twenty-seventh psalm have long been the object of scholarly dispute regarding their relationship to verses 7 through 14 (one of the lectionary readings for next week). Some scholars argue that it is a separate Psalm of Confidence, while verses 7 through 14 represent an Individual Lamentation. Still others feel that the integrity of the psalm is in order and that it is a Royal Psalm when taken in its entirety.*

I prefer the latter position. There are many times in our lives when we call upon our faith consciously and deliberately: "I will sing and make melody to the LORD," only moments later to find ourselves bewailing the pain of our existence: "Hide not thy face from me" (v. 9). It is important for Christians and spiritual sojourners to experience these ambivalent feelings. There are times when our life experiences point simultaneously to despair in living and hope in surviving. The capacity to successfully bridge the abyss between the desperate now and the fulfilled future is a predominant characteristic of spiritual maturity. Fearlessness is not the absence of feeling afraid. It is the act of courageously moving onward. To move onward we must have principles of confidence, beliefs which set our direction. In order to *keep* moving we must face the feelings of fear, isolation, abandonment, and despair. Only then may we set down our load and proceed on the journey of growth and wholeness.

Prayer: *O God, the universe without is amazing enough; yet the universe within us is even more spectacular. Thank you for balance. May this day be one of spiritual pursuit. May my fear rest in you. Amen.*

---

*The New Century Bible Commentary: The Book of Psalms, volume 1, A.A. Anderson (London: Marshall, Morgan and Scoot, 1972), p. 219.

Wednesday, September 18   Read James 3:13-18.

Wisdom's attributes

"Who is wise and understanding among you? By his good life let him show his works in the gentleness* of wisdom." There is wisdom (objective, factual knowledge), and then there is wisdom (the manner in which what we know shapes us). These verses seek to illuminate the differences between the two.

Apparently a dispute has arisen in the church as the result of contradictory teachings among the leadership. How do we know whom to follow? Some of the leaders appeal to their wisdom and in so doing behave condescendingly and with derision. These leaders, says our author, are not truly wise people. Their wisdom is not from God. Its goal is social climbing and personal power. It is demonic and without value to Christian community.

True wisdom—derived from God—is characterized by peace. This community longs for such peace. And so there is need for discernment. In order to determine who the true peacemakers are, one must watch to see how peace is sown. Those who truly seek peace *seek it peaceably,* not deviously. Their wisdom is one of righteousness. It is characterized by sincere love for the household of faith. Such genuine participation in the community of faith renders *teaching* an instrument of peace. If we are to be teachers of the faith we must ultimately be peacemakers—and sow our peace peaceably.

Prayer: *Just for today, Lord, let me set down my fear of not knowing and extend myself to the growth of another. Where there is strife, let me sow love, not facts. Where there is grief, let me sow comfort, not capability. Where there is need, let me extend my hand to help, and not merely point the way. Amen.*

---

*RSV reads "meekness," but "gentleness" is the sense of the term. See *Interpreter's Bible,* volume 12, p 50.

Thursday, September 19   Read Mark 9:30-32.

Wisdom's plan

"But they did not understand the saying, and they were afraid to ask him." It is not difficult to imagine that the disciples were feeling very confused by Jesus' statements about dying and rising. The disciples, however, apparently knew more about politics than religion and like so many of us often confused one for the other. And they seem to have preferred their confusion over risking the embarrassment of appearing ignorant.

Wisdom is *intentional*. Everything that Jesus said and did reflected a long-range sense of purpose, a sense of direction, and a profound sense of meaning.

But we, like the disciples, find it difficult to perceive or plan meaning and direction in our own ministries. Self-doubt, the maze of institutional demands, and the counterproductive relationships which come from our efforts to succeed—all these strap our sense of spiritual purpose and deplete our enthusiasm for living out the calling to serve others.

Yet it is just this calling to serve others to which Jesus is pointing. He warns his followers that he is about to become a living example of servanthood—intentionally, willingly, respectably, peaceably, differently from anybody else. He demonstrates the servant aspects of ministry through every act.

As leaders in the community of faith we must embody the intentionality of Christ. We must seek a thorough understanding of our gifts and our call to ministry. Let us not fall into the trap of the disciples and grope our way to the cross. Let us turn to one another and ask the questions of our hearts.

Prayer: *Holy Spirit, descend on us. Supplant the madness of our status-seeking by nurturing our longing to share our spiritual journey with others. In Jesus' name and by his example, we pray. Amen.*

Friday, September 20   Read Mark 9:33-35; 10:31.

Wisdom's place

"If anyone desires to be first, he shall be last of all and servant of all."* Examining this text in the Greek, I am far less certain now regarding its import for us for daily reflection. The RSV renders the Greek "shall be" as a future indicative used in an imperative sense; hence, "if any one would be first, he *must* be last of all and servant of all." Recognizing the absence of space for scholarly debate, I would like to entertain the possibility that this clause may be a *predictive* use of the verb rather than an imperative. Were this the case, then we have a statement of simple condition: "If you desire to be first you *will* be last of all."

In 10:31, Jesus reinforces the predictive sense of the saying with these words: "But many that are first will be [again, future indicative] last, and the last first." Jesus is warning the disciples against status seeking. He tries to point to the divine aspects of leadership. Such leadership is inclusive (a child is the most important) and directed toward the needs of others ("For the Son of Man . . . came not to be served but to serve . . ." 10:45*a*). In the case of the disciples, the demonic aspects of ambition have skewed their capacity for understanding.

Our own search for status and power skews our understanding and fulfillment of God's call. The result may be that those who now are "last" or least may take a new place in the kingdom of God (we may already occupy it). And those of us in power?

Prayer: *Lord, you are my redeemer. You are also my example. Let me relax my ambitions for this world and exercise my capabilities for serving in your kingdom. May your truth be the glory. Amen.*

---

*George Ricker Berry, *The Interlinear Greek-English New Testament*, (Grand Rapids, Michigan: Zondervan Publishing House, 1972). See literal translation.

Saturday, September 21   Read Mark 9:36-37.

Wisdom enacted

"He said to them, 'Whoever receives one such child in my name receives me.'" Infant baptism is always a source of conflict for me—because I believe in it so strongly. I am deeply persuaded that grace is a gift and not an acquisition or accomplishment and that children may therefore be the only people truly capable of freely experiencing it.

Throughout the New Testament, and powerfully so in this week's readings, we are told of the folly of knowledge and warned against the arrogance of knowing. Yet we turn again and again to our intellect to guide us on our journey to the kingdom.

Could the accoutrements of adulthood be stumbling blocks to the kingdom? I was fifteen when I first felt stirred by God's voice. It was as if a spirit arose within me and empowered me toward a future having one certainty: I would be a minister of the word. Twenty years later I find myself having these same feelings of spiritual strength that had previously propelled me into the future. The years between? At times it was only the *memory* of that inner voice that kept me moving forward.

As a teen I had had no time limits, no goal constraints, and no overwhelming needs beyond life itself. Loving, sharing, and relating were the fuel for my day-to-day existence. In the depths of my soul I am discovering that place again where the moment is more important than the hour; where people are more important than accomplishments; and where generosity is the answer to most of the world's problems. It is to this place that Jesus' words about children direct us.

Prayer: *Everlasting Parent, sustainer of life's longing, fill me today with your graciousness toward all people. May I receive those around me as you receive us. In Christ's name. Amen.*

Sunday, September 22   Read Mark 9:35*a*.

Wisdom for us

Jesus is forever filling in a chosen few as to the real meaning of his words and activities, though often to no avail. As readers we are the eavesdroppers, the overhearers of the truth. We have the privilege of anonymous misunderstanding and/or confusion. We need not be embarrassed by the indignity of misunderstanding, and yet we are still able to witness Jesus' person and humanity in a way that neither the crowds nor the disciples were able to in his very presence.

As overhearers of the word, our burden is great. The words we speak must reflect the truth as we have come to understand it. Our behavior is expected to reflect integrity with the knowledge we have been given. Finally, we are called to make choices based on the values and goals derived from these understandings.

As much as we identify with the twelve, and in spite of the fact that we sometimes feel like one of the crowd, we are neither and yet both. We are neither because we have the inside story and two thousand years of Christianity to inform us. We are both because we are self-seeking like the crowds and self-serving like the disciples. In spite of this, we are also witnessess to our own personal experiences of salvation. These experiences bring life to the scriptures and nurture bonding within Christian community. When we share these experiences with strangers to the household of faith, they become newcomers.

As we witness to our faith—or fail to witness—there are always overhearers and unknown eavesdroppers. In your life day by day, what is being overheard about your faith?

Prayer: *Almighty God, even when I am silent, my life is heard by others. Lord, make my message to others be meaningful and true. Through your Holy Spirit and for Jesus' sake I pray. Amen.*

SEEING THE WONDERFUL

September 23-29, 1991   **Elizabeth Nordquist†**
Monday, September 23   Read Job 42:1-6.

The drama of Job's encounter with God is full of loss, humiliation, bafflement, anger, grief, and suffering. Yet in all this, Job did not charge God with wrong. The key to Job's blamelessness seems to be in his openness to the wonder of God, to allow God to reveal who God is, and then to reveal more and more as the encounter unfolds.

On the basis of Job's history and life experience, he might feel justified in thinking that he knows all about who God is, how God acts, and what one can expect from God. However, Job chooses to wait for the continuing revelation of who God is, against the advice and explanations of his spouse and friends. He looks trustingly to God to explain and to vindicate the events of his life in the context of God's holiness. Job finds that by choosing to experience God on God's terms he enters into a new realm of reality about God. "I had heard of thee by the hearing of the ear, but now my eye sees thee."

We are invited by God into deeper and wider realms of reality about God. It takes determination to stay in the process of interacting with the living God, without withdrawing, without cursing God and dying, without false recrimination, without presuming on past experiences of God's grace.

To wait to see God despite grief, pain, and darkness will result in our seeing the wonder of God in ways we never imagined.

Prayer: *Open my eyes, wonder-full God! Show me more of yourself and more of myself. In Jesus' name. Amen.*

---

†Associate Pastor, St. Peter's by the Sea Presbyterian Church, Rancho Palos Verdes, California.

Tuesday, September 24   Read Psalm 27:1-8.

This psalmist has come through on the other side of Job's dark and trying journey. Yet even the experience of victory over enemies and nurture in God's house doesn't allow the psalmist to presume that there is nothing more to be learned or experienced with God. Persons of faith have a continuous need to respond to God's invitation, "Seek my face."

Experience has demonstrated to this writer God's capacity to protect, to keep someone safe, to cover from harm, to conquer enemies. The relief at having been rescued is evident in the tone of exultation. But along with this trust in God now validated comes another awareness: there is and there will always be more to learn all the days of our human lives.

Sometimes we feel that we know just about all there is to know about God, about ourselves, about our families, about human behavior, and about the ways of the world. Yet, certainly Job was taken completely by surprise when his world was devastated by disaster. The psalmist, too, knows that one dramatic act of salvation by God is not all there is to know. Each of them calls us to keep seeking God's face, to behold God's beauty, to dwell and to inquire in God's house.

We seek God's face by choosing, like Job, to do so, and by developing the skill of seeing God everywhere God is to be found—in the ordinary and in the extraordinary. Seeking God is a habit we can develop in order to learn something of the wonderful nature of God. Both Job and the psalmist proclaim that God will be found by looking for God's face.

Prayer: *I seek your face, O God; teach me to recognize it. In Jesus' name. Amen.*

Wednesday, September 25   Read Psalm 27:9-14.

Discovering the wonderful multifaceted nature of God is delightful and pleasing, and it nourishes our growth as well. The psalmist knows from experience that seeking the wonder of the face of God will not only continue to protect and nourish but will also lead to new behavior in life. Knowing God and God's ways helps us learn how to live ourselves and how to make our own choices for our days.

I have been a teacher all my adult life. I have taught in secondary school classrooms, in church gatherings, in casual settings of people in the neighborhood, and in my own home with my own family. I know a great many teaching techniques; however, I know that my technique is of little use without the attention and intention of the learner. The psalmist wants the Lord of light and salvation to become his teacher; but he knows that for real transformation to take place, he must choose to pay attention. He must be a good listener.

The most important encounter we have as learners is with the character of God. As we learn God's ways in worship and in other places of our lives, we get a glimpse of God's holiness. We also encounter the joy of the Lord and find that it is strength. We learn in worship and in living to exercise trust in the grace of our Maker. In confessing our sins, we experience the forgiving nature of Jesus Christ. As we observe the church calendar year, we learn to hope for the One who will come again.

We learn God's ways when we pay attention to God's character, especially as we see and hear and feel it lifted up in our worshipful living. "Teach us your ways, O God."

Prayer: *Make me teachable and perceptive, O Lord of light. Amen.*

Thursday, September 26   Read James 4:13-17.

Seeing the wonderful in God leads us to a place of humility. We are no longer able to control our future, rewrite our past, or even contain the present moment. Seeing the grandeur and the majesty of God teaches us about the fragile and ephemeral quality of our human lives.

Yet James doesn't discourage planning altogether. He reminds us that our planning must be made with God, insofar as we presently know and comprehend God. We can be secure in the knowledge that no matter what the circumstances, no matter what unanticipated events careen into our world, God will be present in and to all of them—redeeming, guiding, and shaping our lives.

With that kind of openness to and knowledge of the presence of God, we give up arrogance. Arrogance is a besetting temptation of our age. It is so easy to feel as if we can get control of our life and our times. The best-selling biographies and autobiographies are those that chronicle the lives of politicians, entrepreneurs, entertainment celebrities, even religious "successes," who often point more to their own power and deftness than to the work and word of God in their lives. James calls us up short if we are tempted to characterize our own lives that way; he calls it boasting and says it is evil. We are asked to stop clutching tightly to our own designs for our destinies. We need to learn to speak of the influence that God's character and will is making in our planning, to hold the days and times given to us gently but firmly, the way we accept a precious gift—not crushing or overpowering it, but receiving it with gratitude.

Prayer: *Help us, Lord, to order and live our lives in an awareness of the wonder of your power and love. In Jesus' name. Amen.*

Friday, September 27   Read James 5:7-11.

Waiting for the Lord is a great ideal, but the strength to sustain the wait requires patience:

—patience rooted in the belief that Christ will come again

—patience that gives up judgmentalism

—patience that is the style of the prophets

—patience that Job exemplifies

—patience because God is merciful and compassionate

Job was able to move from hearing about God and believing on an intellectual level to seeing God and experiencing things about God that moved him and awed him deeply. James reminds us that we must be patient because we are recipients of the wonderful compassion and mercy of God and God's purpose.

To see God's compassion is to understand that God cares for us—all human beings—flawed and gifted, inept and capable, fragile and strong, foolish and wise. Jesus looked on all kinds of people and loved them. He was moved by their lack of direction, touched by their gestures of love and grace, and brokenhearted by their lack of understanding. God's patience and compassion in Jesus Christ become standards for our own openness to others. We often find it easier to label and categorize the people with whom we work and worship than to see them with the compassion that Jesus would have for them. Look at Jesus' choices for compassion: Zacchaeus, Mary Magdalene, the woman taken in adultery, his sleeping disciples in Gethsemane.

Sometimes our only reference point for patience in living our lives openly is the point at which we realize God's compassionate and merciful patience with us. If God is patient *with* us, we can trust God to work *through* us.

Prayer: *Compassionate, merciful God, help me see people as you see them, and give me patience and compassion. In Jesus' name. Amen.*

Saturday, September 28   Read Mark 9:38-41.

"Whoever is not against us is for us" (NIV). What a wonderful pronouncement by Jesus! Jesus, knowing where he has come from and where he is going, and that God has put all things into his hands, is open to the hearts and intentions of people. Therefore, he can include all sorts of people in his affirmation, far beyond the limits that we set.

Jesus' disciples are concerned that their ministry be done in the right way, by people with the right credentials. When they see acts of dramatic healing take place, they cannot rest with the good news that a person is healed; they question the healer's associations. Jesus, the visible image of the invisible God, knows that their limited view is too small. He tears down the walls they erect to keep their ministry and faith life safe.

In a recent Advent season, I attended an evening of prayer in a retreat center belonging to a church much different from my own in liturgy, in polity, and in emphasis. Yet, as I sat in that circle of Advent watchers, participating with them in listening to the scripture, sharing a common meal, waiting in silence, and praying in the candlelight for healing of the nations, I was at one with the heart of each person there. I was another believer who called Jesus Christ Lord and awaited his appearing.

I do not believe that an outside observer or an internal participant could have distinguished us from one another by our church of origin. Those who were for Jesus Christ and his intended rule were not against him; together we bore the name of Jesus Christ. God surprised us with the wonder of God's inclusiveness.

Prayer: *Lord of the universe, open my eyes to see all those who belong to you, even though they are different from me. Amen.*

Sunday, September 29   Read Mark 9:42-50.

"Have salt in yourselves, and be at peace with one another."
This is the last word from Jesus after a series of powerful
statements about issues of healing, resurrection, power, inclusiveness, and temptation. Jesus tells his disciples to "have
salt," a word for our inner journey, and to "be at peace," a word
about an outward journey.

All this week we have been considering how the wonders of
God transform the inner life of the one who is paying attention.
Here Jesus concludes his discourse by saying that continued
learning of him and his ways makes our lives both stable and
dynamic, centered in our Lord and the things he teaches us.
Looking for the wonders in Christ preserves and enlivens our
souls just as salt preserved and purified food in ancient times.

The salt of the knowledge of God affects our outer relationships as well. A better rendering of this verse might be, "Have
salt in yourself, and then you will be at peace with one another."
The knowledge of God, openness to Christ, leads us to the
possibility of peace with one another. When we are sure of our
place in the loving arms of God, when we have tasted to see that
the Lord is good, when we have sought God's face and caught
glimpses of it, we can also be at peace with our compatriots,
colleagues, friends, and family.

One of the best-preserved saints in our time has been Mother
Teresa of Calcutta. She has been honored, interviewed, ana-
lyzed, and revered in place after place around the world; yet she
speaks consistently of the two axes on which her life is founded.
The first is her love of Jesus, with whom she communes every
morning of her life; the second is her love for the poor, in whose
faces she sees the face of Jesus. Have salt and be at peace.

Prayer: *O God, where I am dry and tasteless within, season me; where
I am hostile, make peace in me. For Jesus' sake. Amen.*

THE FAMILY

September 30–October 6, 1991   **Sally A. Paulsell†**
Monday, September 30   Read Psalm 128.

The importance of the family is a theme which is emphasized throughout the Bible.

In the Old Testament, many of the psalms celebrate the family, asking God for a Jerusalem with God-centered homes. In the New Testament, Jesus often visits in the homes of his followers and shows loving concern for their families' welfare.

The writer of Psalm 128 rejoices that the faithful worship of God brings contentment and enjoyment of the fruits of physical labor and many children. The hope for long life in a prosperous Jerusalem was a common wish among the Israelites. However, after the Babylonian captivity the people were scattered, and family unity was threatened.

Today, the family is no less threatened. Changing moral standards, financial pressures, and lack of time together for solving problems strain family ties. But basing family sharing, praying, and studying in a common commitment to God and God's ways can be a source of stability and joy. As the psalmist wrote, "Happy are those who obey the Lord, who live by his commands" (TEV).

Prayer: *O God, bless families today. Help us overcome the problems which threaten our primary objective—to remain faithful to you. Amen.*

---

†Graduate student, University of Kentucky, Lexington, Kentucky.

Tuesday, October 1   Read Genesis 2:18;
                                                    Psalm 128.

The importance of relationships was established at Creation.

In the Creation story given in the second chapter of Genesis, we learn that God did not create the male and then forget about him; rather, God's love and concern for creation led to the creation of the female as part of humanity.

In the story of the creation of male and female the woman is called *companion*. A companion is a person who is frequently in the company of another—a helpful friend. Although Old Testament women and men lived within a patriarchal culture, our Creator provided for relationships of fellowship and commitment between companions—close relationships that would help both personalities develop to their fullest potential.

In today's society we are still struggling to establish roles for women and men that will reflect God's model for relationships. In addition to the picture of domestic life which the psalmist praises—a child-bearer wife who gives her husband many sons —either or both marriage partners may choose other types of work today.

God's love for us undergirds the love which we feel for one another. Concern for one another, loving commitment to one another, and commitment to common goals within the life of the church make the challenge of living together as helpful companions an achievable reality.

Prayer: *We give you thanks, O God, that you care for your creations. Help us to remain faithfully committed to you and to the companions you have given us. In Jesus' name we pray. Amen.*

Wednesday, October 2   Read Genesis 2:18-24.

The importance of the mutual dependence in relationships is reflected in God's creation of man and woman as equal partners. God said to *both* of them, "Be fruitful . . . subdue [the earth]. Rule over [it]" (Gen. 1:28, NIV).

Nevertheless the male-dominated Jewish culture subordinated woman to man. In Genesis 2:18-24, we read that God created the animals and birds; but although man named these creatures, none was a suitable companion for him. Then, while man slept, God created woman—also made in God's own image—out of man's rib. Finally, man was united with woman.

Woman's interdependence and equality with man is reinforced by Jesus' relationships with women. For example, Jesus discussed matters of faith with women; he trusted them as companions and friends; his first appearance after his resurrection was to women.

Later, Paul wrote, "There is no difference between . . . men and women; you are all one in union with Christ Jesus" (Gal. 3:28, TEV). In First Corinthians 11:11 Paul wrote that "woman is not independent of man, nor is man independent of woman" (TEV).

In spite of the Bible's statement, we will question the equality of men and women. The conflict over inclusive language, for instance, is evidence of the frustration women and men still feel. But increasing acceptance of the equality of men and women in the sight of God adds an exciting dimension to relationships within the Christian family.

Prayer: *Give us the courage, dear God, to live according to your holy will. Amen.*

Thursday, October 3   Read Deuteronomy 24:1-4;
                                                            Mark 10:2-12.

Jesus affirmed the importance of the family when the Pharisees tried to trap him with questions about divorce.

Deuteronomy 24:1-4 sets out a clear procedure by which men could divorce their wives and also rules for subsequent marriage relationships. If a wife did not please her husband, he could present her with divorce papers and put her out of his home. The law of Moses giving men permission to divorce their wives still governed the Jews during Jesus' ministry.

When confronted by the Pharisees, Jesus transferred their questions from the realm of law to the higher realm of the purpose of God. Jesus emphasized the moral and spiritual responsibilities of marriage and in doing so affirmed women as people, not property, and as equal with men in the sight of God. Although Jesus stressed the permanence and sanctity of marriage, his concern was caring for people, not setting down inflexible rules.

People in the twentieth century still struggle about divorce. Ministers and other church leaders are frequently asked what the Bible says about divorce. Should a Christian avoid divorce at all costs? Can a divorced person remarry? Like Jesus, we can affirm God's intention that men and women should approach marriage as a lasting relationship. But also like Jesus, we can strive toward the goal of responding to one another with love and compassion, regardless of marital status.

Prayer: *Dear God, help us to love and support those struggling over the question of divorce. Give us understanding hearts. Amen.*

Friday, October 4   Read Proverbs 17:6;
                                                                    Mark 10:13-16.

The family takes on new possibilities when children are part of it.

The many allusions to children found in the Bible signal their importance. We have read in Psalm 128 that the Lord sends children as a blessing. In Proverbs 17:6 we read that the elderly are proud of their grandchildren. Old Testament stories such as the story of the baby Moses being saved from death by his mother and sister illustrate the love, sacrifice, and care which families give their children.

Jesus, too, loved children and often used stories about parents and children to illustrate his teachings. Mark 10:13-16 tells a story about the disciples becoming irritated because people were bringing their children to Jesus for his blessing. Jesus angrily tells the disciples to let the children come. He says, "I assure you that whoever does not receive the Kingdom of God like a child will never enter it" (TEV). Then Jesus touches the children and blesses them.

Jesus constantly reminds parents and all adults that we can learn from the generous, open, and spontaneous responses of children. All of the children of God (no matter what our ages) can learn from one another. Every individual in the Christian family is important in the eyes of God.

Prayer: *Loving Creator, we thank you for the innocence and eagerness of children. Help us to nurture and teach them according to your will and to learn from them in return. Amen.*

Saturday, October 5   Read Hebrews 2:11-18;
                                                              Mark 3:31-35.

The importance of the family is emphasized in the Bible through the metaphor of believers being God's family.

In both the Old and New Testament the term "children of God" refers to a moral or spiritual relationship to God rather than a physical one; God is our spiritual parent. In the Old Testament, God's chosen people, the Israelites, are called God's children; in the New Testament, those who have come to know God through Jesus Christ are also included as God's children.

Furthermore, the writer of Hebrews tells us that Jesus willingly calls himself a brother to God's children. By sharing our human nature and suffering death on the cross, Jesus freed God's children from death. By taking away our sins, Jesus gave us new life.

In the incident recounted in Mark 3:31-35, Jesus stressed his kinship with humankind. When told that his mother and brothers were outside waiting for him, Jesus looked at the people before him and said, "Whoever does what God wants . . . is my brother, my sister, my mother" (TEV).

As sons and daughters of a loving Creator, we must maintain absolute devotion to God, the source of all goodness. Following Jesus' example, we must extend our Christian concerns beyond the boundaries of our biological family to God's children everywhere.

Prayer: *Source of all goodness, we thank you for your constant, loving presence. Help us to appreciate what it means to be your children. Amen.*

Sunday, October 6   Read Hebrews 2:5-10.

To be included in the family of God is the joy of every Christian.

The designations "children of God" and "family of God" go back to the covenant of God with Israel (described in the Old Testament). This covenant relationship was the foundation on which family unity rested. Strong family identity was Israel's protection against foreign cults and social customs which threatened to undermine their devotion to God.

During the ministry of Jesus, the term "family of God" was used for Christians. The family was the major source of daily religious teaching and activity, and Christians in the early church had their corporate worship in homes. For example, Paul refers to the church in the home of Aquila and Priscilla when he writes to them at Corinth (see 1 Cor. 16:19).

Christian families are still important to the church today, and each member of the family of God is equally important. However, as the family members nurture one another in their devotion to God, they must continually reach out to share God's love with others. In this way, the family of God continues to grow.

We marvel at what we read in Hebrews 2:6-8—that God cared enough for humanity to give us glory and honor and that God created us a little lower than the angels (see Ps. 8). To provide forgiveness for us, God allowed Jesus to suffer and die. Accepting Jesus as our Christ makes him our brother and makes us members of God's family.

Prayer: *Loving God, grant us the joy of a life lived in service to your family. Amen.*

CALLED OUT OF HIDING

October 7-13, 1991   **Lynn W. Gilliam†**
Monday, October 7   Read Genesis 3:8-10.

In this passage from Genesis, God walks in the garden searching for Adam and Eve who, filled with shame, have hidden
themselves from their Creator. To the reader, their hiding seems
ludicrous. We know that we cannot hide from God.

Or do we?

The truth is that many of us, for the most part without even
realizing it, spend a lot of time and energy hiding—from each
other, from ourselves, and, yes, from God. The shelters that
"protect" us are many, as are our reasons for seeking their
protection. This week's readings will suggest some of the places
that we choose for hiding. But our readings will also reveal
God's unfailing response to our hiding.

God was not, as this story from Genesis tells us, content to let
Adam and Eve remain hidden. God searched them out. God
called to them. In the same way, God is not content to allow us to
remain in our hiding places. At all times and in all places, God is
seeking us, calling us out of hiding.

Prayer: *Loving Creator, still our hearts and minds that we may hear
your call to leave our hiding places and live in the fullness of life that
you intend for us. Amen.*

---

†Episcopal laywoman; Assistant Editor, *Weavings, A Journal of the Christian Spiritual Life,* Dickson, Tennessee.

Tuesday, October 8   Read Genesis 3:11-13.

This portion of the story of the Fall of humankind finds Adam and Eve trying desperately to avoid the responsibility for their act of disobedience to God. Adam blames Eve and even God for his actions. Eve, in turn, blames the serpent.

These excuses will not do. God does not accept them from Adam and Eve, and God will not accept them from us. Instead, the One who created us calls us to the often uncomfortable position of accepting the responsibility for our own sinful acts. As comfortable as the blaming of others is and as hard as we try to hide in that blaming, God will not let us get by with it.

Often I wish it were not so. At times I want, just as desperately as Adam and Eve, to blame someone else when I have sinned (a word I don't even like to use in connection with my own behavior). I try to avoid admitting the wrong even to myself; the last thing I want to do is to confess it to God. Yet, over and over, God calls me to leave the blaming behind, to stand in the truth of what I have done, to ask for and receive God's forgiveness.

No matter how often or how skillfully I hide, no matter what I do to forget, God never forgets the person that God created me to be. The person who was created in the image of God, the person who is hidden in Christ, is written on God's heart. And God knows that until I respond to the call to come out of hiding and stand in the truth, I will never know the true reality of my identity in God.

Prayer: *God of truth, we find it hard to leave the places where we have become comfortable hiding. Give us the courage to see ourselves clearly, so that we can become the people you have created us to be. Amen.*

Wednesday, October 9   Read Psalm 90.

The Christian life is full of paradoxes. Christ's burden is light (Matt. 11:30) yet the way is hard (Matt. 7:14). We are free yet we are servants. We worship a God of love and mercy, yet our God is, according to the scriptures, capable of great wrath.

I like that gentle God of love and mercy. But I am decidedly uneasy about the wrathful God portrayed in many of the scriptures, including this psalm. I have never been very comfortable with anger, either my own or that of others. And I certainly have never been comfortable with God's anger.

One of our common responses to anger is to avoid or withdraw from the one who is angry. But this psalm reminds us again of the not-always-welcome truth that ultimately we cannot hide ourselves from God: "Thou hast set our iniquities before thee, our secret sins in the light of thy countenance."

The psalmist also reminds us that God is everlasting. God is always God. Whether we are confronted with God's anger or enfolded in God's mercy (or both), we cling to that truth. The God whose wrath overwhelms us is the same God who created us in love. The God who sets "our secret sins in the light of thy countenance" is the same God who, in Christ, suffered pain, humiliation, and death for those sins. The God whose anger the psalmist says consumes us is the same God who is always searching us out, calling us to a fullness of life beyond our imagining.

Prayer: *Loving God, often we do not understand your ways. Help us trust in your love for us even when we do not understand. In the name of Christ. Amen.*

Thursday, October 10   Read Mark 10:17-22.

Today's reading is one of the most familiar of the Gospel stories, and it names one of the most common of our hiding places.

This is an uncomfortable text in many ways, because this young man seems quite sincere in his desire to serve God. He has observed the commandments all his life (how many of us could make that claim?). And now he has come to Jesus to find out what more he must do to earn eternal life. It seems that he is willing to do anything to serve God.

But the one thing he is not willing to do (at least at this point in his life) is to leave the security of his great wealth. As great as his desire to serve God is, he cannot leave that which makes him feel protected. He does not dare to risk complete trust in God.

Most of us could easily read this text and neglect or refuse to see ourselves in it. Most of us do not have great wealth, at least by the standards of our culture. Yet the truth of the story is the same for us. This is not just a story about giving up possessions (although it is partly about that). This is a story about casting away whatever it is that separates us, that "protects" us from a full and living relationship with God. For the man in this story, his protection is the security of possessions, and for many of us it is the same. But our hiding places are many. And whatever our hiding places, Jesus says that we must leave them behind in order to experience the relationship with our God for which we were created.

Suggestion for meditation: *In a quiet, comfortable place, reread the passage of scripture for today. Then ask Jesus the question asked by the young man, "What must I do to inherit eternal life?" Listen quietly for Jesus' response.*

Friday, October 11   Read Mark 10:21-27.

A young man who has kept the commandments all his life asks Jesus what more he must do to inherit eternal life. Clearly, Jesus' response is not what he expected.

"And Jesus looking upon him loved him. . . ." Jesus loved him enough to name the one thing that kept the young man from full relationship with God. Jesus loved him enough to name his hiding place. Jesus loved him enough to call him out of that hiding place. Jesus loved him enough to invite him to experience the joy of a life lived in intimate communion with God.

The young man "went away sorrowful," perhaps feeling that Jesus had asked him to do something he found impossible. Perhaps he even felt that all he had done in his life to serve God had been in vain.

The disciples were stunned at Jesus' explanation that it is almost impossible for the wealthy to enter the kingdom of God. The prevailing wisdom of the day held that wealth itself was a sign of the favor of God. Hearing this fundamental belief turned inside out, the disciples were "exceedingly astonished" and probably about as discouraged as the young man. Perhaps they also wondered if their efforts to serve God had been in vain. If those who were believed to be favored will find it difficult to enter the kingdom, "then who can be saved?"

Most of us know by heart Jesus' response that although it is impossible in human terms, "all things are possible with God."

With God it is possible for us to trust. With God it is possible for us to risk. With God it is possible for us to have our hiding places with the assurance that, whatever awaits us, we are held in God's love.

Suggestion for meditation: *In a quiet, comfortable place reread Mark 10:27. Contemplate the things that God is making possible in your life.*

Saturday, October 12   Read Hebrews 4:1-3, 9-11.

This portion of the Letter to the Hebrews promises that those who receive the good news of God will enter God's rest. Although this passage appears to refer to an ultimate resting with God in eternity, it also contains a very real truth for our daily lives in the present.

We are reminded that God, following the act of Creation, rested and that we too should have regular times of rest. This is a practice not fully adopted by many of us and certainly not supported or encouraged by our culture. Instead of developing a healthy rhythm of work, leisure, and rest, we are urged to prove and increase our "value" by working more, acquiring more, and even doggedly pursuing "leisure" activities. Thus the frantic pace of our lives becomes one more place to hide from true intimacy with each other and with our Creator.

As God invites us to leave behind all else that separates us from God, we will hear, if we listen, the gentle but insistent beckoning to take time to rest with God.

We would probably all agree that we should take time alone with God. Perhaps we are even aware of our own deep hunger for such times. But we know that finding these times will not be easy. We must remember the promise from yesterday's scripture reading that "all things are possible with God." Perhaps as we respond to God's call to full and intimate communion, finding more time to rest with God will be possible.

Prayer: *O God, you know the frantic pace of our lives. You know the priorities that compete for our time and attention. Help us hear and respond to your call to rest with you. In Christ's name. Amen.*

Sunday, October 13   Read Hebrews 4:9-13.

When my daughter was a little over a year old she liked to "hide" from her father and me by covering her eyes. After we pretended to look for her for a few seconds, she would uncover her eyes and "reveal" herself, delighted to have fooled us. Perhaps this very common form of play for very young children has a parallel in our own lives. Do we unconsciously hope that as long as our eyes are covered, as long as we do not see the many ways in which we have deviated from what God has created us to be, that God cannot see us either?

This brief passage from the Letter to the Hebrews rather sharply removes any hope we may cling to of hiding from God. God knows the thoughts and intentions of our hearts. God knows the difference between what we are and what God created us to be. Before God we are "open and laid bare." This is a somewhat disquieting thought. Indeed, apart from the knowledge of the love and grace of God that we have experienced over and over in our lives, it would be a terrifying thought!

As parents, my husband and I indulged and even enjoyed our daughter's game. We knew that it would do her no harm and that she would soon grow out of it. But our hiding games are not so harmless, and God cannot simply wait for us to grow out of it. Instead God is always pursuing us, revealing the truth to us, calling us out of hiding, and inviting us to glorious intimacy with the One who created us in love.

Prayer: *God of grace, thank you for never giving up on us even when we fail to trust you enough to leave our hiding places. Help us as we try to become more fully the people you created us to be. Amen.*

SERVANT OF ALL

October 14-20, 1991   **Ellen Anthony†**
Monday, October 14   Read Psalm 35:17-20.

The psalmist feels abandoned by God; he is sure God would be on his side against his enemies, and alternately commands and bargains with God to do something. We often face similar situations in our own lives. We see ourselves as right, attacked, and needing protection. We assume that God is on our side and against "them." Or, we *wish* we could assume that God is on our side and against "them." Where do you think God is in relation to pain? Looking on or causing it? Is pain the absence of God, the tool of God, self-created, the glee of our enemies?

Our way of thinking and believing influences how we interpret the events of our lives and how we act. Take some time daily to hold each situation up to the light. New angles, new relationships, new insights may come. Perhaps the outward forms won't change, but perhaps your own attitudes and responses will.

You may know persons who hate you without cause. Take some time to reflect on their reasons. You may hate another person or persons. What are your reasons? How are enemies created? How much of your thinking is black and white, either/or? What is satisfying about being the victim? What is satisfying about hating and conquering? Do you usually see yourself as the wounded one, the righteous wounded one, the victim? Or the victor? Is the position of victim more Christian than that of victor? How do you include or exclude yourself and others from God's protection?

Prayer: *O Light, open my eyes, open my heart to your goodness that is within me. Amen.*

---

†Poet; member of Society of Friends (Quaker), Truro, Massachusetts.

Tuesday, October 15   Read Psalm 35:22-27.

Yesterday's passage ended with "those who are quiet in the land." Today's passage characterizes God as silent and far away, enemies rejoicing, and the psalmist wishing that those who favor his cause would shout for joy.

What comes out of our mouths? How do we show where we stand? Here, the phrase, "those who are quiet in the land" seems to indicate the good guys. *The Living Bible* paraphrases this, "Innocent men who are minding their own business." How am I quiet in the land? Am I minding my own business, respectful? Am I checking my desire to change others, and asking instead to be changed? In AA and Al-Anon the attitude of taking care of ourselves and loving with detachment can work miracles. But this does not mean being uninvolved, noncommital, or avoiding conflict at all costs.

Bishop Desmund Tutu says that if we remain silent in situations of injustice, we have chosen to be on the side of the oppressor. So how do we discern and show where we stand? There is a button that reads "Silence = Death" on a pink triangle, representing the conspiracy of silence around the AIDS epidemic. How do we respond to this cry for help?

The psalmist says "Stir up thyself, and awake to my judgment, even unto my cause, my God and my Lord" (KJV). Is God here passive? pacifist? too quiet? Is the psalmist making an assumption that God agrees with his judgment? Sometimes, in the heat of vindictive ire, we tell God how to act. "Keep not silence: O Lord, be not far from me" (KJV). How do we interpret God's silence? Is God far away? Or are we taking so loudly we can't hear?

Prayer: *Dear God, hold me in that silence that leads to clear thinking, clear action, and your inclusive love. Amen.*

300

Wednesday, October 16   Read Isaiah 53:7-9.

"He was oppressed, and he was afflicted, yet he opened not his mouth." What kind of silence is this? What motivates the servant's silence? Perhaps we have taken the rap for someone else in the past. What do we really think about that sacrifice? Sometimes we ourselves must absorb others' slaps. Or gossip. Or rape. Or toxic dumping. When others are slapped, we respond by distancing ourselves, or we respond in solidarity. Sometimes our actions are inconsistent with our values.

What do we believe about violence and nonviolence? Who is worth absorbing pain for? Who isn't worth such a sacrifice? If we want to change our responses, how do we do it? What kind of help do we need to change?

"For the transgression of my people was he stricken" (KJV). Who are our people? Whom do we belong to? What does it mean to belong to a people? Often we think of shared goods, lineage, history, values, customs, race, class, sexual orientation, region, and occupation. What should you do for your people? How are you available to them when they need you?

"He made his grave with the wicked, and with the rich in his death" (KJV). How comfortable are we with this idea? What would it mean for us to be buried like a criminal? How do we respond to wrong opinions, especially when they affect us directly? Whom do we want to be buried with? Rich? Poor? Wicked? Good? What will the last category be? How do categories make us feel?

Suggestion for meditation: *How do I respond to God's people when they are hurt by others?*

Prayer: *Help me, dear God, to see others as you see them—worthy of my love and care. Amen.*

Thursday, October 17 Read Isaiah 53:10-12.

"Yet it pleased the LORD to bruise him" (KJV). *The Living Bible* says "the Lord's good plan to bruise him." What do I believe about the design of my life? Especially about the design of painful experiences? How is God involved? How do I respond? Do I accept? Do I resist? Why me?

"When thou shalt make his soul an offering for sin, he shall see his seed, he shall prolong his days, and the pleasure of the LORD shall prosper in his hand" (KJV). This passage implies a choice: *when* we do this, *then* this. So how does our choice fit with God's plan? What is the relationship between God's will and mine?

And what does it mean to make my soul "an offering for sin"? To "bear their iniquities"? To "be numbered with the transgressors"? (KJV) What do I think about transgressors? What's my body language? How do I adjust my route? What do I pass on to others?

A reward is offered in all this sacrifice: many children, longevity, prosperity, and a portion with the great "*because* he hath poured out his soul unto death" (KJV). Do I pour out my soul? Do I do it for reward? Do I do it unto death?

Suggestion for meditation: *Reflect on what it would mean for you to respond to the painful experiences of your life in a way that would be different from how you have responded in the past.*

Friday, October 18   Read Hebrews 4:14-16.

"Seeing then . . . let us hold fast our profession. . . . Let us therefore come boldly . . . obtain mercy. . . find grace" (KJV).

These verses are set out like a logical proof: having what we need, let's use it! The tone is one of, "Come on, get going." We have a model, a mentor. What more are we waiting for? We don't have to look around anywhere else. We don't have to make further tests. We don't have to wonder if he knows what we've been through or whether he cares. He does. He does.

It would be easier to see Jesus as inapplicable to my life if he were really other, if he were completely different from me. But he apparently had all the same problems, lures, and diseases, and was "yet without sin." What is sin? If the only thing Jesus did differently was not sin, what does that mean? Perhaps he never really wanted anything other than what happened. He didn't separate himself from nasty people or from God. And he didn't see his will as separate from God's will. So is sin a matter of operating alone, believing we're in control?

We are asked to hold fast to our profession and come boldly to the throne of grace to obtain mercy and find help in time of need. The second step of the twelve steps of the Alcoholics Anonymous organization is, "We came to believe that a Power greater than ourselves could restore us to sanity." This step is sometimes divided into three smaller steps: 1) came: walked, made the effort; 2) came to: woke up; 3) came to believe: began to have faith, emerged into believing.

The Hebrews passage is so strong it reads like a birthright: we belong here, we deserve help. And Jesus is not so heavenly as to be of no earthly use!

Suggestion for meditation: *"Come boldly . . . obtain mercy . . . find grace." Reflect on what these imperatives mean for your life now.*

Saturday, October 19   Read Mark 10:35-40.

"We would that thou shouldest do for us whatsoever we shall desire" (KJV).

This is what I say when I feel sick, when I am two years old, when I am testing someone, or when I am assigning a penance to someone who crossed me. I say this when I want others to fix my life while retaining control of how they fix it, or when I'm trying out someone for the part of God or partner or friend. Or maybe I use this phrase when I want someone to make up for attention I never got, or when I give myself the gift of Queen for a Day: Do whatever I want.

Sometimes it is hard to admit to myself that I do this. I judge this behavior; I judge James and John, as the other disciples did, indignantly. But how else can I encounter this passage? What do you do? To whom do you make this kind of request? How do you feel when someone makes that request of *you*? Just feel. Be each side of that request. Let that question/command search you out. What kind of relationship results?

Jesus answers, "Okay, what do you want?" James and John say, "Glory." Jesus says, "Ye know not what ye ask" and "[Glory] is not mine to give" (KJV).

Perhaps we could paraphrase this passage as follows: Be careful what you ask for; you may get what you want. Or, you may get a lot more than you bargained for. Whatever you do, no one can know the final outcome.

Suggestion for prayer: *Ask God first for wisdom to discern your true desires. Pray for God's will, not yours, to be done always in your life.*

Sunday, October 20   Read Mark 10:41-45.

My copy of the *Revised Standard Version* of the Bible sub-titles verses 35-45 "the ambition of James and John." The root meaning of *ambition* is "to go around, especially to solicit votes." James and John wanted to be separated out, preferred, special. But Jesus says, "But so shall it not be among you . . . whosoever of you will be the chiefest, shall be servant of all" (KJV).

As usual, Jesus turns everything upside-down: however you want others to serve you, forget it. Serve others. I wonder about the meaning of ambition and "chiefest" in the context of serving/ servant. Does it apply?

The issue of specialness is certainly not new. But too often we have believed that *special* relationships, with *special* love, can bring us salvation—that, in fact, separation is salvation. But when we are truly living in the realm of God, no one is special. That is because this kind of specialness—being somehow sepa-rate from others—seems always to be at the expense of, or set against, commonness. God's love is different and inclusive. So much so that we really cannot have a relationship with any of God's children unless we love all God's children equally. In this context, love is not special. Radical, yes! But not special.

These reversals are pofoundly challenging to me. Does it really mean I'm not special? Or does it mean I'm some kind of special that everybody else is too? Different but equal? Does it mean I should hold myself back? How do I feel about noncom-petition for preferential treatment? What about those that have served for centuries and are finally getting uppity? What does it mean to be "servant of *all*"?

Pray: *Great Spirit, teach me. I'm listening. Amen.*

GOD: REDEEMER AND RESTORER

October 21-27, 1991   **Jorge A. González†**
Monday, October 21   Read Jeremiah 31:7.

These words were addressed to the people of the northern kingdom. They come from a time early in Jeremiah's ministry, before the first deportation of the Judean exiles in 597 B.C. As was often the case in the history of the chosen people, realities of the divided kingdom did not obscure the essential unity of the people of God. Therefore, in this passage a prophet of Judah, the southern kingdom, proclaims restoration of the people of the north, the nation of Israel.

The rapid succession of imperatives—"Sing aloud . . . raise shouts . . . proclaim, give praise, and say"—expresses the intensity of the prophet and the urgency of his message. The first half of the verse presents a poetic parallel structure by referring to the northern kingdom both as "Jacob," a favorite poetic name for Israel, and as "the chief of the nations," a proud and popular name for that country. The second half of the verse makes clear the reason for all the rejoicing: the redemption and restoration of "the remnant of Israel" through God's action.

At the time Jeremiah calls for this rejoicing Israel has been swept away by the tide of history. Assyria brought an end to their existence as a nation in 721 B.C., yet Jeremiah calls Israel to celebrate because of his certainty of God's redemption, even in the presence of all evidence to the contrary.

So also are we called to witness through eyes of faith to God's redemption, even in the midst of the darkest hour.

Prayer: *Lord, teach me to discern your redeeming and restoring action, that even in the midst of despair I may rejoice and celebrate your gracious deeds. Amen.*

---

†Fuller E. Callaway Professor of Religion, Berry College, Rome, Georgia.

Tuesday, October 22   Read Jeremiah 31:8.

Jeremiah continues his oracle proclaiming the restoration of Israel. The people will return "from the north country," that is, from Assyria, where they were deported at the time of the fall of Samaria in 721 B.C. The pain of the loss of Israel is to be healed by the redemption and restoration of the remnant.

That remnant shall be "a great company," he says. Still, the return of this people will be made possible not because of their numbers or because of their power. In fact, the company will include the sick and the infirm, pregnant women, and even those in childbirth. No one will be left behind who is part of this remnant. It will be an all-inclusive community made up of all those who have maintained their faith in the midst of their trials and tribulations.

But the wonderful words of the prophet never came to pass, for the people of the northern kingdom became "the lost tribes of Israel," absorbed into the Assyrian Empire which itself disappeared a few years later. Was the prophet wrong in his hope?

Let us remember that those who survived the disaster of 721 B.C. were a very small number, yet Jeremiah speaks of "a great company" that is redeemed and restored. In the Old Testament the remnant referred to: those who survived a calamity (Jer. 8:3), the people of the New Israel restored in their land as the community of the new covenant (Isa. 28:5), and a spiritual Israel that included also the converts of all nations (Isa. 11:10-12).

When Jeremiah speaks of the restored and redeemed remnant, he is using the term to mean a spiritual Israel, the faithful ones of God. Christians claim that the church is such a remnant, brought into being by the restoring and redeeming action of God.

Prayer: *God, help my weakness and my blindness, that I may truly be counted in your faithful remnant. Amen.*

Wednesday, October 23 Read Jeremiah 31:9.

Jeremiah drew upon the imagery of the Exodus to speak of God as the redeemer and restorer of Israel. The "remnant," that "great company" delivered by God, returns to their homeland. As they go on their pilgrimage they do so "with weeping." Yet God leads them in this new exodus "with consolations," tender expressions of loving solicitude toward the faithful ones of God.

This loving care manifests itself now more dramatically than at the time of the Exodus from Egypt. Whereas then they depended on the intermittent flow of water from the rock (Exod. 17:1-7; Num. 20:2-13), now God "will make them walk by brooks of water." While then they had had to cross the rugged Wilderness of Sinai, now God will take them along "a straight path in which they shall not stumble."

Drawing upon an image used earlier by Hosea (11:1-7) and Moses, (Deut. 32:4-9), Jeremiah gives the reason why God is acting thus toward Israel. He says, "I am a father to Israel, and Ephraim is my first-born."

God's being called "father" has nothing to do with masculinity. A gender-related conception of the God of Israel was rejected in biblical religion. Such an understanding of the gods was not part of Israel's faith, in contrast to that of its pagan neighbors. To talk of the God of Israel as "father" is to make not a biological statement but a relational one. Jeremiah does not speak of God as a male being but rather addresses the doctrine of the election of Israel. As God's first-born, Israel stands in that preferential relationship expressed, for instance, in the "double portion" that was the share of the oldest son (Deut. 21:17).

Prayer: *Gracious God, let me see the wonder of your love, the mercy of your grace, and the power of your presence, so that I may share with others the joy of your redemption. Amen.*

Thursday, October 24   Read Psalm 126:1-3.

At the very time that I am writing these meditations the news has come of the opening of the border between East and West Berlin. We have seen on TV crowds surging through the streets, climbing over the Berlin Wall, laughing and crying with joy. Things have changed so fast in these last few days that it is hard to envision what the future will bring. No one can say what will happen between now and the time you will be reading these lines. But we can be certain that we will not forget this one incredible day when The Wall came tumbling down!

The situation must have been very similar on October 13, 539 B.C., when the armies of Persia entered victorious into the city of Babylon. Some days later Cyrus himself entered the city. The one who had been expected to deliver the Judean captives, the one who had been declared to be God's anointed (Isa. 45:1-3), Cyrus of Persia, had finally brought about the end of the Exile. Now the captives were free to return to Jerusalem, to rebuild the ruined city, and to restore the temple, which had been razed to its foundations almost half a century before.

The psalmist exults, remembering that day "when the LORD restored the fortunes of Zion." The people were in a daze, "like those who dream." And what a dream it was! It was a most wonderful, beautiful dream! It was a dream come true! In synonymous parallelism the poet describes the intensity of the emotion: "Our mouth was filled with laughter, and our tongue with shouts of joy."

The long-awaited deliverance has taken place. Like E.T. longing for his home planet, the people have waited and hoped. And now, finally, the time is here. They can go back home.

Prayer: *God, teach me to rejoice in your acts of redemption and restoration. Make me grateful for all your deeds. Amen.*

Friday, October 25   Read Psalm 126:4-6.

The phrase that begins the psalm, "the LORD restored the fortunes . . ." reappears at the beginning of the second stanza: "Restore our fortunes, O LORD." There the phrase looked toward the past restoration; here it looks toward a future deliverance. There it celebrated what God had done; here it hopes and asks for what God can do.

A psalm that began with an affirmation of faith now speaks of the need for a new restoration. It isn't that the psalmist, having begun on a spiritual high, now stands in the midst of depression; rather, though the psalm was composed during troubled times, it was still possible to sing the joyous song we read yesterday.

Such was always the experience of the people of God. In the midst of their distresses they were able to celebrate God's gracious deeds, and this ability enabled them to press on. God can restore us, they said, "like the water courses in the Negeb," those dry riverbeds that mark the parched landscape in the south of the Holy Land, which in winter swell and transform the countryside into beautiful fields of green.

The last two verses are, once again, in parallelism. Their imagery is drawn from the ancient Near Eastern practice of weeping at the time of sowing to ensure the fertility of the seed. This practice was based on the common belief that the fertility gods died and were brought back to life through ritual weeping (Ezek. 8:14).

The psalmist is probably unaware of the origins of the practice of weeping and crying associated with the planting season. Here he uses the image to dramatize the contrast between the present trials and the joy that will be experienced at the time of God's redemption and restoration of Israel.

Prayer: *O God, help me see beyond any present troubles to the past upon which I stand and to the future for which I hope. Amen.*

Saturday, October 26 Read Hebrews 5:1-6.

In the Book of Hebrews the author seeks to present the superiority of Christ over all the institutions of Judaism, including its prophets—even Moses—and its priests. The passage that guides our thinking today comes from the section where a contrast is made between the levitical priesthood of Israel and the priesthood of Christ. Specifically, the writer contrasts the high priest of the Jerusalem Temple and the priesthood of Jesus Christ.

According to Jewish tradition, the high priest of Jerusalem had to be of the tribe of Levi, of the family of Aaron, and of the Zadokite line. Jesus was of the tribe of Judah, of the family of David, and certainly not of the Zadokite line. How then could he be a priest, and a high priest at that?

Rabbinical tradition taught that whatever was not in the Torah did not exist. The author of this book appeals to that principle of Jewish interpretation, well known to the readers. He draws upon the figure of Melchizedek, the priest-king of Salem (later known as Jerusalem), whom Abraham himself acknowledged as a priest (Gen. 14). Since there is no mention in Genesis of his ancestry or any reference to his death, this Melchizedek, who could not possibly be of the Levitical-Aaronic-Zadokite lineage, must be a priest of a different order, "a priest for ever." Such, the author says, is the priesthood of Christ.

While this way of arguing the point seems strange to our ways of thinking, that should not cloud the truth conveyed in this witness. Christ is our priest, our mediator, in a way no other person could possibly be. The uniqueness of his priestly function on our behalf makes him our redeemer and restorer.

Prayer: *O Holy One, you are my Lord, my Christ, my redeemer, my restorer, my God, my all. Amen.*

Sunday, October 27   Read Mark 10:46-52.

The gospel calls him "Bartimaeus . . . son of Timaeus," which is redundant since this is precisely what the name Bartimaeus means. But while the names of most of the other beneficiaries of Jesus' works of power are lost to posterity, his name is emblazoned forever in the annals of Christian history. Since childhood we have heard in Sunday school the story of the blind beggar from Jericho who went to Jesus asking for sight, and how the Master redeemed him and restored his sight.

Bartimaeus was a beggar. He had spent his life with eyes glazed, fixed nowhere, hands stretched out in supplication, asking, pleading in silent submission to his fate. Yet when he heard that it was Jesus of Nazareth who walked by, he put all restraint aside, broke his submissive silence, and began crying aloud, "Jesus, Son of David, have mercy on me!" Others wanted him to show restraint, to keep silent, to go on being the same faceless bundle in the shadow, which they, in their own blindness, couldn't see. Bartimaeus would have none of that! Undaunted, "he cried out all the more, 'Son of David, have mercy on me!'"

And because he did, because he went to Jesus hoping, expecting, believing, saying, "Master, let me receive my sight," Bartimaeus the beggar was redeemed of his blindness and restored to fullness of life. Such is the power that is in Christ—God: Redeemer and Restorer.

Prayer: *God at all times and in all places, you have been at work as Redeemer and Restorer of your people. The scriptures bear abundant witness to the way in which you act for our deliverance. Like Bartimaeus I also raise my cry. Redeem me from my blindness that I may see your love in action in the midst of the community of your people. Restore the vision of my first call to serve you that I may see how, in the service of others, I can meet you in the crowded ways of life. Amen.*

A Heart for God

October 28–November 3, 1991   **Trudy M. Archambeau†**
Monday, October 28   Read Deuteronomy 6:1-4.

A prepared heart

For forty years the nation of Israel had wandered in the desert. Now a new generation was poised and ready to enter the promised land. The wilderness experience had been a training ground, a time of preparation. Now, the clarion call sounded as a challenge across the plains of the River Jordan, "Hear, O Israel. . . ."

A heart for God can be defined as a heart prepared to listen to what the Lord is saying. Before crossing the Jordan to take possession of the promise, the Israelites needed one final word of preparation as a reminder to carry with them. Israel was about to enter Canaan, a land of many gods. They needed to remember that "the Lord our God, the Lord is one." The Lord alone was to be their God. Moses was, in effect, telling them, "You have been prepared to listen to the Lord your God, the only God for you. Make sure your heart remains true and loyal to God."

The reason for these injunctions is clear. They are a plan of action, a way to live, and a way to keep the faith alive for the future. Today, we too have the assurance that wherever we go, whatever place we call home, the Lord is still our God. We are confronted on every side by gods that jostle for space on the altars of our lives: the gods of success or failure . . . acceptance, approval, or rejection . . . fears and hang-ups . . . ambitions and dreams . . . homes and family . . . work and play. But in the face of them all, Jesus Christ issues the call, "Hear, O people, I am the way, the truth and the life. Follow me."

Prayer: *Lord, prepare my heart to follow you this day. Amen.*

---

†Contributing editor, *Michigan Christian Advocate*, Lansing, Michigan.

Tuesday, October 29   Read Deuteronomy 6:4-9.

A faithful heart

The first portion of today's scripture is known as the *Shema* from the Hebrew imperative form of the verb "to hear." It became the Jewish confession of faith and creed and was recited regularly by gathered and individual worshipers. The words were made part of the phylacteries strapped to the foreheads or arms of pious Jews. They were written on scrolls inside the mezuzahs, small wooden or metal boxes affixed to the doorways of houses and rooms. On a recent visit to Jerusalem, I noticed the mezuzahs on the door frames of all the rooms in our hotel.

In such visible ways, the people were reminded of the Lord through all the comings-in and goings-out of their days. God was to be the center of their lives, not an abstract idea or something added as an afterthought. In a culture where education was life-centered rather than information-centered, children were taught about God amid all the normal routines of everyday activities. The author of Deuteronomy urged close and attentive listening to the words of God, constant and diligent teaching in the ways of God, and careful obedience to the instructions of God.

Loving God with all our heart and soul and strength therefore means loving God with our total being, and living out our faith in daily life. A person cannot just stumble into such a close and meaningful relationship with God. It requires effort and time spent in God's company. Loving God with our whole being means being intentional about keeping God central to daily living, developing an awareness of God's unfailing presence in the midst of life, and admitting that sometimes we too need to be reminded that God is with us, no matter what each day brings.

Prayer: *O God, I love you! Keep my heart faithful to you today. Amen.*

Wednesday, October 30   Read Psalm 119:33-40.

A teachable heart

In this section the psalmist expresses an intense desire to learn. "Teach me to follow. . . . Give me understanding. . . . Direct me" (NIV). A heart for God is a teachable heart, a heart willing to listen and learn, a heart thirsty for the next set of instructions, a heart that *expects* to be guided.

The writer here is longing for God's will, yearning for it with the whole heart. In biblical language, the term "heart" refers to the seat of emotions, intellect, and will. "Heart" therefore defines the entire personality, the total self. In Old Testament terminology, it was the heart, the innermost and authentic being, which dictated and motivated all outward actions.

Not only does the psalmist long for the will of God to be revealed, but he longs to obey it, recognizing that God's will is worthy of being followed. He wants to do God's will with undivided attention. A heart for God is a heart willing to ask for God's advice, and then willing to act on the counsel given.

A heart for God is willing to be led in positive and productive paths and away from negative, harmful ones. "Turn my eyes away from worthless things" (NIV), the psalmist prays. This is an honest admission of distraction. There are times when each one of us needs to admit that we get sidetracked. We stray from God one small step at a time, until we discover we have lost our way.

Like the psalmist, we need to be careful about the condition of our heart. Are we becoming complacent on our spiritual journey? Are we beginning to let lesser things distract us? Are we allowing the second-best to crowd out God's best for us?

A heart for God is constantly in the process of becoming, continually learning, stretching, changing, growing.

Prayer: *O God, teach me, for I am willing to be taught. Amen.*

315

Thursday, October 31   Read Psalm 119:41-48.

A joyful heart

Today's scripture speaks to us of a heart that is happy. The psalmist gives us several reasons for joy. A heart for God is a joyful heart because of God's unfailing love. God's love is unconditional and never-ending. God accepts us just as we are. God affirms us with a smile of divine pleasure. Our worth and identity are defined by the creating, re-creating love of God, and because of such a love, we are offered abundant life.

A heart for God is a joyful heart because God's word is trustworthy. God's promises were not made to be broken. God is faithful to us. God will not give up on us. No matter what happens, God is there for us. Therefore, our joy is complete because of who God is.

A heart for God is a joyful heart because God teaches us about freedom. We are free to celebrate God's involvement in our lives. We are released from prisons of inadequacy and insecurity; from bondage to crippling fear and bitterness; from destructive habits that paralyze our potential. We are set free to walk in friendship with God!

Finally, the psalmist tell us, "I delight in your commands because I love them" (NIV). This, too, is a declaration of joy. There is a certain excitement that resides in the heart of those who follow God's way.

A heart for God is a heart in love with God; and a heart in love is a heart alive to the laughter of wind and rain . . . a heart in tune with the lingering song of life's soft and gentle moments . . . a heart confident of living above the things that try to pull it down . . . a heart free to roam the fields and grasses of life with the Holy Spirit of God as its guide.

Prayer: *Joyful and loving God, pursue my heart with your smile today. Amen.*

Friday, November 1   Read Hebrews 7:23-28.

An obedient heart

The Old Testament sacrificial system was established to provide forgiveness for the sin of disobedient and rebellious people. Once a year, on the Day of Atonement, the high priest would offer sacrifice for his own sins first and then, being forgiven himself, would sacrifice for the entire nation. Since the priests were themselves sinful and imperfect, they needed to be cleansed before they could make intercession for the people.

The writer to the Hebrews tells us that no longer is this imperfect system necessary. Jesus Christ has become the perfect sacrifice and the perfect high priest. Jesus meets the needs of a holy God and meets the needs of a people searching for healing and forgiveness. The Levitical priests were imperfect; their work was incomplete. Now, Jesus stands with us in the completeness and perfection that was foreshadowed in the Old Testament.

A heart for God is an obedient heart. Yet, there is not one of us who can claim perfect obedience. In our own strength and merit, we are unable to approach the holiness of God. No matter how hard we try to obey, still we fall short . . . we miss the mark . . . we fail . . . we sin. But Jesus Christ provides the answer to our dilemma. Being completely obedient, Jesus is able to meet us where we are and minister to us in our imperfection.

Because of Christ, we can come to God with confidence. Jesus opens the way for all who are lost to find their way back to God. Jesus is forever our mediator and advocate, interceding continually on our behalf. A heart for God chooses to submit all of life to the Lordship of Christ. A heart for God depends on the power of Christ in order to walk in obedience to God's will.

Prayer: *Lord Jesus, whatever comes my way today, keep me aware that you are praying for me! Amen.*

Saturday, November 2　　　　　Read Mark 12:28-31.

A loving heart

The rabbis were fond of expanding the law and adding minute points that covered every facet of life. But, at the same time, they enjoyed playing a mental game entitled, "Which commandment is the greatest?" They tried to simplify the law and reduce it to its lowest terms. This is the game the teacher of the law was trying to play with Jesus in today's scripture.

Rabbis had calculated that the law contained 365 prohibitions, plus 248 positive commands. It was of these 613 statements of law that the teachers tried to determine which was the greatest. They had been playing this game, which we might label "trivial pursuit," for years, and now it was Jesus' turn.

Jesus surprised them by combining the beloved *Shema* with the statement from Leviticus about loving your neighbor as yourself (Lev. 19:18). It was a unique combination. Jesus was in effect saying that God's requirement for holy living is more than adherence to a set of rules; it is relationship—with God first, then with other people.

A heart for God is a loving heart. To love God with all our heart and soul and mind and strength involves our total self. It means reaching toward and responding to God in every area of our lives. Then, because God is love, a heart for God loves others. It tries to see them from God's perspective . . . to accept them as they are . . . to affirm their worth . . . to help them grow . . . to call forth the best in them . . . to forgive them when they fail . . . and finally, to treat them as we ourselves want to be treated.

It takes time, effort, practice, and patience for our love to be perfected. The Spirit of the Lord is our teacher, helping us day by day to grow in love.

Prayer: *God of love, love someone else through me today. Amen.*

Sunday, November 3   Read Mark 12:32-34.

An understanding heart

I imagine that Jesus looked with love at the teacher who now praises his answer to the difficult question. Perhaps there is also a hint of humor in Jesus' eyes at hearing, "Well said. . . . You are right" (NIV). In any case, Jesus saw that the man had grasped the point: that heartfelt longing to obey God is better than mechanical compliance to rules.

The man understood that it is the inner condition of the heart that makes a difference in the way we live. It is easy to pretend to worship, even when the heart is really far from God. It is easy to put on a mask and let it pass for the authentic self. But the teacher realizes that loving God is more important than forms of worship. True worship is a way of life where relationship with God is primary. Our daily walk with the Lord exceeds the importance of our church attendance, committee membership, and even our ministry and service, although all these things are valuable and should rank high in priority.

In its original context, the Levitical concept of love of neighbor was meant only for Jews. It did not extend to non-Jews, for it was not intended to be an inclusive philosophy of loving. But when it came from Jesus, the man sensed a difference. He may even have caught a glimpse of Jesus' all-embracing love.

Jesus told the man that he was not far from the kingdom of God. He had attained a degree of wisdom. A heart for God is an understanding heart, even if it is only beginning to understand. It is a heart that allows God's wisdom to soak into it, shaping it, changing it, helping it grow and mature along the journey of faith. It is a heart on pilgrimage.

Prayer: *By your grace, Lord, may my life be defined as having "a heart for God." Amen.*

THE GIFTS OF GOD FOR THE PEOPLE OF GOD

November 4-10, 1991   **Lawrence H. Tyler Wayman†**
Monday, November 4   Read 1 Kings 17:8-13.

Elijah had run out of food. He had no water. He was on the road again, listening for God and looking for help.

Elijah found an unlikely savior. She was alone, outside the city gates, picking up sticks. Her intent was to survive until death came for her and for her son. She had no time for Elijah, and she certainly had no food. But what could she do? She was a woman and a widow, and she was outside the city gates. He was a man and a stranger, yet hospitality required her not to refuse his request. Also, he was speaking as if God were commanding him.

In this encounter between Elijah and the widow we see two possibilities in her response: one represents a statement and the other represents a question.

"How can I possibly help you! I am hungry! I am poor! I am tired! I am waiting to die!" The widow's woes are convincing. It seems strange that God would direct Elijah to her.

"How can I possibly help you? I am hungry also; like you, I am alone and weary; I don't know if I can live another day." The widow's questions are practical. Elijah's reply equals and embraces her practicality. "Fear not." But he does not stop there. "Make me a little cake first." But he does not stop there, either. "Make one for yourself and your son also."

Elijah offers the widow a choice. She may continue to pick up sticks and wait for death, or she may accept the invitation to contain her fear and feed another one despite her poverty.

Prayer: *Seeking God, contain our fear within your invitation. Amen.*

---

†Clergy member of California Pacific Annual Conference of The United Methodist Church, now active in community environmental ministries, Nashville, Tennessee.

Tuesday, November 5   Read 1 Kings 17:14-16.

Does God expect no more from us than we can give? Is God's grace adequate, reliable, and sufficient for our daily needs? How effective, efficient, and realistic is the faith that calls us to "trust and obey"?

Our memory is the warehouse for our visions of the past. It stores, reminds, reclaims, and reinterprets events that have moved us. The hindsight from past events of God's grace provides us with foresight for the present and the future.

Do you know people who have said, "There was no way that we could have survived, let alone prevailed; however, somehow, God brought us through"? Such a God-inclusive vision illumines our memories; it serves as the spark that lights our present and future paths.

Elijah, fleeing for his life, and the widow, waiting to die, sparked each other's memories of past God-inclusive visions. They trusted and obeyed their enlightened memories of God's grace. Once again they discovered God's faithfulness.

Trust and obedience require active thoughtfulness. We cannot be mindful of the needs of others or even of ourselves without active reflection. Elijah and the widow searched actively for God in the events of their living with each other. Somehow, faithfulness moved them from famine to family.

Devotional exercise: *Neither famine nor family are easy lifestyles. In famine we long for what we lack. In family we often get more than we want. In your memory, ignite a spark of a past event in which God did indeed provide for you sufficient grace or asked of you no more than you could give. Apply that spark to your present and future concerns. Think and pray. Share with another. Act together in response to a renewed vision of trust.*

Wednesday, November 6   Read Psalm 146:1-8.

No! Definitely not! Victimization is not forever!

Psalmists don't sing unless they have a reason. The reason for this song rests in the assurance of God's creative justice. God provides freedom, sight, power, and love—the gifts of God for the people of God. What more do we need?

When someone celebrates, shouts for joy, or just smiles a lot, we are sometimes suspicious. The cheshire cat from Lewis Carroll's *Alice in Wonderland* comes to mind. We wonder, "What does he or she really think?" "This is too good to be true." "They're simply not facing up to reality."

A close look at the content of this psalm will show that the psalmist is not an innocent in the world. In fact, realism is both the subject and the principle of this song. The reality is this: the world and its ways will perish eventually; God and God's movement will prevail forever.

We can find comfort in knowing that peace and justice and hope and love do not depend ultimately on human faithfulness. Ultimately, God will be faithful.

The psalm is an ultimate song for less-than-ultimate times. Constantly in the scriptures—in the witness of faithful people and in the experience of seemingly defeated nations—cries of gratitude echo from dark valleys. Injustice cannot endure. Sorrow's tears will be dried. Hunger does not last. God's faithfulness will feed us.

Is God's faithfulness sufficient for us now? The psalmist sings, "Yes!" Despite the fact that hunger persists, "Yes!" Although the wicked seem to prosper, "Yes!" Even though unfairness and injustice overpower us, "Yes, yes, yes!"

Prayer: *Watch over me; I am a stranger in your love. Uphold me by your wings, Mighty Dove. Amen.*

Thursday, November 7   Read Psalm 146:7-10.

When the manna stopped, the people started. They started to feed themselves. However, some people needed assistance. Their need gave birth to the concepts of law, custom, and justice.

The law required that harvested fields be opened to those who could not plant or reap. The law required families to care for their orphans, widows, and elderly. The law required persons to watch for others in need. The law demanded justice in the face of need.

Custom both included and surpassed law. Travelers could expect hospitality from those they encountered. Elijah's request of the widow was not out of line, and the widow was obligated to respond according to custom. Also according to custom, Elijah could ask of her no more than she could give.

The consequence of watchful law and hospitable custom is insistent justice. Such insistence crumbles prison walls like those of Jericho. "Justice" is the cry echoed by the temple stones in a Jerusalem that withheld hospitality from Jesus' saving presence. God gives sight to those who have eyes for justice. God stiffens the backbone of those whom injustice seeks to bend. God empowers by a righteous hand those whose hands have been tied by the binding of constricting need.

Humanity is a band upheld by God's own hand. The psalmist sings the music and marks the rhythm to which the band shall march. The rhythm moves to the beat of liberation, insight, power, and love, and it resounds throughout the generations.

Suggestion for meditation:
> *Fear not, I am with thee, O be not dismayed,*
> *For I am thy God and will still give thee aid;*
> *I'll strengthen and help thee, and cause thee to stand*
> *Upheld by my righteous, omnipotent hand.**

---

*"How Firm a Foundation," *The United Methodist Hymnal,* no. 529.

Friday, November 8   Read Hebrews 9:24-28.

We can know something of God by means of fate. The fate of one who eats bad food is an upset stomach. The fate of those who gossip about others is usually their being gossiped about themselves. The fate of those who live as if there were no tomorrow is often the discovery that their assumption is true. God can be found in fate, in rational, cause-and-effect experiences, and in natural patterns. In fateful time we live, laugh, weep, and die.

A word has been spoken, however, that declares fate to be groundless, the Word grown from the Ground of God—Jesus Christ. Christ has fulfilled the requirements of fateful time, and he has contained death in life. Christ has saved fateful time.

The writer of Hebrews confidently declares our faith to be beyond fate. God has never left us. Jesus Christ saves us. The Holy Spirit continually moves our souls. The Word that has been with us from the beginning is the Word that has no end.

God attends to us. From the widow waiting to die, Elijah asked for food and drink. His hunger and thirst were satisfied. From his disciples, Jesus asked for food to feed the multitude. The people were filled. From a parent exhausted at the close of the day, a child asks for love. Love renews the one who gives as much as the one who receives. From a person who has lost hope, a stranger asks for direction. The presence of a companion often makes clear the way we will go.

Christ comes to us in our need, and our "cup overflows." Christ our companion walks with us as no one has walked before, and our fate no longer prevails. Christ has saved us in time.

Devotional exercise: *When you receive Communion, watch for Christ's love in the act of giving as well as in the elements that are given. The act is our salvation. We are broken. Yet in the breaking of the bread and in the filling of the cup, we are made whole.*

Saturday, November 9   Read Mark 12:38-43.

What kind of value system praises suffering and poverty? What kind of faith encourages want and need as if they were divinely ordained?

Jesus never approved of poverty. When he spoke of the poor in spirit, he was not encouraging physical or spiritual suicide. He was referring to those who knew their need for God.

Mark's account of Jesus teaching in the temple underscores how threatening Jesus was to those who profited from perfunctory religious practices. Jesus' criticism is not of the practices themselves but rather of those who use them for their own prestige and power. Although we gain much from going to church, we don't go merely for our own sakes. We go for God. We worship God for the sake of God. God's being is not limited by our church practices, nor does the love of Jesus Christ depend upon the manner or frequency of our worship.

Jesus' purpose is to awaken us from our slumber so that we can receive the salvation God offers. Jesus therefore warns us to watch out for our pride in our tithing. He cautions us to take care in seeking the most prestigious chair. He calls to our attention the danger of overlooking our roots in the manger.

Jesus does not praise or encourage the widow's poverty. He warns those who think her gift is of less value than theirs. But Jesus may be warning the widow, also. Beware, lest you believe the judgments of the powerful about your lack of value.

Devotional exercise: *Reflect on how you regard those who are poor, hungry, ill, unemployed, or in prison. If you transformed your judgment into a gift to be offered in worship, would you find yourself among those who seek the best chairs? those disciples listening to Jesus? those who equate their poverty with an absence of value? What word would Jesus want to speak to you?*

Sunday, November 10   Read Mark 12:41-44.

Mark's story of the rich people and the widow is well known. Traditionally, we have interpreted the story to be a warning from Jesus to those who measure the size of their faith by the size of their tithe. Jesus is also emphasizing the value of gifts given out of poverty over those given out of abundance. But there may be more to the story when it is taken in context with verse 40. There Jesus warns against those who "devour widows' houses." This warning is given not only to individuals but to institutions as well, including religious institutions.

The widow has given her whole living. It might make one wonder: Has she been encouraged to believe that God expects the temple treasury to be filled at the expense of those whose need is great? Has "poor in spirit" been redefined to mean "poor in pocket"? Could organized religion be one of the institutions "devour(ing) widows' houses"?

The event of Jesus Christ clarifies afresh the meaning of "poor in spirit." The gift of Christ is one in which God's grace embraces and enlivens all people. When we give to God, our intent is to strengthen and empower *all* of us. All that impoverishes our ability to be sons and daughters of God—and that includes the greed and complacency that allow such poverty as the widow knew to exist—stands exposed before God's justice.

Jesus' gift to us has saved the world. In turn, God requires of us the gift of our response to what God has done in Jesus. This gift is not greater than our ability to give. When walking with God, we remove our worn-out shoes of pride and privilege; we discard our cloak of fateful resignation; and we step forward on paths of justice and loving-kindness.

Prayer: *Gracious God, warn us if our giving impoverishes our power to live as faithful people in your sustaining love. Amen.*

LIVING ON THE EDGE OF VISION

November 11-17, 1991 **Betsy Schwarzentraub†**
Monday, November 11 Read Daniel 7:9-12.

This scripture comes in the strange words of apocalyptic writing: dramatic images of God's intervention and rule at the end of history, when God's will at last will be done on earth. From the second century B.C. the Book of Daniel was written to those forced to worship their government and its head of state.

The point of Daniel is this: no matter how evil our rulers may be, God is in charge! It is the same God who is the Ancient of Days, who has always been on the throne, no matter how despairing our situation. Finally everyone will see God's rule of justice lived out in their midst.

Our age desperately needs this vision! While not all of us relate easily to kings and thrones, we find ourselves in the midst of demanding governments that present themselves in super-human terms, destructive influences in our society, and popu-larized atheism or nominal religion.

What good does it do to know that God is in charge? God's rule gives us a vision of God's sovereign fire already at work. This ruling fire pours forth justice and mercy on all who come to live in God's reign; it is a renewing fire that cleanses all God's people and brings them together before God; it is a discerning fire that destroys self-serving myths and the beastly rule of evil.

This same fiery vision of God's rule fuels our daily living. God's vision is not meant to wait until a far-off endtime. We are to live on the edge of God's vision for us now.

Suggestion for meditation: *Where can I see God's sovereign fire between the lines of today's news? How can I help it grow?*

---

†Senior Pastor, First United Methodist Church, Marysville, California.

Tuesday, November 12   Read Daniel 7:13-14.

Sometimes we can be so desperate for a vision that we do not think about whose eyes we are using to seek the vision. Many claim God's eyesight and see themselves as true followers of Christ. But not everyone who makes a show of being a follower has a real relationship with Jesus (see Matt. 7:21). How do we distinguish the true vision of God for us from our own self-styled dreams? We should look with the eyes of Jesus. That is, we should look upon all that is around and within us with human eyes, as Jesus did.

Jesus did not come to us as unbeatable conqueror or super-human miracle-worker. He came into life as you and I did: vulnerable, fragile, dependent upon others. As he grew in maturity he grew in solidarity with those less powerful in worldly terms: the unnoticed, uncounted, uncared for; those who are "expendable" and "the least" in our midst (see Matt. 25:31-46).

One title for Jesus is "Son of man," used in the generic sense to mean "human being." Jesus chose this term for himself: a term of humility, of mortality, and of solidarity with us.

What difference does it make that the One who is sovereign sees through human eyes? It means that, through Christ, God comes not to rule over us but to rule with us; not to have power over us but to empower us. God's eyes look from the underside of all this world's power balances, whether among nations or between persons. Because of the incarnation, God knows first-hand what it is to be oppressed and on the bottom.

Daniel saw that God's vision looks at justice through human eyes. Little did he know that one day Jesus would come as this human being, to actually live in our midst!

Suggestion for meditation: *How does God see what is happening with me and with the world today? What does this vision say about the way I am to live?*

Wednesday, November 13   Read Psalm 145:8-13.

Today's scripture describes the quality of God's vision for us. God's role is one that shows "compassion": God's "passion" is both *with* and *for* us in every moment.

Through both the Old and the New Testaments we have known God as Emmanuel—God with us. This is what the Law and the Prophets of the old covenant proclaim, and what Jesus came to embody in the new covenant with creation.

But it is not enough to know that God is with us. The good news is that the One who is with us is full of compassion: that God cares for us and for all creation and is not a god of vengeance or indifference toward the human condition. This is the quality of God's vision for all humanity which Jesus lived out, which he embodied in dying for us, and which God showed us supremely through Jesus' resurrection.

One Hebrew word for compassion comes from the word for "womb." Although we find that God carries us through the times when we are utterly helpless, the Bible says more than this. God carries us from womb to our old age. As surely as God has given birth to us, God will carry and save us (see Isa. 46:3-4). God's steadfast love—*covenant loyalty*—continues to see us through.

This was great news to the psalmist, who was living through a difficult time. The psalms are our living repertoire of praise and prayer hymns, meant for corporate worship. They give us words for both suffering and thanksgiving, a way to protest our innocence and yet to turn all our pretensions over to God in one giant "Nevertheless!" "Nevertheless," we praise you, O God, despite the ambiguity of our lives, for you have borne us all along. Your rule, your compassion, is endless!

Suggestion for meditation: *How has God carried me through good times and bad? How can I show God's compassion to others today?*

Thursday, November 14　　　　　Read Hebrews 10:11-17.

The Bible is full of covenants between God and God's people. A covenant is a personal agreement, a treaty of loyalty, an intimate vow or promise.

It all began with God's covenant with Abraham: I will be your God, and you shall be my people (see Gen. 12:1-3). This was God's vision, repeated to Isaac, Jacob, and each generation in turn, from the Old Testament to the New, culminating in God's promise for the endtime (see Rev. 21:3-4).

Jesus said, "This is my blood of the covenant," (Matt. 26:28) as he lifted up the cup at the Last Supper, knowing he would shed his own blood on the cross the next day. Thus he is greater than any of Israel's priests, who offered up the blood of perfect animals in ancient Hebrew sacrifice.

Here the writer of Hebrews speaks to Christian Jews, who know their scriptures well. The writer recalls the new covenant promised by Jeremiah (31:31-34): "This is the covenant which I will make with the house of Israel . . . I will put my law within them, and I will write it upon their hearts."

The basic term for "law" in the Old Testament is Torah. Torah means "teaching" or "instruction." One day, we are told, God's teachings will not have to be taught from one person to another. They will already be within our minds and hearts!

Hebrew rabbis stood up to read and sat down to teach. Thus the Book of Hebrews says that Christ has already stood to proclaim God's word through the ultimate offering of his life. That sacrifice now made, Christ is seated at the right hand of God and continues to teach. What he teaches is a covenant of grace, made with us long ago, and lasting to the end of time.

Suggestion for meditation: *Where have I experienced God's promises in my life? Where are they challenging me to learn and grow?*

Friday, November 15   Read Hebrews 10:15-18.

God's fiery vision of compassionate sovereignty sees with the eyes of the least among us and promises continued growth. Yet far more important is the fact that God's covenant is built upon a foundation of forgiveness!

Graciousness is one thing, but forgiveness is another. A family member or dear friend may show compassion toward us many times over, despite our betrayals. Yet even among the best of us there comes an end to such generosity. When Jesus told us to forgive seventy times seven, he set a standard that is impossible for us if based merely upon human effort.

So it is with God's covenant. God's sovereignty is real. Our continued growth is a blessing—but without the solid foundation of God's complete forgiveness, God's whole human household would fall in ruins. The writer of Hebrews recounts God's promise to his torn and shattered people: "I will remember their sins and their misdeeds no more."

Here we see the contrast between any human intercessors and Christ. While offerings were made repeatedly in the temple, Jesus Christ has made one offering, once for all time. In his ultimate sacrifice, he has done away with any further need for sacrifice. Human acts of atonement are useless. Either we stand squarely upon God's full forgiveness, or we despair.

This message is both good news and bad news. It is bad news to those who are still trying to make amends, to do penance, to become more acceptable to God. However, the message of Hebrews is good news to those who know that God's love has gone before us, laying a foundation of forgiveness! It is good news for all who believe God's victory is already won.

Suggestion for meditation: *When have I secretly tried to earn my way toward God? Do I really believe that I am forgiven?*

Saturday, November 16   Read Mark 13:24:27.

When all goes well for us, we do not mind a long life and a seemingly endless future. On the other hand, mere survival can feel like a curse if we are in the agony of illness, grief, poverty, war or despair, and we may wish for life's speedy end.

The early Christians must have felt this way, under tyrannical persecution and great personal fear. Yet Mark tells us that there will be an end to the time of tribulation, and that this end will bring a glorious new beginning!

We are not meant to waste our energy asking when and how Christ will finally come to rule at the end of time. What is important is to know that he will come, just as he comes in countless ways in this meantime: in the face of a stranger; in the challenge to act justly, to demonstrate caring, to act with kindness (see Matt. 25:35-40). Mark's assurance does not focus on a remote endpoint in history, but on the here and now. There is yet an urgent task before us: that of following Jesus in a deeply fractured and troubled world.

What can be done in this world depends on how I live my life. All of time is God's time, and I am given each moment to drink deeply of God's love and to share it with others. Those who are content plan their days from the present into the future. But those who suffer take one day, one moment, at a time.

This is God's time, the *kairos* of each moment rather than the *chronos* of numbered days. No matter what our tribulation, Christ comes with great power and glory! We are assured that God is really in charge, and that before God is through, every one of God's chosen people will be gathered together in Christ.

Suggestion for meditation: *How am I living God's vision now? Am I expressing Christ's victory for myself and for others?*

Sunday, November 17   Read Mark 13:28-32.

This week we conclude with the apocalyptic imagery with which we began: an affirmation of God's vision for human society and for each person's life. This belief is focused on the coming of Christ as the Son of man, a human being, who comes with a sovereign fire and compassionate human vision, in a covenant relationship of forgiving grace and growing glory.

The intent of such writing is not to frighten us about who is in and who is out of God's circle. Rather, Mark means to give us hope. No matter what our struggles, oppression, failures, or burdens, in Christ, God is the suffering Sovereign, our righteous Ruler, the compassionate Judge who is to come. This is the One who is very near, and even now is at our front gate.

From the fig tree we can learn a lesson of timeliness and inner life. Through each season it grows, gathering its vitality within until it suddenly bursts with new life in the spring. Then follows the summer, when its fruitfulness becomes visible to all. At last comes the fall harvest, its final vindication.

So it is with us as the people of God. No matter which season we find ourselves in now, we are to be filled with life in Christ. Jesus promised us life that is both abundant and eternal (see John 1:4; 10:10; 20:31). No one knows when the final fall harvest will come for us, either individually or as a group, but it comes to each one of us and to every generation as our fulfillment.

Thus the promised future harvest points us back to our meantime living. No matter what the wintry appearances of our present time, God's vision is forming before and through us, by the promise and power of God.

Prayer: *O God of all times and of our time, grant us, we pray, the faith to live always on the edge of your vision, as channels of your transforming power. This we pray by your grace shown us in Jesus. Amen.*

LIVING IN TWO WORLDS

November 18-24, 1991   **Dennis R. Keller†**
Monday, November 18   Read John 18:33-37.

It was a meeting of representatives from different worlds, this meeting of Pontius Pilate and Jesus Christ. Pilate was a symbol of earthly authority. By his decree, policies could be initiated that would affect the lives of all in Judea. Soldiers wielding weapons of violence would respond to his every command. With a word, Pilate could condemn Jesus to death.

In Pilate's hall of judgment, surrounded by symbols of earthly power, Jesus must have seemed a humble figure. Dressed in tattered garments, he had been brought to the praetorium by his enemies. He had no sword-wielding servants to carry out his policies. His authority was seen not in his physical prowess but in his compassion for those who suffered and his self-giving love. When Pilate questioned him about his authority, Jesus answered simply, "My kingship is not of this world."

As you meditate upon the scripture readings for this week, I invite you to consider that the people of God always live in two worlds. In this encounter between Pilate and Jesus we see that while we live in a world enamored with power, we also are called to live under the reign of God. In the present world, human worth often is determined by how much influence or wealth or success a person has attained. But as citizens of a kingdom not of this world, we are called to regard all persons as valuable because they are children of God.

Prayer: *God of truth, who has called me in Jesus Christ to citizenship in a different kind of kingdom, grant me an awareness of your presence amid the realities of daily life. Reign in me that I may be compassionate and self-giving as I relate to others today. Amen.*

---

†Pastor, Grace United Methodist Church, Centre Hall, Pennsylvania.

Tuesday, November 19   Read Psalm 93.

Assurance in a world of uncertainty

It was late in autumn. The people of Israel were gathered for worship as another new year was about to begin. Once again the cycle of planting and cultivating, harvesting and storing away had been completed. Some years they had reaped a bountiful harvest. Other years, because of drought, flooding, or the plundering of crops by their enemies, the land had yielded little. Life for these agrarian people was filled with uncertainties. They wrestled with many evils that were beyond their control, threatening their very existence. Often they knew firsthand the chaos that seemed like "the thunders of many waters."

Whether the previous year had been one of bounty or scarcity, the people of God came to worship. In their liturgy they acknowledged their weakness in the face of threatening circumstances. But their own frailties were not the primary focus of their worship. At each new year a song of trust could be heard resounding from their synagogues: "The LORD reigns." They did not know if the coming year would be a time of plenty or poverty, of peace or turmoil. But they did know that no matter what they encountered, they could trust in God's care. No powers, however mighty, could separate them from God, who reigned over all.

Like those who first sang this psalm, we live a precarious existence. But we also live under the reign of God, from whose love nothing can separate us. The evils that threaten us are legion. Yet we have this assurance that whatever we face, God cares for us. The psalmist invites us to affirm our trust in God amid a world of uncertainty by proclaiming, "The LORD reigns."

Devotional exercise: *Several times during the day today call to mind these words: "the LORD reigns." Consider what difference it makes in your life when you affirm God's reign amid uncertainties.*

Wednesday, November 20   Read Jeremiah 23:1-2.

Confrontation in a world of complacency

In times of prosperity and times of scarcity the people of God are called to proclaim that "the LORD reigns." Living under the reign of God invites us to a growing awareness of God's care for us amid life's uncertainties. But our reading for today reminds us that there is another dimension to our life in God. It is also confrontive, challenging our complacency in a world of injustices.

The days before their nation was plundered by the Babylonians were days of complacency for the people of Judah. Outwardly they were practicing the rituals of their faith, claiming with their lips that "the LORD reigns." But in life outside of their sanctuaries many turned from God, supporting leaders who built luxurious palaces while trampling upon the poor and persecuting the faithful. They preferred the comforting message of popular prophets who announced that Judah was on the brink of a new age. They ignored the cutting words of Jeremiah, who challenged them to face the reality of their coming destruction.

In this text, Jeremiah looks at the people of Judah in exile and sees the consequences of their complacency. "Destroyed," "scattered," "driven away," they are like sheep without a shepherd.

It is not enough for the people of God simply to proclaim with their lips, "the LORD reigns," in a world where we see many injustices. God's reign confronts our complacency, calling us to acts of love and justice on behalf of those who have been "destroyed," "scattered," and "driven away."

Suggestion for reflection: *As you consider the present world, what do you see as the greatest injustices? To what specific acts is God calling you in response to these injustices?*

Thursday, November 21   Read Jeremiah 23:3-4.

Community in a world of exile

> By the waters of Babylon, there we sat down and wept, when we
> remembered Zion (Ps. 137:1).

Their nation had been plundered by the Babylonian armies. Their community of faith had been scattered about, a few remaining amid the spoils of Judah, others carried off to a strange land. They lamented as they longed for home, remembering how precious life was when they were together singing the Lord's songs in Zion. Giving up hope of ever being restored, they sat down and wept. These were a people in exile.

The experience of being in exile is a common one. A homeless woman, carrying all of her earthly possessions in a paper bag, digs through a trash can for a morsel of food. Alone, she is resigned to the fact that poverty will be her plight for life. A young man lies in traction in a hospital room following a serious accident. Members of the hospital staff are always nearby. Friends and family members come for occasional visits. Yet he feels depressed and lonely as his recovery drags on. All of us can know the brokenness and isolation of being in exile.

Jeremiah offers a vision of community to exiled people. He declares that those who have been scattered will be gathered together into a flock under the reign of God. Life in this new community will be marked not by isolation but by mutual concern, peace, and a sense of belonging.

In a world where people experience separation, the church is called to be a supportive community. We glimpse the reign of God among us as we join in caring relationships with others.

Suggestion for reflection: *When have you experienced exile? What do you learn from Jeremiah's vision of community about the ministry of the church?*

Friday, November 22 Read Jeremiah 23:5-6.

Loyalty in a world of idolatry

The experience of exile is an oppressive one. But in the midst of brokenness, opportunities for rebuilding can arise. Before their days of captivity the people of Judah had looked to institutions, kings, and powerful neighbors to bring them salvation. Now that their nation had been plundered at the hands of the Babylonians, everything to which they had previously given loyalty was swept away. The exile was a time for God's people to see that they could trust in God alone for salvation. This breaking down of false foundations would pave the way for a new age.

As we grow in our awareness of the reign of God we can experience times of sweeping away and times of rebuilding. In the process we realize that the things in which we often place our loyalty are feeble indeed. God desires for us to discover the truth of these words: "The Lord is our righteousness."

Many things would claim our allegiance in this world. There is much that we can put in the place of God. Such things as career, money, governments, food, television, exercise, and romance can become idols for us. The problem with idols is that rather than fulfilling us, they lead us further into bondage. Rather than enabling us to grow in our relationships with God and others, they create barriers between us.

God calls us, in a world of idolatry, to claim, "The Lord is our righteousness." Putting our trust in God, we catch glimpses of the new age, where we live in harmony with God and with others.

Suggestion for reflection: *What do you put in the place of God at the present time in your life? Where do you see sweeping away and rebuilding taking place in your life; in your community; in the world?*

Saturday, November 23   Read Revelation 1:4*b*-6.

Identity in an alienating world

The end of the first century was a time for struggle for Christians in Asia Minor. Harassed by their brothers and sisters of Jewish descent, they were excluded from the synagogue. Persecuted by the Roman authorities, they feared imprisonment and even death. Often the faithful felt like aliens in a hostile world. Some were beginning to question the validity of their faith and leaving the church.

Claiming loyalty to Christ can lead to alienation for his followers in this world. When we act for peace in a world enamored with power, or defend the poor in a world of complacent consumption, or try to build community in a divided world we encounter hostility. The reign of Christ stands over against the powers of this age.

In his letter to the churches in Asia Minor, John, the visionary, gives a message of encouragement. He reminds the faithful that while they feel like aliens in this world, they have a greater identity in "him who loves us and has freed us from our sins by his blood and made us a kingdom, priests to his God and Father." We belong not to this world, but to Jesus Christ. And those who belong to Christ also belong to each other, fellow citizens in his kingdom.

As we discover our true identity in Christ and his church, we have a growing awareness that we are loved, even in the face of hostility. Living as people who belong to Christ, we are offered freedom, even under the weight of suffering. Christ invites us to receive a new identity that an alienating world can never take away from us.

Prayer: *Lord Jesus Christ, in whom we find our true identity, grant us a growing awareness of your love for us, that we may be faithful in the midst of adversity. Amen.*

Sunday, November 24   Read Revelation 1:7-8.

Experiencing eternity in a mortal world

In the face of hostility and persecution, first-century Christians in Asia Minor struggled with perplexing questions. If Jesus Christ is Lord, then why do his followers continue to suffer? Why has he not yet returned to free us from our plight?

When we see the reality of human suffering, our faith is put to the test. It is not always easy to talk about a God of love and care in the face of evils which can afflict innocent people indiscriminately. If God reigns, why does suffering persist?

If John encouraged the faithful with a reminder of their identity in the present, he also gave them hope in the world of eternity. Though we catch glimpses of God's reign in the present time, the powers of evil still raise their heads to challenge God's reign. Suffering may persist in the present, but it will ultimately be defeated. For God's reign is eternal. "'I am the Alpha and the Omega,' says the Lord God, who is and who was and who is to come, the Almighty."

Today in our churches we celebrate "Christ the King." We proclaim the reign of Christ over the powers that threaten our human wholeness. We can experience his reign in this life, with its uncertainties and limitations. As participants in his kingdom, we also look forward to the fulfillment of his purposes in us and in our world, as he reigns eternally.

Prayer: *Almighty God, your reign is eternal, but you desire to respond to our suffering in the present. Reign in me, that I may participate in your ministry of offering hope in a suffering world. Amen.*

Devotional exercise: *Think of someone you know who is confronted by the reality of his or her limitations at the present time. What could you do today to offer that person hope amid suffering?*

GOD'S PROMISE AND OUR RESPONSE

November 25–December 1, 1991   **Jiro Mizuno†**
Monday, November 25   Read Jeremiah 23:5-6; 33:14-16;
                                              Amos 5:21-24.

Jeremiah's expectations for the future are based upon the word of God, which is more than mere human hope. In this passage Jeremiah is very clear about two things: that God will fulfill God's own promise (33:14) and that God will, through David, bring justice and righteousness in the land. In the many centuries since the time of Jeremiah, the house of Israel and the house of Judah have been plagued by bitter strife, bigotry, and hatred. When politically motivated solutions fail and human ingenuity seems to get no place, we tend to lose our hope altogether. It seems humanly impossible ever to bring peace among people who live in the land where the Prince of Peace was born.

In many parts of the world today people have been forced to flee their own lands. They do not know what freedom means. There are people today who live under constant fear of death because of war. They do not know what peace means.

In the midst of despair we need to be reminded of the faith of Jeremiah, who believed that our final destiny is in God's hands. Jeremiah reminds us that the reign of God will eventually prevail and that real salvation and security are found only when God's justice and righteousness have been established in the universe (33:15). This is the promise of God, and we, during Advent, anticipate its fulfillment while we faithfully examine ourselves to see if we are ready and fit to receive the Son of God.

Suggestion for meditation: *Read Amos 5:21-24 and reflect especially on verse 24.*

---

†Assistant General Secretary, World Division, General Board of Global Ministries, The United Methodist Church, New York, New York.

Tuesday, November 26   Read Psalm 25:1-10;
                                        Rom. 8:26; Matthew 6:5-6.

The Psalms contain many different kinds of prayers. There are beautiful prayers, such as that of Psalm 23, that are much treasured by many as prayers of eternal comfort. There are other psalms that are less universal because they are more narrowly focused and personal. Both types of psalms are the very nature of our prayers; some are for public use, while others are spontaneous outcries of individual souls toward God.

In Psalm 25 the psalmist pours out his soul and spells out his needs before God. His honesty and sincerity come across in his prayers because he knows that there is nothing he can hide from God. He praises and gives thanks to God, confesses his sins, and makes his supplication to God openly. Just like the psalmist, we should open our souls to God through our prayers.

Very often, we feel inadequate to pray because we feel that we do not know how to express properly our deep thoughts and inner needs through prayers. During such times, it is well that we be reminded of the words of Paul in his letter to the Romans: "The Spirit helps us in our weakness; for we do not know how to pray as we ought, but the Spirit himself intercedes for us with sighs too deep for words." While we sometimes think that there are certain words, phrases, and expressions that make our prayers acceptable in the eyes of others, it is well that we be reminded of Jesus' teachings regarding prayer (Matt. 6:5-6).

Prayer is one of the ways we keep in touch with God. It is not so much how we pray that is important; what matters is that we be sincere and honest in our pleas. Through God's steadfast love, our prayers will always be heard (Ps. 25:10), no matter how poorly we may express ourselves to God.

Suggestion for meditation: *Read Matthew 6:5-6 and reflect on your prayer life in light of these words of Jesus.*

Wednesday, November 27   Read 1 Thessalonians 3:1-10.

The Thessalonian congregation had gone through very difficult, trying times. Paul was fully aware of the stress and strain
under which the church was carrying out its ministry. Seeing that
they were totally vulnerable to tempters and troublemakers, Paul
feared that the Thessalonians would lose faith. Out of this deep
concern and anxiety he sent Timothy to the Thessalonian church
to assess its spiritual status. If Timothy were to find that the
faithful were being overcome by temptations, he was expected to
strengthen and encourage them to restore their faith. Finally, he
was to return to Paul and Silas and report what he had witnessed.

Now you can fully appreciate the joy expressed here as a result
of the wonderful report by Timothy that the Thessalonian Christians had been faithful to the Lord in spite of all their adversity.
Paul praises God for this group of loyal and faithful Christians.

We have seen a similar example of such faithfulness in modern times. For many years, since 1949, Christians in China had
gone through an incredible amount of suffering, persecution,
and hardship under the Communist regime. The Christian
church in China had been totally isolated from the rest of the
world for almost 30 years. Other Christians had no way of
knowing whether the Chinese church had been totally destroyed
and the Christians eliminated. When China was eventually re-
opened in the late 1970s, it became clear that the faithful
remnant of the Christian community had not only survived but
remained as a dynamic and caring community of the people of
God. What a joy and an inspiration that has been to Christians
everywhere!

Suggestion for meditation: *Reflect on those who continue to witness
for Christ under severe persecution. Pray for their safety and strength.*

343

Thursday, November 28   Read 1 Thessalonians 3:11-12;
Matthew 5:43-48.

Although Timothy returned with good news regarding the Thessalonian congregation, Paul still prays that he may visit that congregation again. There are many new converts in the faith, and Paul knows that the church needs continuing support and nourishment. In the face of constant pressures from outside, those new members need to be protected and guided with great love and care.

The mutual support that comes from being with fellow Christians is especially valuable in time of need. It has been said by those Christians in difficult situations that the physical presence of other Christians has given them more encouragement than any other form of solidarity. For example, several years ago, student and company workers in Korea demonstrated against their government for not allowing the workers to form a union to protect their rights. Many Christians joined the effort for basic human rights and fair labor laws. The government responded by employing police and security forces to enforce repressive measures, causing violent confrontations between the security forces and the demonstrators. When some were arrested on false charges and tried in court as communists, Korean Christians appealed to their Christian friends around the world to send delegations who could actually be present in court to express their support for those being tried. Such mutual support helps Christians to protest injustice and to stand in love not only for each other but for *all* people. Jesus said, "You have heard that it was said, 'You shall love your neighbor and hate your enemy.' But I say to you, Love your enemies and pray for those who persecute you."

Suggestion for meditation: *Pray for one person with whom you have a less than friendly relationship.*

Friday, November 29   Read 1 Thess. 3:12-13; 4:13-18.

Since most of the Thessalonian Christians were converts from pagan backgrounds, many of the religious teachings and concepts they learned in the church were new and strange to them. Perhaps one of the strangest among these was the church's belief in the *Parousia,* the second coming of Christ (1 Thess. 4:16-17). It seems reasonably certain that the early Christians expected the second coming of Christ in the very near future. In fact, in both his letters to the Thessalonians, Paul brings up this matter several times so that those who believe in Christ may be ready for the occasion (see 1 Thess. 1:10; 2:19; 4:15; 5:2,23; 2 Thess. 1:7; 2:1, 8). Christ is to return to earth to set up his kingdom, to judge his enemies, and to reward the faithful. Firmly believing that the Lord will return thus, Paul urges the Thessalonian Christians to be "holy and faultless" (NEB) before God.

Paul's letter to the new converts in the Thessalonian church compares to contemporary mission work in several ways. As Christian missionaries work in non-Christian environments, they have to deal with customs, practices, and ideas which are not only different from but at times diametrically opposed to Christian norms. God has used many dedicated missionaries such as Paul to share the good news of salvation through Jesus Christ in these settings.

Many churches around the world today, now dynamic and reaching out, were once like the church of Thessalonica, born as the result of missionary endeavors. Through the action of the Holy Spirit and the witness and hard work of countless faithful Christians, those former "receiving" churches are now missionary churches, sending their own missionaries throughout the world, proclaiming the good news of Jesus Christ.

Suggestion for meditation: *Read and reflect on Luke 4:18-20.*

Saturday, November 30   Read Luke 21:25-33;
                                                    John 8:31-32.

The scenario described in this passage from Luke is part of the eschatology prevalent among early Christians. They believed that a new age was to break in at any moment and usher in the kingdom of God, the total reign of the Son of Man.

The *eschaton,* or the end of time, has been the subject of study by biblical scholars, who have given many different interpretations and views on it. But it seems that in times of uncertainty there are more predictions and speculations made about the present and the future. These speculations provoke fears in some people, who, to ease those fears, tend to grab at whatever security and promises are offered them by false prophets and self-appointed messiahs.

The fig tree in today's lesson is a timely reminder when we become vulnerable to such hysteria. First, the parable teaches that we must always be alert to signs of the kingdom of God in our world. Jesus gave the same warning to the Pharisees and Sadducees (see Matt. 16:1-4). He said that in all the changes taking place around us it is important for us to understand the deeper meaning of current events, to interpret "the signs of the times," and to prepare ourselves for the future.

Second, today's lesson speaks to us of the dependability of God's word in times of constant change (Luke 21:33). Very often changes—even changes for good as we have seen recently in a number of countries—result in confusion. How important it is to have something that never changes! Jesus promised that "if you continue in my word, you are truly my disciples, and you will know the truth, and the truth will make you free."

Suggestion for meditation: *Select a country which has gone through drastic changes recently and pray for its people.*

Sunday, December 1   Read Luke 21:34-36;
                                          Revelation 22:1-5.

The world created by God, once blessed as good, is no longer completely good because sin has since entered into it. The world is full of those evil elements described by Luke (21:34); some religions in the world consider the world basically evil, saying that those who wish to remain clean and pure should disassociate themselves from the world.

Jesus, however, was born in a stable and grew up in a carpenter's family. He carried out his mission and called his disciples from the common people of his time. He lived, ate, and taught in a marketplace and out in the field. He mingled with people and was part of the ordinary life of his time. Jesus was not *of the world*, but he was certainly *in the world*.

Jesus chose to be part of the world because his primary mission was to discern God's presence and work in the world. In spite of all the distortions and evils caused by human sin, God continues to affirm the divine presence in the world. God continues to work diligently with humans and through every possible means available in order to fulfill God's ultimate goal. It is the primary task of Christians to participate in this mission, to discern God's presence and work for the fulfillment of God's purpose in the world.

When we discern the presence of God in the world—no matter how polluted the world may seem—it gives us the assurance that beyond the disasters described by Luke, God will ultimately fulfill the ancient promise and bring about the total reign of love and mercy (Rev. 22:3-5). The conscious search for God's presence in our daily devotional life is a response to this promise.

Suggestion for meditation: *Think of one particular example in which you can clearly discern God's presence. Give thanks to God for it.*

WAITING FOR THE LORD

December 2-8, 1991   **Julie D. Hammonds†**
Monday, December 2   Read Malachi 3:1-4.

In the first years following the return of the Jews from exile (some four hundred years before the birth of Jesus), the temple was built in Jerusalem and the people prospered. Hope was theirs: the hope of good harvests, the hope of peace, the hope of existing as a people in their own land with their own God.

Then, as the years passed and the memory of their triumphant return faded, the rosy glow of the good life faded as well. Drought threatened the livelihood of the farmers. Class differences grew, and the rich began to oppress the poor, seemingly with impunity. As social conditions worsened, the people began to fear that their God favored the lawless. For they saw that the fortunes of the dishonest prospered, while the crops of honest people failed in the field.

The prophet Malachi renewed the hope of his people by promising that the Lord would return to the temple. The priests would be purified and their offerings would be made acceptable to the Lord. But his words were also words of warning, as he queried, "Who can endure the day of his coming?" (NIV) The people were not to be idle in their wait; rather, they were to prepare for the fires that would purify them like gold and silver.

Suggestion for meditation: *As Christians, we too are people waiting for the Lord during difficult times. We await the Lord's return, and we await evidence of God in our daily lives. As we wait, are we preparing for God's coming? Are we ready to be purified like gold?*

---

†Free-lance writer; active in environmental ministries, Fresno, California.

Tuesday, December 3   Read Malachi 3:1-4.

Malachi's words conveyed a message of warning and of hope to a group of people who were waiting for some good news. Let us now explore this same passage in light of some later events.

"My messenger . . . will prepare the way before me" (NIV). In these words we meet "the messenger" John the Baptist, the voice of one calling in the desert (see Isa. 40:3), whose ministry prepared the people for Christ's coming and who himself baptized Jesus in the Jordan.

"Then suddenly the Lord you are seeking will come to his temple . . ." (NIV). Jesus visited the temple in Jerusalem several times. Mary and Joseph took him there to consecrate him, their firstborn son, to the Lord. Later, during his ministry, he returned and drove the money changers from its courtyard.

"He will be like a refiner's fire . . ." (NIV). We picture a refiner's fire as a physical place—a hot, bleak foundry where bins of ore are dumped into a furnace. Jesus, who for three years walked the dusty roads of Palestine preaching a message of forgiveness, hardly conjures the same image. Yet his gentle questions, his sure, peaceful answers, his steadfast refusal to give anyone an easy answer surely sent hundreds of people back to their homes with questions that would not let them sleep.

For two thousand years after his death people have read about Jesus' ministry and have been changed. Surely everyone who has come in contact with this gentle man and his teachings has been refined like gold and silver, the pure ore of our souls separated from the dross. And those who have been through the fire are acceptable to the Lord. Our offerings are brought in righteousness; our covenant is restored.

Suggestion for meditation: *As we await the return of our Lord, let us ponder his ministry as a refiner and purifier of the silver of our souls.*

Wednesday, December 4   Read Psalm 126:1-4.

The first three verses of this psalm serve as a reminder to the Jews of God's goodness. The Jews were captives in another land and the Lord restored them to Zion. Upon their return, the people sang songs of joy and rejoiced in their good fortune.

As we read in the fourth verse, however, this psalm was not written during the first flush of good fortune. Rather, it was written later, after the memory of the triumphant return had faded and the harsh reality of living, with its injustice and misfortune, had set in. In the first three verses, the psalmist reminds his hearers to remember what the Lord has done. In the fourth verse, he asks the Lord to restore their fortunes.

What has the Lord done for us that we can remember with a smile, even in the darkest times of our lives? There may be a thousand things to remember, yet we may recall few if any because of our poor powers of perception and memory. The one sure memory we all share is that of our own triumphal return to Zion. At one time or another, we too have been like captives in another land, feeling abandoned by God even as the Lord laid plans for our return. When you finally came into the presence of the Lord, do you remember that first feeling of overwhelming, joy? Do you remember the weight lifted from your shoulders, the sudden release of care, the burden of sin melting away?

Even when times are bleak, when the harvest we've sown in the earth or in the hearts of our friends withers and seems to die, when it seems that the ungodly prosper while the godly go to ruin, take heart. Wait for the Lord, remember God's goodness, and sing a song of joy. Peace comes; peace comes. Our fortunes, too, will be restored.

Prayer: *Gracious God, sustain our hope that those who sow in tears will reap with shouts of joy. Amen.*

Thursday, December 5 Read Psalm 126:5-6.

The psalmist wrote this passage during a time of widespread crop failure. The expected rains failed to materialize, and the plants withered in the ground. The farmers were in despair. This psalm is a prayer that God will restore the fortunes of farmers and of the whole community whose life depends on their harvest.

In our own spiritual lives, at times the expected rain does not fall and the seeds we planted die in the ground. Perhaps the words of the gospel, spoken in hope to non-Christian friends, seem to have no effect on their lives. Or maybe, try as we might to read the Bible daily and attend church regularly, our own behavior may not yield the fruits of this nurture. Our fields grow to weeds, or they do not grow at all.

The grace of the Lord poured out like rain brings forth shoots from our spiritual fields. God's grace, as far from our control as sunlight, is the necessary ingredient in the spiritual harvest.

We are waiting for the Lord. But this psalmist does more than wait; he acts. First, he remembers the past—the triumphant return to Zion which, in Christian terms, signifies repentance and return to God. Then, with boldness the psalmist asks the Lord to fill his need, sending rain for a bountiful harvest. The rain we need is God's grace that the seeds we plant will grow. Or perhaps we have other needs, more personal needs. Like the psalmist, we need not be afraid to ask. Finally, the psalmist dreams of the time to come, the harvest time, the time of plenty. "He who goes out weeping, carrying seed to sow, will return with songs of joy, carrying sheaves with him" (NIV).

Devotional exercise: *Psalms are songs. Try singing this psalm in any tune you like, either familiar or newly created. If you don't like the sound of your singing voice, try chanting.*

Friday, December 6   Read Philippians 1:3-6.

Most of us will never know the experience of being jailed for our beliefs. At least, we will never know the horror and deprivation of being physically jailed. However, we do have walls around us that are not of our own making, walls that curtail our sphere of action as surely as the concrete cells of a prison. We may have walls of misconceptions people hold about us because of our gender, race, or age. We may have walls of expectations others hold for our behavior. We may even have defensive walls people build against us for our open profession of Christianity.

Paul sat inside the walls of his prison and prayed for his friends. Even in that oppressive atmosphere, he remembered to thank the Lord for those he cared about. We, too, trapped within walls, would do well to pray for our friends as we wait.

Like Paul, let us pray with joy. I like to think of prayer as a secret giving of gifts, a discussion with the Lord in which we bring the highest and best possibilities of those we care about to the attention of One with the power to bring them into being. Praying for our friends also brings them close to us in thought, and they comfort us as we sit within our walls.

Friends are people who have seen our walls and have seen past them to the person inside. Even as we sit on our cots praying for friends, the walls weaken, become transparent, and fade away. Suddenly our prisons, which once seemed so substantial, are dissolved.

As we wait for the Lord, let us pray, remembering with special joy those relationships that allow no walls to be built.

Suggestion for prayer: *As you pray, think of three people who are very close to you in spirit. Pray for them with joy, especially for any specific needs you know. And remember to give the Lord a special thanks, for friends in spirit are treasures indeed!*

Saturday, December 7   Read Philippians 1:7-11.

"I have you in my heart" (NIV) wrote Paul, and we also carry in our hearts an image of the community of believers. That image of community can be as small as the inner circle of our church friends, or as large as that unknowable number of people who strive to know God in their secret hearts. Our feelings toward them, no matter who they are, should be, like Paul's, "the affection of Christ Jesus" (NIV). Thoughts of these believers can encourage us as we wait for the return of the Lord. After all, they also wait, and though we cannot always be with them nor can we always speak aloud of our common vigil, we can keep them in our prayers, and so be encouraged.

Paul requests for his friends a knowledge and depth of insight that will set them apart from the crowd. He asks that God give them a spiritual maturity that will help them discern what is best among a number of choices. He prays that they will be filled with the "fruit of righteousness" (NIV), not like a basket of fruit picked for eating, but like a tree which, after many seasons of growth, brings forth the proof of its discipline. This passage evokes the vision of a community of people rooted and grounded in Christ, bearing the fruit of the new creation for the nourishment of the world. And all this sharing, all these fruits of spiritual maturity, are to the glory and praise of God.

Suggestion for prayer: *As we wait for God, let us remember in our prayers the community of believers. Such thoughts encourage us when we feel alone in our vigil for the return of the Lord. These believers bind the community together, reminding us of our common denominator, Jesus Christ. Let us pray for the other trees in our spiritual orchard, that the time of waiting might also be a time of maturing, to the glory of God.*

Sunday, December 8   Read Luke 3:1-6.

This week we have explored the meaning of waiting for the Lord. We have seen how hope of the Lord's return can be renewed in a people struggling with social and environmental crises, and how those crises can be turned to joy with the help of the Lord's grace. We have also seen how prayer can help us.

. In today's verses we meet John the son of Zechariah, a man whose wait for the Lord was amply rewarded. The first two verses present a marvelous contrast: on the one hand, the powerful rulers Caesar and Herod arrayed in their splendor and the high priests Annas and Caiaphas, and then, on the other hand, "the word of God came to John son of Zechariah in the desert" (NIV). Despite the power those rulers wielded, the word of the Lord came to a man wandering the desert. John possessed something that set him apart from the powerful rulers of his time: he waited for the Lord. What he waited for, he received.

We, too, wait for the Lord. We wait for the Second Coming, the return of Jesus for those faithful of the Lord. We also wait for evidence of God's power in our daily lives: for answers to prayer, for change in our habits, for spiritual growth leading to maturity. The example of John encourages us. John waited, and the word of God came to him.

The words of Isaiah fulfilled in John's ministry are also a call to us as we await the Lord's return. Whatever makes the road between us and Jesus rough must be removed, and the paths to our hearts must be prepared for his coming. Our commitment to this task must be renewed daily, for we seek a reward that cannot be won in a day—the reward of a life of spiritual growth and maturity. When God returns, we will be ready.

Prayer: *May our strength be renewed and our spirits refreshed daily as we wait for you, O Lord. Amen.*

NOW AND NOT YET

December 9-15, 1991 **Avery Brooke†**
Monday, December 9 Read Luke 21:25-31;
Isa. 12:2-6.

In the Bible, time is often *kairos,* not *chronos. Chronos* is the time of our clocks, while *kairos* is like the fig tree and all the other trees coming into leaf. They leaf out when the time is ripe. They have an interior clock, and their time is *kairos* not *chronos.*

Looking forward to the end of the world is not easy, nor do we like to think that the time is near. We do not want to faint with fear or see "signs in sun and moon and stars," or have the nations any more distressed than they already are. And yet we should not fear, for Jesus said that these signs foretell "the Son of man coming in a cloud with power and great glory." When all is at its darkest we should not fear, but rather raise our heads; for our redemption is near.

As with all great images in the Bible, this terrible and wonderful vision speaks to us in many ways. One of these ways has to do with our own personal worlds rather than that of the whole universe. We may see signs that our marriage is in jeopardy, our child is in trouble, our job is threatened, our sins are destroying us, or our health is deteriorating. Sometimes everything seems to come at once. Darkness comes upon us. We despair. And it is just then that Christ says we should look up and have faith, because our Redeemer is near.

Prayer: *Dear Lord, when darkness surrounds us, when no light shines where we must walk, grant us the faith to know that you are always with us and that your light and love await us at the end. Amen.*

---

†Author, retreat leader, and spiritual director, Noroton, Connecticut.

355

Tuesday, December 10 Read Luke 3:7-9;
21:34-36.

How are we to act when signs proclaim that the end of the world is drawing near? Do we escape into earthly joys or earthly work and try to forget? We all do that sometimes, but "take heed to yourselves," says Jesus. No matter how clear the signs, the day will come suddenly. "Watch at all times."

To watch means to keep our eyes open. What do we watch? Ourselves. We do not go sit on a hill and relinquish all responsibility. We live our lives. But we are to live them in faith and in the constant awareness that suddenly, unexpectedly, we will have to stand before the Son of man.

Of all the sinful situations in which our Lord might find us, Jesus mentions only "dissipation and drunkenness and cares of this life." Why? Perhaps because these situations represent the major ways that we most often neglect and forget God. To be dissipated means to use up our resources, our time, and our energy on pleasure. And drunkenness, of course, is not limited to alcohol. We can be "drunk" in many ways. When drunk or dissipated, we forget God. But how about the "cares of this life"? Ah! This is the subtle one. We tell ourselves that we are too busy to pray. We are tired, confused, weighed down with cares. But Jesus knows. "Come to me, all who labor and are heavy laden, and I will give you rest" (Matt. 11:28). Come to Jesus in those moments of time between work. Give to God the very work itself and all your cares, and you will be refreshed.

To be aware that at any moment we could be called to stand before Christ gives life an immediacy it does not otherwise have. Surely, this is the kind of watching that Christ calls us to do.

Prayer: *Lord Jesus, help us live all our lives as if you were coming at any moment. Amen.*

Wednesday, December 11   Read 1 Thessalonians 3:9-13;
                                   Philippians 4:4-9.

Paul's letter to the young church in Thessalonica was written only twenty years after the crucifixion, yet his thoughts and feelings come through to us as if the letter were written yesterday. Timothy had just brought Paul good news of the welfare of the Thessalonians, and Paul poured out his joy and thanksgiving on paper.

Yet, in spite of his joy, Paul is not fully satisfied. He does not see Christians as standing still. They must grow. He prays to see the Thessalonians face to face and "supply what is lacking" in their faith.

Paul had not known the Thessalonians long. We can read his statement as meaning simply that he wanted to teach them more. Faith is primarily a matter of heart and will, but it has content too—teachable content. Yet Paul doesn't mention teaching. He wanted to see them, to be with them, and the tone of the letter implies a deep friendship in Christ.

The word *fellowship* has been used so often that it has lost its meaning. The meeting of a "Christian Fellowship" or other church organization today seldom implies the same kind of deep and joyous Christian friendship that Paul's letter reveals. I am not suggesting that all church meetings should be so intense. But it is in the face-to-face sharing of our faith that it grows—both when we hear how God has acted in other Christians' lives and when we share how God has acted in our own lives. If we wish our faith to grow, we should seek that kind of fellowship.

Prayer: *Jesus, grant us the grace of deep Christian friendships where we may grow in faith and love. Amen.*

Thursday, December 12   Read Jeremiah 33:14-16;
Zephaniah 3:14-18.

The days of justice, says Jeremiah, are *coming*. In this passage the prophet says nothing of the lack of justice in his own time, except by implication. But he makes it clear that justice was *not yet*. Justice will come, he says, with "a righteous Branch" and "will be called 'the LORD is our righteousness.'"

For Christians the Lord of righteousness came almost two thousand years ago, yet Jerusalem still does not dwell securely and the world is still an unjust place. We both suffer and cause injustice. The system is so complex and so corrupt that we despair. Where, then, is the Lord who is over righteousness? Is he here? Or is he to come? And the answer, of course, is both now and not yet. Christ is here within the church, within us, and yet Christ is to come.

If Christ were not here, we would have no hope. His righteousness is our only righteousness. Our imperfection is redeemed in his perfection. Nor is this just a matter of being redeemed in the end. There is a nowness to Christ's justice. With Christ's light we may see our particular paths of justice in the complexities of our unjust world. With Christ's strength we may walk them. When we fall, Christ's love forgives us and brings us to our feet to try again. And when we ourselves suffer injustice, we gain strength from Christ's cross.

Suggestion for meditation: *Search your mind for cases of injustice that you have read or heard about. Pick one injustice and think about it deeply. Put yourself in the shoes of those who suffer from it. Imagine their circumstances and feelings, and pray for them.*

Think of some small step that you can take to alleviate either this particular injustice or one related to it. Resolve to take this step. Pray for God's help in keeping your resolution.

Friday, December 13   Read Psalm 25:1-3;
                                           Zeph. 3:19-20.

Everyone feels shame. It is a human emotion as old as Adam and Eve, who felt shame when they realized their nakedness. Shame is something we feel after we have disobeyed. We want to hide, to cover up, to pretend it didn't happen. Little children first feel shame when they disobey and try to hide it. Their attempt to hide is often comic (to us, not to them). They hold the cookie behind their backs, stand awkwardly, and assume an expression of innocence that seldom fools anyone.

"O my God, in thee I trust, let me not be put to shame; let not my enemies exult over me," says Psalm 25. Our enemies are both inner and outer. We feel shame, for instance, if we lose a job, even if it is through no fault of our own. We pray that we will never feel such unearned shame. Yet we remember the mocking that Jesus suffered. Already scourged and knowing what lies ahead, Jesus is derided: "You say you are a King, do you? Well, here's your crown." And the ring of thorns is pressed on his head, a reed stuck in his hand for a scepter. When we are unjustly shamed, Jesus knows how it feels.

There is a public quality about shame. Like the lesser word *embarrassment,* we experience our shame in the full light of day. Parents, friends, family, and a world of judges look at us in our shame, and we must look too. And at the end of time, it will be in the light of Christ that we feel the greatest shame.

Our inner enemies are many and strong. We battle them. We pray for God's help in the battle. But when we fail, we know that we do not have to be shamed. What is called for is not denial but penitence and the joy of remembering our redemption.

Prayer: *Lord Jesus, help us never to deny our sins and always to remember our redemption. Amen.*

Saturday, December 14   Read Psalm 25:4-5.

We wait for God "all the day long." We know that God is with us and yet we wait. God is with us now, but not yet fully with us.

To wait for God we must already have found God. But we see, as Paul said, "in a mirror dimly" (1 Cor. 13:12). We yearn to see more, to know God better than we do. And God puts impatience in our hearts. We do not want to be idle while we wait. We want to journey toward God, and with the psalmist we beseech heaven, "Make me"; "teach me"; lead me."

The psalmist knew his own weakness. At the moment of prayer, he wanted to know God's ways. But would he still want to know God's ways in a few hours? How often we are sincere and even passionate in our prayers, only to forget in a short time what we have prayed for. And so the psalmist prays, "Make me to know thy ways." Don't just leave it up to me.

"Teach me thy paths." We can learn much about the paths of the Lord from reading the Bible and from listening to human teachers. But without the teaching of the Spirit, we will not know those paths as we need to know them. The Spirit is the ultimate, and in one sense the only, teacher of prayer, and without prayer we may not hope to learn the paths of the Lord.

The last imperative of the psalmist is, "Lead me in thy truth." Even if we had before us a wonderful map of the way that we should go (and, in a sense, we have such a map in scripture), even if Jesus' words "I am the way, and the truth, and the life" (John 14:6) have come fully home to us, we need Jesus to take us by the hand and lead us. For although God's truth is the same for all, each of us is unique. We look toward God from different vantage points, but we all share with the psalmist that yearning for "the God of my salvation."

Prayer: *O Lord, take my hand and lead me in the way that I should go. Amen.*

Sunday, December 15   Read Psalm 25:8-10.

The psalms have a way of turning back upon themselves. If we really listen and let the words enter our mind and heart, we find our thoughts and feelings tossed to and fro like tree branches in a storm. Sometimes the wind blows in one direction for several lines before it shifts and blows in another. Sometimes, from one verse to another, we are called from joy to despair. But at other times the change is very subtle, and we don't even see it unless we look closely. Such a change comes in the last verse of today's reading.

For several verses the psalmist has been praising God. The Lord is "good and upright." He "instructs sinners" and "leads the humble." The first half of verse 10 continues in this vein. "All the paths of the LORD are steadfast love and faithfulness." We feel supported, protected, cared for. But then in the second half of verse 10, the psalmist says, "For those who keep his covenant and his testimonies," and we are brought up short. Do we keep God's covenant and testimonies? And suddenly we remember all the times that we forgot to listen to and obey the Lord. The paths of the Lord are offered to us, but we must know and accept and follow the Lord's way to be able to walk them.

Looking at the psalm from a Christian perspective, we are conscious that we are people of the new covenant. This situation changes the scripture for us because we know we are forgiven. We stumble and forget where we are, just as the psalmist did. But we need only to acknowledge our sin and remember our redemption, and we know God's love and faithfulness once again.

Prayer: *O Christ, help us to be penitent rather than arrogant, and to rejoice in our forgiveness. Amen.*

361

WAITING ON GOD'S PROMISE

December 16-22, 1991   **Janet R. McNish†**
Monday, December 16   Read Micah 5:2-5*a*; 7:1-7.

Advent lectionary readings traditionally include Micah 5 because the Gospel writers saw in verse 2 a foretelling of the birth
of Jesus in Bethlehem (see Matt. 2:6; John 7:42). However,
biblical scholars generally agree that in verse 2 Micah is speaking of the past as if it were the future. God is represented as
speaking to Israel using future tenses at the time David was being
anointed king. Micah, writing between 737 and 686 B.C., then
turns to the future in verses 3-5, foretelling difficult times for
Judah until God chooses to raise up another king who will make
Israel a united and safe nation again.

Perhaps in attending to these verses alone, we miss the greater
message Micah holds for us—a message of confident, active
waiting on God to act and of unshakable faith in God's ultimate
goodness and mercy. Micah looks around and sees injustice and
dishonesty everywhere: "Listen to me, you rulers of Israel, you
that hate justice and turn right into wrong" (3:9, TEV). Instead of
despairing, Micah waits confidently for God. And while waiting, he never ceases trying to make people see that injustice and
honesty are not part of God's will.

What does Micah's example of active, confident waiting say
to us today as we move through another Advent season when
people are homeless, children are malnourished and underedu-
cated, the elderly find medical care unaffordable, and our planet
is in danger of dying?

Prayer: *God of hope, instill in me an attitude of active, confident
waiting during this season of new beginnings. Amen.*

---

†Editor, *Pockets,* the magazine for children published by The Upper Room,
Nashville, Tennessee.

Tuesday, December 17　　　　　　　Read Micah 5:2-5*a*; 6:8.

What does God want of us? In Micah 6:8, the prophet tells us in no uncertain terms. And he tells the people of Israel that this is exactly what they have *not* been doing. "Your rich men exploit the poor, and all of you are liars" (6:12, TEV). "There is not an honest person left in the land. . . . Everyone hunts down his fellow countryman. . . . They are all experts at doing evil" (7:2-3, TEV). And so, according to Micah, God will punish them. But even in that punishment there is promise—the promise of a leader who will rule not by worldly power but by the power that comes from the Lord. His rule will be the Lord's rule, a rule in which God will teach the people the just way and they will follow, a rule in which the great powers "will hammer their swords into plows and their spears into pruning knives" and "nations will never again go to war" (4:3, TEV).

What does God want of *us*—we who are living in the last decade of the twentieth century, so far removed from those people of seventh-century B.C. Jerusalem—or are we? The homeless walk the streets, many people are without adequate health care, 20 percent of our children live in poverty, our prisons are overflowing, young people turn to drugs, and military spending far outstrips spending for human welfare. All this poverty exists in the midst of great wealth, and in spite of the fact that we have something the people of Micah's day did not have: God's full revelation in Jesus, whose birthday we are about to celebrate. Indeed, this Advent, this preparation time, is a good time to ask again: What does God require of us . . . of me?

Prayer: *Holy God, help me to do what is just, to show constant love, and to live in humble fellowship with you. Amen.*

Wednesday, December 18   Read Psalm 80:1-7.

I prefer not to read this kind of scripture passage during Advent. I would much rather read the wonderful Isaiah passages that hold so much promise—passages about preparing a road in the wilderness for the Lord (40:3), or people who have walked in darkness now seeing a great light (9:2), or the absence of harm and evil on God's holy mountain (11:9), or deserts singing and shouting for joy (35:1-2). But, "You have given us sorrow to eat, a large cup of tears to drink"—I don't want to read that during the Advent season. But then, I must ask myself, How can I experience great joy over the birth of the Christ Child if I do not understand and, indeed, experience for myself the cry for help and the need for deliverance?

As we see in the Psalms, over and over again in its history Israel cried for help and asked for deliverance. Of the 150 psalms, just over one-third are lament psalms—psalms that invoke God's name, cry for hearing and help, state the nature and cause of a particular misfortune, and pray for deliverance. Of these lament psalms, thirteen are community laments; that is, they are expressions of national sorrow brought on by a sense of the nation's sin. In this particular community lament, the people see a military defeat as a sign of God's wrath and so ask, "How much longer, Lord God Almighty, will you be angry with your people's prayers?" (TEV)

What are our national sins? Misuse and overuse of natural resources? Unspoken, yet pervasive racism? Far from equal distribution of wealth? Faith in a glorified military machine? Consumerism? As a nation whose motto is "In God We Trust," we must name our sin before we can cry, "How much longer, Lord God?"

Prayer: *Come, Lord Jesus, to all nations. Amen.*

Thursday, December 19   Read Luke 1:39-45.

Elizabeth is somewhat overlooked in the Christmas cast of characters, I think. Her husband, Zechariah, steals the scene from her when he, not Elizabeth, receives Gabriel's announcement that a special son will be born to the couple. And although the scripture doesn't tell us so, Zechariah's inability to speak as a result of his unbelief probably remained as much a topic of conversation among the townfolk as did Elizabeth's pregnancy.

But if we take time to ponder Elizabeth's words before moving on to Mary's beautiful song of praise and thanksgiving in verses 46-55, we see something special about Elizabeth. She recognized the long-foretold messiah, even before his birth. Without proof of mighty and miraculous deeds, face to face with a young, unmarried, pregnant cousin who, like her, was "just ordinary folks," she recognized the Savior of her people.

What does it take to recognize our Savior in such unlikely circumstances? Elizabeth must have been a woman of great faith, believing deep within herself that if the Lord had promised a deliverer, then the Lord would indeed send a deliverer. But Elizabeth had more than what might be called "blind faith." She had an openness to the Holy Spirit's activity in the world. Thus, when presented with evidence of the Holy Spirit's ultimate intervention in the affairs of the world, she herself was "filled with the Holy Spirit" and could say in wonder and humility, "Why should this great thing happen to me?"

Elizabeth is another example of confident waiting and openness to God's intervention. Let that confidence, patience, and receptivity be ours this Advent season.

Suggestion for prayer: *Think about where God might be intervening in your life. Ask God to give you the kind of faith, patience, and receptivity Elizabeth demonstrated.*

365

Friday, December 20   Read Luke 1:29-38, 46-49.

What if Mary had said No—"No, I do not want to do this thing"? We could hardly have blamed her. To say yes meant risking her very life. Or, if she was spared her life, she would have to live in disgrace the rest of her life. She might not have had a man to provide for her, in a society in which most women had no identity and no possessions outside their father's house and later outside their husband's house.

But Mary, like her cousin Elizabeth, believed in a God who kept promises. And a long time ago that same God had promised her people a deliverer, one who would rule "with the strength that comes from the LORD" (Mic. 5:4, TEV). That God was a God who worked through common, ordinary people to intervene in history. That God was a God who gave strength and courage to those who allowed themselves to be instruments of God's will. And so Mary said, "Yes, I'll do it."

Mary's yes was not a halfhearted, begrudging, resigned one. It was a joyful yes, a thankful yes, a faith-filled yes. The tenor of Mary's willingness is beautifully clear in her response to Elizabeth in verses 46-55. These verses are known as the "Magnificat," so-named after the first word in the Latin translation, and have become one of the great hymns of the church.

We, like Mary, are ordinary people. But, like Mary, we can be powerful instruments to help bring about God's will, whether that will pertains to saving our planet, combatting racism, feeding the hungry, clothing the naked, ministering to the sick, visiting the imprisoned, or raising our children with a keen sense of peace with justice. Are we saying yes to God's call to us to be instruments of God's love and mercy? Do we respond to God out of thankful, joyful, faith-filled hearts?

Prayer: *Loving God, help us to say yes to you this holy season. Amen.*

Saturday, December 21 Read Luke 1:46-55.

In words and cadence strikingly similar to Hannah's song in First Samuel 2:1-10, Mary depicts a God who champions the cause of society's powerless ones. Mary's words have been called revolutionary—and they are, but no more so than those of Hannah or the psalmist or the prophets Amos, Isaiah, and Micah. God's message has always been one of *shalom,* well-being for all people. That message is difficult to see when it becomes entangled in a people's understanding of their place in the world's power struggle, but the message is there nevertheless.

Hannah was an object of scorn because she was childless in a society that counted a woman's worthiness by the number of sons she delivered. Mary was young and pregnant out of wedlock. That this message of shalom is heralded so beautifully and so emphatically by two women centuries apart is perhaps indicative of its sustaining power. Similarly, faith in God's revolutionary message has its strongest voice today not in U.S. and Western European pulpits, but in the base communities of Latin America and among the oppressed people of color in South Africa. Faced with a daily poverty most of us cannot conceive of and in constant danger of physical violence, these people are able to say, "How wonderful it is to live threatened with Resurrection! . . . and to know yourself already Risen!"*

God's revolutionary message has power for those of us for whom poverty, oppression, and extreme violence are not part of our daily existence. It calls us to a passion for justice for all the poor and oppressed people of the world, a passion that may result in our sacrificing material wealth, power, or influence.

Devotional exercise: *Consider the question: Where does God's revolutionary message call me?*

---

*From the poem "We Dream Awake" by Julia Esquivel.

Sunday, December 22   Read Hebrews 10:5-10.

How often have we heard the statement, "Without Easter, Christmas would have no meaning"? Today's passage reminds us that there is more to Christmas than the birth of a special baby. It calls us to an obedience to God's will so complete that it becomes a dangerous challenge to the world's will and so results in the ultimate sacrifice. Ultimate because the sacrifice was that of a person's life, and ultimate because it was the full and perfect sacrifice that abolished the Old Testament system of sacrifice. Jesus offered himself in faithful love and obedience to do God's will, whatever that required. That sacrifice bridged humanity's alienation from God for all time.

So we can begin to understand the nature of God's promise to us. It is not a promise of military might, or monetary riches, or fame. It is a promise that the way to God is forever open. It is a promise of a God who will always be with us—Immanuel.

Each Advent gives us the opportunity to examine anew our response to God's fulfillment of the divine promise in Jesus. Centuries ago, Micah gave us one response: "To do what is just, to show constant love, and to live in humble fellowship with our God" (6:8, TEV). People around us today are also responding to God's promise. Joyce Hollyday tells about the woman who runs the soup kitchen for the Sojourners Community every Saturday morning. Each Saturday she prays the same prayer that includes this line: "Lord, you're coming through this line today, so help us to treat you right. Yes, Lord, help us to treat you right."*

Prayer: *Dear Jesus, again we are about to celebrate your coming. Help us to treat you right. Amen.*

---

*Joyce Hollyday, *Turning toward Home* (San Francisco: Harper & Row Publishers, 1989), p. 264.

CHRISTMAS IS INCARNATIONAL LOVE

December 23-29, 1991   **Calvin D. McConnell†**
Monday, December 23   Read Mark 10:17-22.

Receiving God's gift

Christmas week is exciting! It warms my relationships, mellows my moods, and fills me with awe. But in spite of the "song in the air and the star in the sky," I have to deal with another feeling: Christmas carries some disappointment as well. I have never gotten for Christmas what I want. The reason is in me. As much as I enjoy opening the colorfully wrapped packages, I know that no gifts like these will satisfy the deep yearnings of my life. My expectancy and need are too vast. I know that the gift I need most can be given only by God.

Aren't we all like the rich young ruler? He was the original yuppie, who had much and wanted more. In spite of his riches he found life to be somewhat lacking in meaning and purpose. When Jesus came to his town, the young man found in him a new way to look at his life. In God's eternal meaning and purpose for humanity he found larger and more inclusive understandings of himself, his possessions, and his relationships.

That is the gift we all want for Christmas, isn't it? God has promised, not as some ubiquitous Santa Claus, to send us one who will share God's eternity with us now in useful and life-transforming ways. The One who is Alpha and Omega, the Beginning and the End, knows what gift we need and bestows it upon those who will receive it.

Suggestion for reflection: *What gifts do you expect? Are your wants too shallow, secular, materialistic, or unrealistic? What do you desire most from God?*

---

†Bishop, The Seattle Area, The United Methodist Church, Seattle, Washington.

Tuesday, December 24   Read Colossians 3:12-17.

Defining incarnational love

Imagine yourself being stopped on the street and asked the question, "What is one word which describes Christmas?" What would you say? Many Christians would select "love." The apostle Paul could be counted on to agree with you. Today's text is but one of many references he makes to the primacy of love. The best known one is "So faith, hope, love abide, these three; but the greatest of these is love."

Love, to be most effective, continually needs to be made new and persuasive. The definition of love of which I am most fond is one offered years ago by the late U.S. Senator Paul Douglas: "What the world needs most is love, or energized goodwill, which if given a chance and practiced with devotion can in most cases melt antagonisms and reconcile opposites." Isn't "energized goodwill" a fitting description of love? Doesn't it define the way in which Jesus lived among us in his earthly pilgrimage? Love with energy is sometimes the only way in which we can cope with some persons or harsh realities. Love is the only force strong enough to break walls that divide persons. It is the goodwill whereby things can change. God energized love in the gift of Jesus to humanity. John Wesley writes of the importance of love in this way: "Let love not visit you as a transient guest, but be the constant temper of your soul. . . . See that your heart is filled at all times and on all occasions with real undissembled benevolence. Let it pant in your heart, let it sparkle in your eyes, let it shine in your actions. Whenever you open your lips let it be with love; and let there be on your tongue the law of kindness."*

Suggestion for reflection: _How is the love of God as known in Jesus Christ seen through your reconciling and peacemaking acts of love?_

---

*John Wesley's sermon "Pleasing All Men."

Wednesday, December 25 (Christmas)
Read Luke 2:1-20.

Incarnational love is always on the way.

> At the right time He came.
> Clocks do not count this time,
>   nor do night and day.
> Every tense is present tense.
> Every place is here.
> Every time is now.
> He comes when earth is ready,
>   and we are needy.
> Every person has their fullness of time,
>   and that is exactly when He comes.
> Precisely.
> He is always on the way.*

Why Christmas? Why this God of compassion and determination? Laron Hall, a spiritual mentor of mine, wrote:

> I do not understand Christmas, why it is that God should come to us and come to us like this. The only explanation is Love, and how does one understand Love? But our part is not to understand it, for what good is that? Our part is to respond to it, to let that Love shape us.**

Though we may not be able to explain the mystery of Christmas, the mystery will sustain us. We each have our fullness of time when we are open to God's nurturing. That is when Christ comes. We can count on it.

Thought for Christmas Day: *May the blessings of Christmas etch your days with meanings too mysterious to be fully fathomed but clear enough to be understood with grateful appreciation.*

---

*Used by permission of Sacred Design Associates, Inc., Minnetonka, Minnesota.
**Used by permission of H. Laron Hall.

Thursday, December 26   Read Psalm 111.

Imitating God's incarnational love

I stopped at a signal light recently behind a car in which a boy three or four years old was standing on the seat looking out the back window. He appeared to be bored. I waved at him. He dropped from view. Cautiously his head appeared above the seat. I made a "bunny" with my fingers and hopped across the dashboard. He laughed and made a bunny which he hopped across the back seat. We had quite a conversation for several blocks. When I had to turn, I waved good-bye. He waved back. The last I saw of him he was waving to the person in the car now behind him, hoping to have another "conversation."

I thought of the Incarnation. Isn't that what God is doing with us in Jesus Christ? Getting acquainted with us where we are, carrying on conversation in a language we can understand, showing us how to live and love, and encouraging us to imitate the example set for us. Jesus leads us in examples of peacemaking, supportive relationships, and the way of oneness with God. We are called to be "imitators of Christ."

Urban T. Holmes III has coined the word "mystagogue"* to define the Christian who stands with others at the intersection of the human and sacred and seeks to understand the encounter and how it transforms life into religious vocation. When Christ has entered into our lives, we are invited to be "mystagogues" who share him with others by words and acts which can be imitated. In this way the kingdom of God grows among us. What a challenge! What a gift we have received and can offer to others!

Suggestion for reflection: *Reflect on those persons, ideas, causes which guide you. How are you a "mystagogue" to others?*

---

*Urban T. Holmes III, "An Outline of Our Intentional Theory of Ministry," St. Luke's *Journal of Theology* 20 (March 1977), p. 93.

Friday, December 27   Read Isaiah 9:2-7.

Incarnational love in the midst of the storm

A legend tells of the king of a make-believe kingdom. He was weary of war, tired of the squabbling of discontented people, and worn-out from the heavy responsibilities of governing. He longed for a special room where he could get away from people and quiet his frazzled spirit. The main feature of such a room was to be a painting which could give him peace. Inviting the best artist of the realm to the palace, he described his needs. The artist accepted the challenge and came back in a few weeks with a magnificent pastoral landscape—a summer scene with a stream flowing lazily out of snow-capped peaks and through a green meadow, large fluffy clouds in a blue sky, and sunshine illuminating it all. The king looked at it a moment, took out his sword and slashed it to bits, and sent the befuddled artist running out of the room, demanding that he come up with something describing peace better than that. Weeks went by before the artist returned, bringing another painting. The king gazed at the same pastoral scene, but one that was marked this time by a wild summer storm. Strong winds lashed the trees, clouds were ominous, the stream was at flood stage, lightning slashed the darkness. The focal point was a bird sitting in the top of one of the storm-tossed trees in the only shaft of sunlight in the dark stormy scene, singing in spite of the storm. The king looked a long time, sighed deeply, and said, "Yes, this is the peace I seek—the ability to sing in the midst of the storm."

As Wonderful Counselor, as Mighty God, and Everlasting Parent, Christ comes to us with peace, whereby we can sing in the midst of the storms that rage within and around us.

Suggestion for reflection: *God does not promise life without storms. Through Christ we receive the grace to live hopefully and to sing in the midst of the storms.*

Saturday, December 28   Read Psalm 96.

Incarnational love as salvation

It is all so simple. God's gift of salvation through Jesus. How can anything so simple be made so cumbersome, complicated, and confusing? Our theological systems, ecclesiastical and ecclesiological structures are but elucidations of the simple fact of salvation. All that is required on our part is acceptance of the way of salvation and our commitment to letting God do for us what only God can do. The psalmist spells it out in four steps.

Step one (vv. 1-4): Recognize the newness that comes from divine sources. God is creator and continual creator. When life opens up in new ways with creative possibilities, we should not take it for granted but sing a new song. Life cannot be lived in the same old ruts anymore.

Step two (vv. 7-8): Give credit where it is due. Our ability to sing the new song is because of God's love and power and not just ours. We are not self-made people; our inventions and creations are not of our own making. It is remarkable what God and we can co-create. But it is even more humbling and exciting to recognize what God can do without our assistance!

Step three (vv. 8-9): Worship God, bring offerings that are indicative of our gratitude. It is easy to be seduced into thinking we've done it by ourselves in our marvelous technological, workaholic, can-do society. Acknowledge God's part, and sing praises of gratitude and awe.

Step four (v. 10): Witness to the newness to others. God's mighty works of salvation should not be kept secret. Salvation is very personal, but it is not exclusively a private experience. "Go tell it on the mountain."

Suggestion for reflection: *What difference does it make that God is continually re-creating? Where do you need re-creation? Where does our world need newness that could make us sing?*

Sunday, December 29 Read Titus 2:11-14.

Incarnational love is unforgettable

Every Christmas I remember a skit performed by the youth at the church where I first pastored. Each youth portrayed one of the characters in the crèche, or nativity scene. As figurines, they did not move as they engaged in conversation with each other. The setting was a few days after Christmas. The set was somewhat in disarray because a little child had been playing with it. The characters were waiting for "The Hand" that would come and put them back into the box in which they would be stored for another "Long Time." It becomes evident that they do not know who they are or what their special significance is. Balthazar, one of the magi, wonders grumpily why the "child" is the only one who has a light around his head. A shepherd is distressed to learn the donkey's broken leg has not been mended. Mary is curious as to why she is the only woman. As "The Hand" reaches out to shove them hurriedly back into the box, they bid each other a "Happy Long Time." Then Mary whispers the closing line with deep wistfulness, "Perhaps next time we'll find out what Christmas is and why we are brought out of the box for such a 'short time.'"

It is only a children's Sunday school skit, but its meaning haunts me. Why are we in such a hurry to put Christmas away and move on—almost as if nothing had ever happened? Paul's letter to Titus makes the meaning clear: Grace has come for our salvation. We are urged to accept the gift and let it do its saving work in us. What is expected of Christians today? That which has always been expected; only to do it "more steadily, more enthusiastically, and more single-mindedly."

Suggestion for reflection: *What difference would it make to use the gifts of Christmas "more steadily, enthusiastically, and single-mindedly"?*

GOD'S PURPOSE FOR LIFE ON EARTH

December 30-31, 1991   **J. Artley Leatherman†**
Monday, December 30   Read Jeremiah 31:7-14.

These words of comfort from Jeremiah are sandwiched between two major themes. First, the lamentations chastise the people for their disobedience, especially for breaking the covenant with their God. After this section, there is the marvelous vision of a new covenant: "I will write [my law] upon their hearts; and I will be their God, and they shall be my people" (v. 33). Bridging those two major streams of the prophetic message is the tender compassion of God: "My people have been exiles in foreign lands long enough. I am bringing them home!" (AP)

These words of comfort provided strength and courage were necessary for restoration. Gathered from "the farthest parts of earth," God's people will come home weeping and singing! Even better than coming home for Christmas, families that have never seen all their children will be gathered together. No matter how much we deserve punishment for our sins, when our hearts are broken we desperately need comfort in order to pick up the pieces and go forward again. For Jeremiah, God's "everlasting love" (31:3) is always drawing the chosen people homeward.

Today, the prophet would surely not limit God's promise of restoration. He would appeal to *all* nations, saying something like: "O people of the earth, have done with hatred and violence that bring only destruction and mourning. Come home to a new relationship with God and with all your brothers and sisters."

Suggestion for reflection: *"Blessed are you who know the meaning of sorrow; you shall be comforted" (based on Matt. 5:4).*

---

†Minister, former pastor and district superintendent, Iowa Annual Conference, The United Methodist Church, Elkhart County, Indiana.

Tuesday, December 31   Read Psalm 147.

As pastor on a college campus, I was privileged to have cherished friends among the science professors. With space exploration expanding, I listened intently to my physicist-astronomer friend on the faculty. One day when we were alone I risked asking my simple, childlike question: "What is beyond? When we explore the farthest reaches of space, probe as far as the telescope can see, or reach the edge of the universe, what is beyond?" His answer was disarmingly simple: "As far as we know," he said, "just more of the same." My mind is not big enough to manage the concept of infinite space without borders, with no beginning or ending. Yet, with the psalmist I dare to believe there is One who can call the stars by name!

One difficulty with travel in outer space is that even when traveling at the speed of light a human being doesn't live long enough to make the trip in one lifetime, even to the stars we have named!

The psalmist is equally impressed by God's care for the children of the earth, sending peace and plenty, splendid crops, and blessings according to our needs. Just when we think we can't stand the cold any longer, God sends the warm winds. The ice breaks up, and the waters flow again. God is involved in this world. Not even a sparrow falls to the ground, Jesus said, without God taking notice.

That the Creator of this vast universe should also be interested in the intimate details of my life elicits profound gratitude and prompts a loving response of accountability.

Suggestion for meditation: *Recall the ways in which God has met your basic needs during the past year, and be thankful. Use a hymn like "Great Is Thy Faithfulness," and let it be your psalm of praise.*

The Common Lectionary 1991
(*Disciplines* Edition)

January 1-6
Epiphany

Isaiah 60:1-6
Psalm 72:1-14
Ephesians 3:1-12
Matthew 2:1-12

January 7-13

Genesis 1:1-5
Psalm 29
Acts 19:1-7
Mark 1:4-11

January 14-20

1 Samuel 3:1-10 (or 20)
Psalm 63:1-8
1 Corinthians 6:12-20
John 1:35-42

January 21-27

Jonah 3:1-5, 10
Psalm 62:5-12
1 Corinthians 7:29-35
Mark 1:14-20

January 28–February 3

Deuteronomy 18:15-20
Psalm 111
1 Corinthians 8:1-13
Mark 1:21-28

February 4-10

2 Kings 2:1-12*a*
Psalm 50:1-6
2 Corinthians 4:3-6
Mark 9:2-9

February 11-17
First Sunday in Lent

Genesis 9:8-17
Psalm 25:1-10
1 Peter 3:18-22
Mark 1:9-15
**(Includes these lections
for Ash Wednesday)**
    Joel 2:1-2, 12-17*a*
    Psalm 51:1-12
    2 Corinthians 5:20*b*–6:2
    Matthew 6:1-6, 16

February 18-24

Genesis 17:1-10, 15-19
Psalm 105:1-11
Romans 4:16-25
Mark 8:31-38

February 25–March 3

Exodus 20:1-17
Psalm 19:7-14
1 Corinthians 1:22-25
John 2:13-22

March 4-10

2 Chronicles 36:14-23
Psalm 137:1-6
Ephesians 2:4-10
John 3:14-21

March 11-17

Jeremiah 31:31-34
Psalm 51:10-17
Hebrews 5:7-10
John 12:20-33

March 18-24
  Passion/Palm

Isaiah 50:4-9*a*
Psalm 31:9-16
Psalm 118:19-29
Mark 11:1-11

March 25-31
  Easter

Isaiah 52:13–53:12
Psalm 22:1-18
Psalm 118:14-24
Acts 10:34-43
Hebrews 4:14-16; 5:7-9
Mark 14:12-26
John 19:17-30
John 20:1-18

April 1-7

Acts 4:32-35
Psalm 133
1 John 1:1–2:2
John 20:19-31

April 8-14

Acts 3:12-19
Psalm 4
1 John 3:1-7
Luke 24:35-48

April 15-21

Acts 4:8-12
Psalm 23
1 John 3:18-24
John 10:11-18

April 22-28

Acts 8:26-40
Psalm 22:25-31
1 John 4:7-12
John 15:1-8

April 29–May 5

Acts 10:44-48
Psalm 98
1 John 5:1-6
John 15:9-17

May 6-12

Acts 1:15-17, 21-26
Psalm 1
1 John 5:9-13
John 17:11*b*-19

May 13-19
  Pentecost

Acts 2:1-21
  (or Ezekiel 37:1-14)
Psalm 104:24-34
Romans 8:22-27
John 15:26-27; 16:4*b*-15

May 20-26
  Trinity

Isaiah 6:1-8
Psalm 29
Romans 8:12-17
John 3:1-17

May 27–June 2

1 Samuel 16:1-13
Psalm 20
2 Corinthians 4:5-12
Mark 2:23–3:6

June 3-9

1 Samuel 16:14-23
Psalm 57
2 Corinthians 4:13–5:1
Mark 3:20-35

June 10-16

2 Samuel 1:1, 17-27
Psalm 46
2 Corinthians 5:6-10, 14-17
Mark 4:26-34

June 17-23

2 Samuel 5:1-12
Psalm 48
2 Corinthians 5:18–6:2
Mark 4:35-41

June 24-30

2 Samuel 6:1-15
Psalm 24
2 Corinthians 8:7-15
Mark 5:21-43

July 1-7

2 Samuel 7:1-17
Psalm 89:20-37
2 Corinthians 12:1-10
Mark 6:1-6

July 8-14

2 Samuel 7:18-29
Psalm 132:11-18
Ephesians 1:1-10
Mark 6:7-13

July 15-21

2 Samuel 11:1-15
Psalm 53
Ephesians 2:11-22
Mark 6:30-44

July 22-28

2 Samuel 12:1-14
Psalm 32
Ephesians 3:14-21
John 6:1-15

July 29–August 4

2 Samuel 12:15b-24
Psalm 34:11-22
Ephesians 4:1-6
John 6:24-35

August 5-11

2 Samuel 18:1, 5, 9-15
Psalm 143:1-8
Ephesians 4:25–5:2
John 6:35, 41-51

August 12-18

2 Samuel 18:24-33
Psalm 102:1-12
Ephesians 5:15-20
John 6:51-58

August 19-25

2 Samuel 23:1-7
Psalm 67
Ephesians 5:21-33
John 6:55-69

August 26–September 1

1 Kings 2:1-4, 10-12
Psalm 121
Ephesians 6:10-20
Mark 7:1-8, 14-15, 21-23

September 2-8

Proverbs 2:1-8
Psalm 119:129-136
James 1:17-27
Mark 7:31-37

September 9-15

Proverbs 22:1-2, 8-9
Psalm 125
James 2:1-5, 8-10, 14-17
Mark 8:27-38

September 16-22

Job 28:20-28
Psalm 27:1-6
James 3:13-18
Mark 9:30-37

September 23-29

Job 42:1-6
Psalm 27:7-14
James 4:13-17; 5:7-11
Mark 9:38-50

September 30–October 6

Genesis 2:18-24
Psalm 128
Hebrews 1:1-4; 2:9-11
Mark 10:2-16

October 7-13

Genesis 3:8-19
Psalm 90:1-12
Hebrews 4:1-3, 9-13
Mark 10:17-30

October 14-20

Isaiah 53:7-12
Psalm 35:17-28
Hebrews 4:14-16
Mark 10:35-45

October 21-27

Jeremiah 31:7-9
Psalm 126
Hebrews 5:1-6
Mark 10:46-52

October 28–November 3

Deuteronomy 6:1-9
Psalm 119:33-48
Hebrews 7:23-28
Mark 12:28-34

November 4-10

1 Kings 17:8-16
Psalm 146
Hebrews 9:24-28
Mark 12:38-44

November 11-17

Daniel 7:9-14
Psalm 145:8-13
Hebrews 10:11-18
Mark 13:24-32

November 18-24

Jeremiah 23:1-6
Psalm 93
Revelation 1:4b-8
John 18:33-37

November 25–December 1
First Sunday in Advent

Jeremiah 33:14-16
Psalm 25:1-10
1 Thessalonians 3:9-13
Luke 21:25-36

December 2-8

Malachi 3:1-4
Psalm 126
Philippians 1:3-11
Luke 3:1-6

December 9-15

Zephaniah 3:14-20
Isaiah 12:2-6
Philippians 4:4-9
Luke 3:7-18

December 16-22

Micah 5:2-5*a*
Psalm 80:1-7
Hebrews 10:5-10
Luke 1:39-55

December 23-29
Christmas

1 Samuel 2:18-20, 26
Psalm 111
Colossians 3:12-17
Luke 2:41-52

December 30–January 5, 1992

Jeremiah 31:7-14
Psalm 147:12-20
Ephesians 1:3-6, 15-18
John 1:1-18